Because I Love You

The Silent Shadow of Child Sexual Abuse

Joyce Allan

vfh
PRESS

Virginia Foundation for the Humanities Press

Acknowledgments

Trying to tell a very personal story such as this requires family and friends to offer both strength and gentleness. I have been helped and blessed by these two gifts in many ways, and I want to express my gratitude to:

Mom, Joe, Jenny and Dorene
for having the courage to face our shared history and
for being my steadfast companions on this journey;

Henry, Dan, Gabe and Rick
for their faithful support while traveling with us through all the stories;

Pat Arnold and B Wardlaw,
providers of wisdom and generosity, for helping me focus on healing the hearts and relationships in our family and for knowing the book would grow from that process;

Mark Heinicke and Lisa Lefferts,
who were with me from the beginning,
for offering encouragement and shelter from the storm;

**Chris Schriner, Marilyn Saunders, Carolyn Kelly,
Ted Siedlecki, Bob Rannigan and Cathie Platt,**
therapists, for being willing to go with me into the darkness
and for keeping the light shining;

Greg Lehne,
my advisor at Antioch University,
for awakening my mind to cross-cultural perspectives on child development
and for helping me discover the pleasure of a well-written paper.

I am grateful to the many
friends, colleagues, healers, and teachers
who formed my emotional and spiritual community during these years.

I also thank my
clients and other survivors
who, by sharing the impact of silence and abuse in their lives,
continue to inspire and teach me.

The actual creation and production of this book has involved extensive collaborative effort. For invaluable assistance with this project, I wish to thank:

The brave and compassionate individuals
who agreed to be interviewed and to share their memories and stories;

The Virginia Foundation for the Humanities and its President,
Robert Vaughan;
the Institute on Violence, Culture and Survival directed by
Roberta Culbertson;
and their intellectually stimulating and creative staff and Fellows,
for an environment which was simultaneously challenging and nurturing;

Marjorie Sunflower Sargent,
Project Director and godmother, who first imagined the artistic and publishing
possibilities and guided me gently but firmly to the reality;

Angela Daniel SilverStar
for dedicating her vision and talent in graphic design to bring to life
the words in the story, balancing the sorrow with beauty and tenderness;

Kara Garbe,
editor extraordinaire, for believing in the book and insisting
that I could find my voice and tell the story;

Trisha Orr
for permission to include prints of her exquisite paintings, which help convey the
complex relationships of pain and beauty, artifact and transcendence;

Michelle Stultz, R.N., L.P.C.,
my clinical research associate, for patience, efficiency, insightful suggestions and never
blinking at my requests;

Sue Stanley,
versatile and competent administrative assistant and provider
of facts, lists, details, order, humor and friendship;

Liz Hart,
of Brookside Services,
for transcribing hours of difficult interview tapes into invaluable printed documents;

Ruth Salzberg
for single-handedly researching and obtaining copyright permissions
for the numerous quotes which enrich the text.

Lastly, this book owes everything to
my beloved partner and devoted co-creator,
Freeman Allan,
for encouraging me to speak, to dance, and to sing out loud.

To
everything
there is a season,
and a time
to every purpose
under the heaven;
A time to
keep silence,
and a...

time to speak.

Ecclesiastes 3: 1 & 7

Because I Love You:
The Silent Shadow of Child Sexual Abuse.

Publisher: Virginia Foundation for the Humanities Press

Printed in the United States of America.

First American Edition

Published in 2002 by the
Virginia Foundation for the Humanities Press, Charlottesville, VA

Designed by Angela Daniel SilverStar, SilverStar Graphics

Front Cover Photo from Family Photo Album

Color Illustrations by Trisha Orr

This book is printed on recycled acid free paper.

Set in Goudy font.

Library of Congress Cataloging-in-Publication Data
ISBN 0-9668919-4-5

Child Development Resource Center

P.O. Box 4222, Charlottesville, Virginia 22905 • Phone: 434-823-5673 • E-mail: speak@cville.net

Dedicated

to my mother,

Marjorie Forehand Walls,

and all those who offer protection

and unconditional love to children;

to my brother,

Gary Richard Culbertson,

and all those who live and die

with their stories untold.

Mom, Gary and Me

Contents

Silent Valley

*"There is only one child in the world
and the child's name is All Children."*

– Carl Sandburg

Author's Note

This book is based on the life of my father. It is a true story of child sexual abuse which spans five generations. My father was a pedophile. He molested me throughout my childhood. Years later, he abused my children. He sexually violated dozens of other children throughout his life. Some friends and relatives knew of his behaviors, and others did not. Of all the many people who knew that my father was a sex offender, no one spoke out to protect other children from his assaults.

It has taken me seven years to research and write this book. His surviving hospital records, letters from and to him, and more than one hundred and fifty interviews form the basis of this story.

My father asked us children to remain silent because he loved us. As a family, we remained silent because we loved him. Friends kept the silence because they loved our family. We all believed that not speaking about "it" was the best thing to do, the loving thing to do. However, these silences about his offenses allowed my father's sexual assaults on children to continue for almost forty years.

Because I love my own children and my family, as well as children who are not my own, because I also love my father, today I no longer keep silent. I have written this book to encourage child sexual abuse survivors and their families and friends to join me in speaking out.

It is time to break silence about the perpetrators we know and, equally important, to tell what happened when we began to talk with each other. It is time to speak.

Daddy's Family

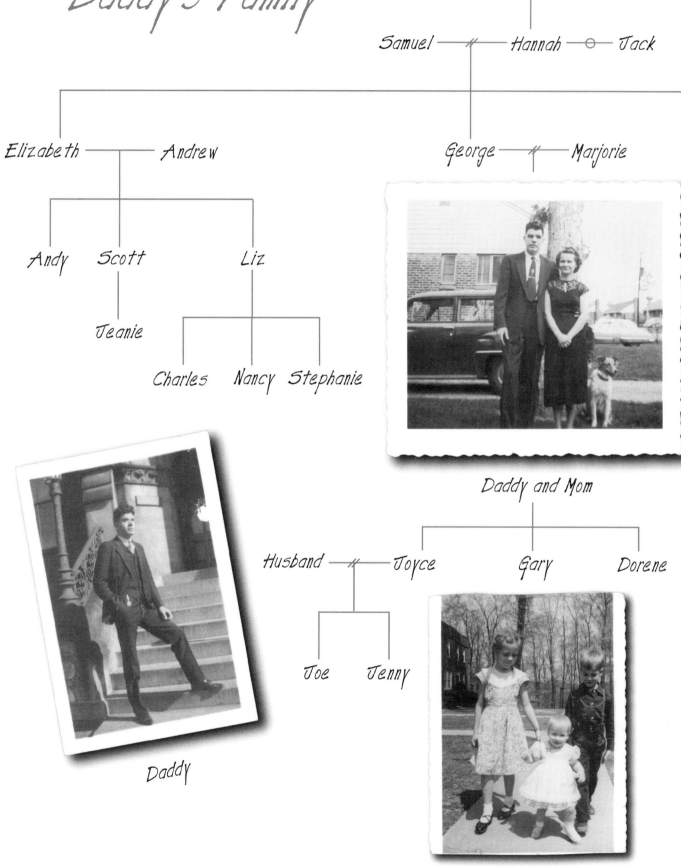

Samuel —||— Hannah —o— Jack

Elizabeth ——— Andrew

George —||— Marjorie

Andy   Scott   Liz

Jeanie

Charles   Nancy   Stephanie

Daddy and Mom

Daddy

Husband —||— Joyce   Gary   Dorene

Joe   Jenny

Daddy's Children

Maude —— Ralph

Hilda ——┬—— Husband

Brad ——┬—— Wife

Five Children

Eleanor ——┬—— Stuart

Wendy

Karen ——//—— William

Brian

Bruce

Paul ——//—— Wife

Josh   Jeremy

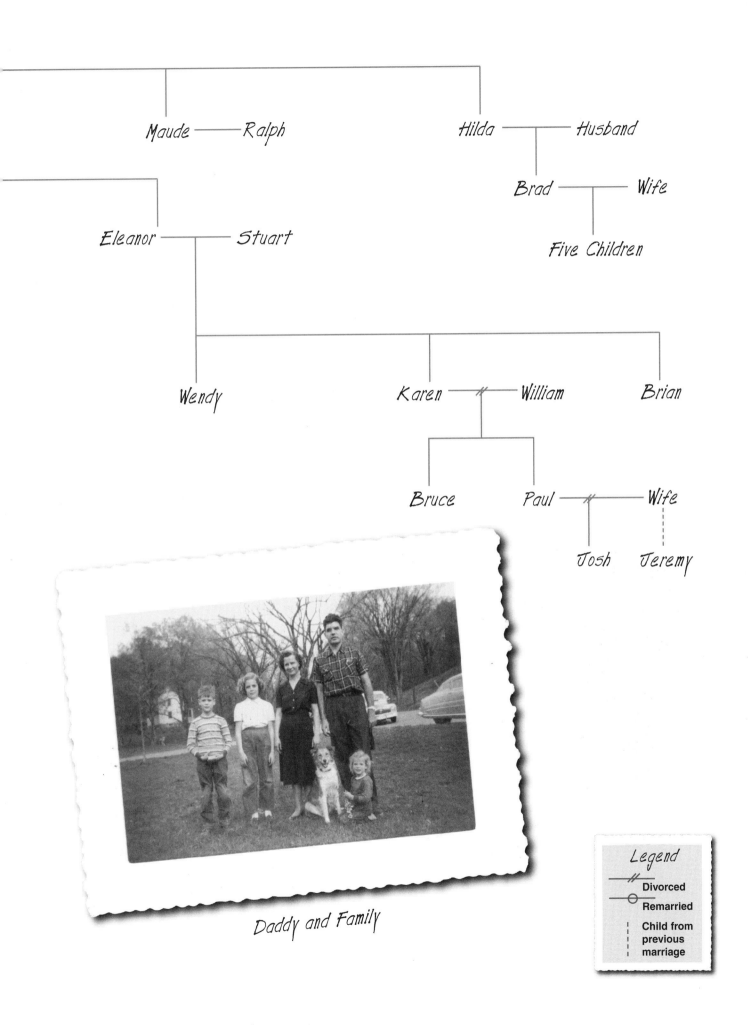

Daddy and Family

Mom and Joe

Foreword

By Dr. Roberta Culbertson

Those who hurt are often also those who loved, and whom one loved.

Some years ago, as part of my professional responsibilities at the Institute on Violence, Culture, and Survival of the Virginia Foundation for the Humanities, I heard Joyce Allan speak at a meeting of survivors of child sexual abuse. She presented the most cogent description of traumatic memory I had ever heard, and in accessible words. She was powerful, calm, and clear about the effects of abuse. She was neither strident nor harsh; she understood that abuse, particularly by family members, is complicated. Those who hurt are often also those who love, and whom one loves.

I was totally intimidated by both the manner and content of Joyce's presentation. Here was a woman highly articulate about things most people did not dare breathe. She spoke confidently and rationally about abuse as the therapist she was, and then said that she was a victim as well. No excuses, no apologies, not even rage or distress: just the fact, and its effects.

I was immersed in the study of the causes and effects of violence, but from a relatively distant, academic perspective. As I listened, I began to believe that Joyce's approach might be better. It might be the only way in which survivors, normally disempowered by events and then by social secrecy surrounding abuse, could be heard by those who need to know. Joyce's balanced language, I saw, allowed thinking about solutions instead of agonizing about what had happened. I was not yet able to talk about what I knew in these same ways, and was afraid to ask Joyce how she did it. She seemed light years ahead of me.

Joyce remains light years ahead of many of us. In this book, she describes her role in a system of abuse five generations deep, extending before and after her. She does not mince words, nor linger over them. She presents a clear, solidly documented story of her own abuse and the silence that surrounded it. Over many years, Joyce made many difficult trips; she visited nearly every living relative, friend, descendant, and colleague of her father, and reviewed his credentials, records, and school yearbooks. She returned to her father's home at his death, and to every other place he had lived. Most painfully, she retraced her own years of alcoholism and depression as she suffered the effects of a secret she did not yet know – a series of symptoms she could not define. She traced the abuse of her own children and their cousins and friends at her father's hands.

Through it all, she remains firm and sturdy about the dangers and terrible consequences of child violation, but somehow she is without rancor. She does not attack or blame those who – like most of us, I am afraid – said nothing, or very little, about the sexual abuses of which they had knowledge. Instead, Joyce wants to understand these silences. She wants to understand how the needs of children always seemed to take second place to her father's needs, and to her father's reputation. Until the evidence was overwhelming, people decided in favor of him; his decency, loneliness, sadness, competence, and even good looks seemed to weigh more in people's decisions than the possible sufferings of children.

Joyce also wants to understand how the violence of abuse is passed down by the children's own suffering. Sometimes, unable to bear the role of victim any longer, children assume that they are themselves to blame, or they normalize what is done to them and become abusers themselves. We learn what we are taught. Joyce traces this as not only a theory, but as an intergenerational fact; from uncle to father to child to nephew to cousin to child.

Suddenly it is very hard to find where to fix blame in Joyce's family. On her father, who was himself abused? On Joyce, who could not comprehend that her own father would abuse her children? On the dozens of friends, coworkers, and family who said nothing? Haven't we all sometimes turned our heads when child abuse is rumored? Haven't we put family stability and a person's stellar reputation over the murmurings of children?

Suddenly it is very hard to find where to fix blame.

But there are heroes in Joyce's story; in particular, her mother, who made the difficult decision to divorce her husband and demand treatment for him in a time when neither was done. And Joyce herself, who has the courage to name her affliction and her mistakes, and to call us all to more accountability for what goes on around us.

Nevertheless, there is one major source of blame in Joyce's story, in which nearly all of us participate. We live within a social structure and cultural values that put family loyalty over the protection of children, secrecy over openness, adults' needs over children's. We live in a culture that sexualizes children and then wonders at people who use them as sexual objects. We live in a culture of isolation and denial that allows one to do what one wants in the privacy of one's own home. We do not want to presume.

Joyce asks us to understand, and to begin, with her, to speak.

We have no decent mechanisms to help those who hurt children. We can only imprison or ignore them. When the cost of helping Joyce's father was his incarceration as a criminal, many people felt the punishment did not fit the crime – and perhaps they were right. Can we simply keep imprisoning our fathers, mothers, brothers, and sisters for something that they perhaps learned at someone else's hands? Does this solution even work? Joyce's story suggests that it does not, or may, but at a cost that is perhaps too great. Is there any other way?

Because I Love You suggests there is another way: the way of social responsibility, education, and alternative forms of treatment. We must be able to see and understand, at all levels of our culture, that just as children should not be forced to work as child laborers, they should not be forced to be sexual partners – the consequences for them and for society are too high. We must be able to find ways to take responsibility for listening to children and confronting abusers.

We must all speak what we know. If this makes us targets of questioning, we must learn how to explain ourselves without feeling morally and personally sullied by someone else's concern that our behavior is not appropriate.

Joyce Allan is a psychiatric clinical nurse specialist and therapist with thirty-five years of experience working in areas related to sexual abuse. She is a regional activist on issues pertaining to child development, sexual victimization, and treatment of trauma. For two years, she pursued her work under an endowed fellowship at the Institute on Violence, Culture, and Survival.

Joyce relates this tale of her family with great feeling and passion, but also with a clinician's trained eye. She tells us about our culture, about what is happening to our children. She asks us to look and help, but not only by blaming and punishing. She asks us to understand, and to begin, with her, to speak.

Preface

Gary and Me

My father was a pedophile. He sexually abused me regularly from the time I was three, often following bedtime prayers and tuck-ins. He also abused my younger brother and sister, who shared my bedroom. He abused my playmates.

When I was ten, my father's incest activities were discovered and he was taken to a psychiatric hospital. After his release, he moved back to his boyhood home in the Rocky Mountains, and lived the remaining twenty-seven years of his life among his large extended family and their wide circle of friends. He molested dozens of other children – relatives, neighbors, and strangers – during this period. When my own children spent summers with their grandfather, he molested them as well. He spent time in jail and on parole, and learned to use periods of psychiatric care to protect himself from prosecution. Finally, with charges of child abuse pending yet again, my father at age sixty-nine committed suicide.

Some of Daddy's friends and family members knew of his history as an abuser; others did not. None of them spoke about it.

I came to understand in both my mind and in my body that my father's sexual abuse of me had been tremendously damaging throughout my entire life. I began to identify, feel, express and release feelings of terror, disgust, shame and rage.

In August of 1994, I made my first healing pilgrimage to Colorado to explore my father's life and origins. In the course of the next seven years, I traveled to Colorado five times. I drove to dozens of places in Virginia and Maryland. I received numerous letters, e-mails and phone calls. In all, I interviewed over one hundred and fifty relatives, childhood friends, neighbors, co-workers, and mental health and legal professionals who knew my father.

In addition, I had the sad opportunity to identify over two dozen of my father's victims, and to interview many of these adults whom he had molested as children. One interviewee asked me, "What did your father say to you when he was molesting you?"

"What did your father say to you when he was molesting you?"

I answered, "He said, 'I'm doing this because I love you.'"

As I researched my life and my father's, I came to accept that a book was being born. The book needed to include all the manifestations of love, friendship and loyalty I had discovered. It also needed to explore the shadow side of love – fear, shame, guilt and grief.

For my own healing, the journey required me to learn how I could have been so confused about love that I sent my children, for six summers, to be with the father who had molested me for so many years.

For my family, I hope that an open dialogue and sharing of memories and feelings will mend and strengthen our trust and love.

I answered, "He said, 'I'm doing this because I love you.'"

As a psychiatric nurse and therapist, I hope that for my clients and colleagues this personal, more intricate view of the world of childhood sexual abuse may enhance their understanding of and commitment to effective treatment.

I also envision writing about the family and community of those who loved, respected, cared for, and even suffered at the hands of my father. I want to stimulate a dialogue among survivors, and clinicians, as well as within families and communities all across our country who love and care about victims and perpetrators.

Every incest perpetrator, every pedophile, is someone's child, sibling, spouse, parent, friend or neighbor.

In my fifties, I interviewed relatives and friends to gather information for this book. With much initial resistance, I began to recognize unexpected and conflicted feelings toward my father – feelings of tenderness, respect and compassion.

I also saw that just as his predatory invasions of other children's bodies had damaged his victims' souls, they had damaged his own soul as well. My father has emerged in this search as a remarkably complex, unhappy and lonely man.

I began talking with my family about how I would explore these issues. Because my stepson, Daniel, easily creates strong visual images, I asked him to help describe my story in pictures.

"Your book is a story about shadows," he says. Closing his eyes for a few moments to allow the images to appear, he elaborates. "Everyone has a shadow," he says. "Some people are afraid of their shadows, but mostly people see the shadow; they know it's there.

He continues, "The shadow is dark and silent. It follows you wherever you go, but it won't hurt you. It's like a storage place to put things people don't want to talk about. We can look at our shadows and talk about them anytime. We can choose to bring things out of the shadow. But some people just don't."

Daniel pauses to consider. "People are used to having their shadow. We don't pay attention to it. We only see what we want to see. We have our image that we show to other people. Usually we don't show them our shadow. The shadow is flat, dark, without emotion. It's just there."

He closes his eyes again. "For you and your book, I see you coming out of a dark cave. There is a fire burning in the cave behind you and it casts a long, dark shadow in front of you as you go out into the light." Daniel opens his eyes and looks at me with an expression I have seen in my own mirror. He says, "You might be walking toward an abyss, or to a mountain peak. But you're facing your shadow as you walk."

My intention, with this book, is to face the shadow, to initiate a much wider cultural conversation about pedophilia and child sexual abuse.

The story of my father, our family, and his friends and community is a mirror of the larger problem our culture faces in accepting and responding to the realities of incest and pedophilia.

I am certain it is only through this active speaking that we will finally dissipate the social silence nearly all of us maintain as a way to keep from thinking about incest. I hope that by telling my father's story, the story of silence within our family and within his social and work communities, I can discover and reveal patterns that all of us can avoid. I believe our active speaking of what we know about perpetrators will keep children safe from violation and the often life-long effects of sexual abuse.

It is our own silence that is betraying our children.

It is our own silence that is betraying our children.

Me and My Shadow

Introduction

My mother discovered Daddy abusing me when I was ten, which led to their immediate separation and later divorce. I seldom saw him during the last three decades of his life. However, his compulsive behavior took a severe psychological and physical toll on my adult life and the lives of my siblings, my children, and many others.

As I discovered through my research into my father's life, silence was the medium that allowed him to molest dozens of children.

The ultimate focus of this book is not on just these victims and survivors, not on just the perpetrator, but also on the rest of us. This is a book about the rules and beliefs that govern our silence. It is about our own participation in child sexual abuse.

A poignant source of information about my father, George Culbertson, is his own words. In October of 2000, I was able to locate and obtain permission to view the microfilm records from my father's months as a psychiatric inpatient, committed to the Spring Grove Hospital (SGH) in Catonsville, Maryland.

He was admitted to the hospital in October of 1955 for "sexual perversion." Throughout parts of this book, quotes attributed to my father come directly from this medical record. Remarkably, my father confirms and sometimes expands on the story that I discovered in my interviews as I undertook my healing pilgrimage into his life's history.

To respect the privacy of the many people who, through their interviews and memories, have contributed to this book, I have changed the names of everyone except the members of my immediate family. I have also changed the location of most residences and events in Colorado.

This story has not been easy to write. Parts of it may not be easy to read. Pay attention to the part of you that wants to turn away from the problems raised by this book, the part that doesn't want to connect them with your own life, or with the lives of people you know so well.

This story has not been easy to write.

Take care of yourself, and pace your reading. This book is designed to be read either as a whole, or in separate pieces, and to be meditated over in the heart. If this book raises difficult or confusing thoughts for you, talk with someone you trust.

Parts of it may not be easy to read.

People, places and dates tell the story of my father's childhood and early adult life. Through interviews, anecdotes, school yearbooks, photographs and personal letters, we begin to know the boy and later the man who was described as well liked, respected, hard working, and friendly.

But these bits and pieces also pose a mystery. How does any person become a child molester? What historical factors contribute to the occurrence of incest in a family? How do relatives, friends and neighbors see the abuser in their daily contacts with him? How can they keep silent about what they know? How is it possible that a documented "good" person can cause so much pain to his own family and others?

I invite you to join me as I assemble the pieces of what is known and explore the mystery of what is unknown – about incest, about pedophilia, about my Daddy.

Silent Valley

Daddy

Chapter One

Return to Silent Valley

(November, 1985)

You've got to walk this lonesome valley.
You've got to walk it by yourself.

– Traditional song

We've all been down this road before – so many times – in the back of the truck, on the motorcycle, on horseback, even sitting on a sled Daddy made out of the rusted hood of a car and that he pulled behind his truck with a chain. Two generations of children have spent our summer vacations here at Silent Valley. My brother, Gary, and I, with our sister Dorene, spent six summers here more than twenty-five years ago. My son, Joe, and my daughter, Jenny, have come here each summer for the past six years. This curving, rutted dirt road is where we all learned to steer, clutch, shift gears, and step on the brake. We sat up tall behind the steering wheel of the rusted and dented green Ford pick-up with Daddy on the right, insisting that he had learned to drive when he was a kid, and we could do it, too.

Today, in mid-November, 1985, Gary, Joe, Jenny and I drive up in our shiny rented green Toyota sedan with an automatic transmission, stop our car in front of Daddy's weathered house trailer and get out. Up behind the trailer, I see the tall rocks where I used to climb as a teenager to sit alone, looking out over Silent Valley, wondering and not understanding.

Pointing to a large iron lock that has been fastened to the door of the trailer, I say, "This must be where they found his body."

Daddy's Trailer at Silent Valley

Three days before, Monday afternoon, the phone had rung at the home I shared with my two children in Washington, D.C., interrupting my determination to spend the afternoon dealing with a basket of clothes needing ironing. Joe and Jenny were home after school and we were discussing Christmas plans. Jenny, twelve years old, was sitting on the kitchen counter as the phone rang. She picked it up and said, "It's for you, Mom."

I was at the sink trying to clean the corroded steam iron. Handing the iron to Joe, a lanky sixteen-year-old, who was leaning against the stove, I took the call. My father's older sister, Elizabeth, spoke gently across two thousand miles. "I'm sorry to have to tell you this," she said, "but they say your father committed suicide. He shot himself with a gun."

She was called by the sheriff with news that Daddy had been found dead in his trailer. Now she wonders if I and my brother and sister want to come to Colorado to go through his belongings?

Though this unexpected news should be startling, I experience no emotion. I tell her we will take care of whatever needs to be done.

As I hang up the phone, there are no tears. "Grampy killed himself," I tell my children. "I need to go to Colorado."

Joe and Jenny have known their grandfather since they were babies when he would come from Colorado to visit us. They have sent him drawings and letters, birthday and Father's Day cards. When they were little, I once took them to Colorado to visit their Grampy. Other times, he came east in his truck or on his motorcycle to visit us. And for the six summers previous to this year, Joe and Jenny traveled, on their own, to spend summers with him at Silent Valley. They want to go with me now to be part of this final journey.

I move naturally and efficiently into my familiar "taking care of business" mode. I call the hospital where I work, to say I will be away, start the laundry so there will be clean clothes for the trip, begin to boil water for macaroni and cheese for dinner, and drink a cup of coffee.

As soon as these tasks are done, I call Gary, my brother, who is just a year-and-a-half younger and is my favorite and closest family member. I tell him the news, and ask if he will come to Washington and fly to Colorado with me. Gary is a Vietnam era veteran who used his GI education benefit to learn welding. He now lives near the ocean in North Carolina with his wife Laura, and works as a welder for a small boat building yard in the backwaters of Wanchese, North

Carolina. He agrees to come to D.C. tomorrow by bus, and says, "I guess it's all over now, isn't it?" Our conversation has the familiar flat emptiness of all conversations that mention our father. No emotion, no adjectives, no expletives. Just the facts.

Our sister, Dorene, who is now thirty-four, five years younger than Gary, lives with her new husband, Rick, in Ohio. They do not yet have a telephone so I call the local police department to ask for help. A police officer leaves a note on her door to call the police department. When Dorene calls, the officer tells her, "We have a message for you. Your father is dead."

Dorene immediately calls me and, when she hears the news of Daddy's suicide, declines the invitation to go to Colorado with us. Her quick response is, "He left the family when I was just four. Except for our summer visits, I don't even know him. He's not part of my life." She says she will get a phone installed tomorrow and call me with her new number.

As I put down the phone, I find myself wondering how Dorene's life has been affected by Daddy's absence and by the fact that she never knew why he was absent. I wonder about Dorene saying she has no childhood memories of her first four years when Daddy did live with us. Reluctantly, I accept her decision not to participate in the trip.

Then I call my mother to tell her the news. She divorced my father almost thirty years ago, but I know she will want to know about his death. Mom lives just twenty minutes away from us, in suburban Maryland, but she is out of town this week, visiting her sister. I wish I could tell her in person and see her face.

Because my mother is deaf, I must call her on an electronic teletype machine. I connect my telephone to the "teletype device for the deaf," the TDD, and dial the number at Mom's sister's home. When my aunt answers, I ask her to have my mother connect the phone to the portable TDD Mom has taken with her on her trip. When our two phone receivers are connected through this electronic system, I begin to type. My message will print out digitally on Mom's small screen.

I type, "Daddy's sister Elizabeth called to tell us that he committed suicide. Gary is coming, and he and I and Joe and Jenny will fly to Colorado on Wednesday to take care of the belongings."

"He must have been terribly lonely," I read on my screen as she responds. "I'm sorry you all have to go through this. I love you. Have a safe trip." I wish we could hug each other.

Then I call Freeman, a kind and gentle man I have known just two weeks, but who already seems important in my life. He comes immediately from his apartment, which is only ten minutes away. Now, late at night, dishes done, plane reservations made, clothes packed and children asleep, I seek comfort in his embrace. Finally, in

Our conversation has the familiar flat emptiness of all conversations that mention our father.

25

his arms, I cry. Freeman stays and holds me through the night.

On Tuesday morning, waiting at home for Gary to arrive, I get another phone call from Colorado. I am alone in the kitchen this time. Joe and Jenny have gone to school for the day. Just coming from the shower, I am wearing my green terry cloth robe; water drips from my hair onto my cheeks. A woman speaks carefully.

"You don't know me," she says, "but I heard that your father died. Some people here are starting ugly rumors, saying that he killed himself because he was going to be charged with molesting a little child and he might have had to go to jail. I just want to tell you that I know he was a good man and that it's not true what they're saying."

Not true. How I wish it could be not true, I think to myself. I search the walls, the counters, the tiny piece of sky visible above the curtain over the window for guidance, for the right thing to say. All I see is a list of tasks to do before our trip: stop paper, stop mail, get Mom to tell Daddy's friends about his death, give milk and other perishables to a neighbor.

"My father molested me all through my childhood," I tell her. "He molested other children, too."

My response comes from an unexpected deep place of knowing. "My father molested me all through my childhood," I tell her. "He molested other children, too. I'm sure what the people are telling you is true. He did molest that child."

There is a heavy, empty silence. The woman hangs up. I never receive any other calls or letters about the child and the accusations. I wish I knew the child and could say that I'm sorry about what my father did, and that his suicide is not her fault.

After this phone call, I am flooded with waves of nausea. My eyes will not focus and I cannot will myself to continue my tasks. The kitchen adjoins my bedroom and I take the few steps necessary to go and lie down on my bed. When I close my eyes I see a circle, like a woven wreath, of limp penises. These are not the kinds of feelings and images a daughter should have when her father dies, I tell myself.

I cannot stay alone very long with these sensations. Opening my eyes, I search the room to reassure myself that I am in my safe adult life. I can see my double bed, with its flowered quilt; the worn but sturdy oak dresser with my collection of hair barrettes on top; my diary and pen carefully placed on the shelf next to the bed. I get dressed, walk back to the kitchen, and focus on my list of tasks.

Gary arrives that afternoon and we go for a walk along the sidewalks of my busy urban neighborhood. He listens quietly as always. As people on bicycles and in cars rush past us, I tell my brother, "I'm glad Daddy is dead. He hurt too many people, especially too many children." I tell Gary how I've been wondering for years what would happen when Daddy got old – if either of us would have been willing to take care of him. I tell Gary I'm glad we don't have to deal with that. I say, "It feels like killing himself is the first responsible thing he's done for us."

Gary meets my gaze with soft directness, but he makes no comment. His dark, sad eyes say all he is able to say.

On Wednesday morning, Gary, Joe, Jenny and I are up early to go to the airport. Freeman comes by briefly to tell me good-bye. He shakes Gary's hand and says he looks forward to getting to know him better when we return. I can tell they will like each other and I am pleased.

We drive to the airport and leave the car in the long-term parking lot. Numbness and exhaustion are settling in, and the flight to Colorado is a blur. When our plane lands in Colorado Springs, I realize I have never been to this familiar place in winter before. There is snow on the ground and the mountains are frosted. This is not a summer vacation.

My father was born and raised in Colorado. He was the middle child and had two sisters. His older sister, Elizabeth, and his younger sister, Eleanor, have lived here most of their lives. During our childhood summer visits, we would spend time with these aunts and with their children, our cousins. I have always appreciated the playfulness and affection of this wonderful part of my extended family.

A tearful and distressed Eleanor meets us at the airport and takes us to her home for the night. Tall and slender, her brown hair now graying, Eleanor has always been the worrier in the family. She says she didn't know her brother was so depressed, thinks his arthritis was getting worse, thinks she should have visited him more often, was planning to invite him for Thanksgiving next week.

After sleeping fitfully at Eleanor's, Gary, Joe, Jenny and I go over to Elizabeth's home for breakfast. Elizabeth and her husband, Andrew, give us hugs and agree with Eleanor that Daddy's arthritis must have been the reason for his suicide. "He loved being active outdoors and had been increasingly in pain with his swollen ankles. He must have felt there was no reason to go on, and he wouldn't have wanted to be dependent on anyone else." I don't tell them about the anonymous phone call. There's no need to add to their pain, and I am used to keeping secrets.

Andrew insists on taking a picture of Gary, Joe, Jenny and me together before we go. Elizabeth and Andrew have albums full of family photos, dated and labeled, and they haven't seen us in such a long time. We pose together, four tired, long-haired relatives, dressed in jeans and flannel shirts, attempting our best obedient smiles. I wish Dorene were with us so she could be in the picture, too.

Elizabeth gives us a pot of homemade soup and a loaf of bread. "Don't forget," she says, "your Daddy and Grampy loved you." With a round of tears and hugs we are on our way back to Silent Valley.

Twenty-five years ago, Daddy bought and named forty acres of beautiful land near the

It feels like killing himself is the first responsible thing he's done for us.

Jenny, Me, Joe and Gary

Rocky Mountain National Forest. He christened it Silent Valley because he was deaf and could not hear its sounds. As we make the trip from Elizabeth and Eleanor's town to Daddy's home, we also make the trip to Daddy's world of secrets and silences. The series of wooden arrows, with the words "Silent Valley" or "SILVA" hand-painted in red with white lettering, guide us ever higher up the rutted dirt roads, which have never seemed so ugly before.

Finally the road begins its descent into the familiar grove of aspens and the valley opens up before us. Ahead on the right is the small pond created in the middle of a stream by a beaver dam. As I slow the car, we see Daddy's weathered red and white aluminum house trailer, with its wood-framed addition, and the tall rocks that loom behind it.

Gary studies the lock on the trailer door. Daddy didn't believe in locks. The sheriff must have put it on after they came to get his body. Gary tries a hammer, then a screwdriver, and Joe and Jenny attempt to open windows they could crawl through. Silently, Gary walks over to the tool shed and conducts a search. He runs a long extension cord from the tool shed to the trailer, connects it to Daddy's electric welding torch and kneels in front of the lock. Slowly and carefully, he softens the iron clasp until, finally, the lock splits and the trailer door swings open.

Pleased with his success, Gary looks up at me and says, "I think this time Daddy finally would have been proud of me." He smiles hopefully.

The trailer is cold and lonely and lifeless. Across the room from the door is Daddy's bed. Blood is spattered on the sheets, the pillow and the wall. We cannot not look at it. The image of him lying there, face up, with his pistol inside his mouth, will not go away. I notice my fear and horror, but I also feel a strange relief that his death has become tangibly real.

He has left everything in order. Daddy used to say to us, "a place for everything and everything in its place." The dishes are done, the trash is emptied, and the magazines are in a neat pile. The note he left in his newspaper box four days before is on the kitchen table. "When you find this note, I will be dead by my own hand. Please notify the authorities – and cancel my subscription to the paper."

Ever careful with details.

Neatly placed on the table are the keys to his truck and the signed title. "This is all I own," the note says. "Try to sell it to pay for expenses." Another paper left for us is his good-bye note: "I love you all so very much and I'm truly sorry I feel that what I'm about to do is necessary and best. Please don't regret – just forgive." No explanations to his three children.

It is time for us to start settling the final affairs of this man, my father, who – as I am still to learn – has abused and wounded so many.

Joe and Jenny gather photo albums, papers, books, knickknacks and other items from the large room. Gary clears out the bathroom, dresser and closet. I empty kitchen cabinets and drawers. In a few hours, we collect all of Daddy's household possessions into a dozen cardboard boxes. There are no hidden secrets or surprises, no revealing diaries or collections, nothing to help us know or understand the inner world and mysteries of this complicated man. The only visible signs of emotions or relationships are the numerous photos of his children and grandchildren, and a few pictures of his beloved Colorado that have been cut out of magazines.

Going outside alone, I walk across the dam of the beaver pond to the cottage where we will spend the night. The owners use this place only in the summer and my aunts have obtained permission for us to stay here. I find the key outside as they had explained, go inside and turn on the electric heat, unpack our suitcases, make up the beds, and warm the soup Elizabeth made for us.

Gary, Joe and Jenny stay behind and begin work on sorting through Daddy's tool shed and then, as the sky turns dark, they join me in the cottage. Joe and Jenny take their soup to the living room and the comfortable ritual of Thursday night television with Bill Cosby.

Gary and I sit at the small kitchen table – tired, confused, and characteristically quiet. We plan to get up in the morning and go to the coroner's office to get Daddy's ashes. He had always said he wanted to be cremated and to have his ashes scattered here at Silent Valley. Tonight there seems to be nothing left to say, nothing that can be put into words. I'm grateful that Gary is here with me and I treasure the safe comfort of his presence.

"I guess it's times like this – just sitting quietly with someone – that you miss the most when they're gone," I murmur.

"Yeah, guess so." He seems tired and far away. "Think I'll go on to sleep," he sighs.

After he leaves, I join the children in front of the television: news, sports, weather, the usual. How remarkably unaffected the world is by our tragedy. How remarkably unaffected we seem, too. We floss and brush and hug good night. Tonight, though, I don't say "sweet dreams."

I am used to keeping secrets.

Inevitably the morning comes. I start the coffee in the tin percolator, see that Joe and Jenny are already dressed and are eating their cereal, and go to the nearby bedroom to get Gary.

"Wake up, Gary." I call from the doorway. No answer. I walk closer and shake his shoulder. "Wake up, Gary." And then, screaming, "Wake up, Gary! Wake up!" But my brother doesn't move. After that the blur, the numbness, the excruciating pain, the scream: "No! Gary, No!"

I lay my head on Gary's motionless chest. There is no heartbeat. His eyes are closed. His hands are cold. Joe and Jenny have heard my screams and are standing behind me. I look into their eyes and say it out loud, "Gary's dead." I wrap my arms around my lifeless brother. My children hold me as I sob.

Gary, you can't leave me. You're the only one who's been with me the whole time – the only one who knows the whole story. Don't leave me alone here in this remote and lonely place. I should be helping the children. They shouldn't have to be taking care of me.

"Oh, please, Gary, No!"

Raising my head, as a driver might lift her head from the steering wheel after realizing she has survived a car crash, I turn and embrace my children. It feels like we are the only three survivors of this three-generation nightmare. We must notify people, we must find out what to do about Gary's body, we must finish packing up Grampy's things, we must get out of Silent Valley and go home.

It is so hard to believe that Gary is gone. He was only thirty-nine years old. We have come here to bury Grampy, not Gary. I phone 911: "My brother is dead."

The sheriff knows where Silent Valley is: he was here five days ago to get my father's body. He will call the coroner.

Next, I speak with my aunts, Elizabeth and Eleanor, who cry and say they will send my cousins to help.

I call my sister Dorene and say, "Is Rick with you?" I am glad that she has a husband to comfort her.

"What happened?" she asks, knowing something is wrong. "Are your children okay?"

"Gary is dead," I tell her.

"Oh, my God," she screams. "No. We can't lose Gary. I don't believe it!" We cry together. She wants to fly out to help, but I assure her we will be out of here by tomorrow and I will see her at Gary's funeral.

I call my old friend, Pat, and my new friend, Freeman. I call Joe and Jenny's father, John, so he can talk to his children. Then, with a renewed sense of heartbreak, I ask John to go to my mother's house to break this news to her in person. I can't use teletype to tell her that her son has died.

How can I break this news to Gary's wife, Laura, in North Carolina? Just a few years ago, she and Gary had their first and only baby, a daughter, who died when she was only three months old. Laura and Gary had held each other and cried together at their baby's funeral.

I don't want Laura to be alone when she gets this heart-breaking news, so I call Gary's best friend Dennis. He is grief-stricken, but agrees that he will go at once to inform her in the gentlest way possible, as well as alerting their community to prepare for Gary's funeral. I am grateful Dennis and Gary's many friends can help Laura, while I try to support the rest of the family in our loss.

Stunned and shaken, I complete all these phone calls and go outside to look for Joe and Jenny. I see them across the valley by the tool shed. On their own, they are sorting, organizing and boxing all Grampy's tools, nails, ropes, camping gear – everything. He had trained his grandchildren well during their summer visits.

The children rejoin me in the cottage when the sheriff arrives. He tries to be sympathetic as he writes down the facts about Gary – name, age, address, medical conditions. He examines the body and looks through the cottage before he leaves.

The coroner drives up next to pick up Gary's body. He thinks it was probably a heart attack, but there will have to be an autopsy. The body will be shipped home to North Carolina where his wife is waiting; she will arrange the funeral. I sign the papers.

"Oh, by the way," the coroner says, "I thought I'd save you a trip into town. Here are your father's ashes."

He hands me a small round tin can, and leaves, heading back out of the mountains with Gary's body. The can holding my father's ashes feels so light. There is almost nothing left. What is there to do now but finish? Gary is gone. Joe and Jenny and I will scatter the ashes, pack up Daddy's things and go home. Again, I wish my sister were here with me.

Now it is time. I had asked Gary yesterday and he agreed. Before we scatter Daddy's ashes I want to tell Joe and Jenny about the incest, so I can break the silence about my father and bury that memory along with the others in this ritual of release. Maybe it's too much now, after Gary's death. But everything is too much now.

Sitting on a soft and comforting sofa, looking out through one of the cottage's large windows, we can see Silent Valley, the pond and beaver dam, Daddy's little house trailer, the weathered tool shed, the distant "sitting rocks." Joe and Jenny's faces look frozen. I remember we have missed lunch. We are confused, stunned, tired. Is there ever a right time to talk about incest?

"Grampy molested me when I was a child," I tell them. "I think you are old enough now to know, and I need to include this part of my childhood in my 'Good-bye' to him. I'm sorry to have to add this to all the other sadness. Do you have any questions you want to ask me?"

Am I devoid of feeling or overwhelmed with feeling? The words ease flatly and

Is there ever a right time to talk about incest?

calmly into spoken reality.

Joe and Jenny – their eyes meeting mine directly and then, again, gazing out over Silent Valley – answer my revelation with silence. I am too tired and too broken by events to pursue the conversation further.

We take the can of Daddy's ashes to the top of the hill behind the trailer. Starting at the base of the sitting rocks, we take turns scooping out handfuls of ashes, twirling ourselves around to release them in a circle, and naming something we remember about him – about my father, their grandfather.

"Chocolate ice cream. Hand-made toys. Motorcycle rides. Incest. Reader's Digest jokes."

We are twirling down the hill, feeling lighter, even beginning to laugh.

"Generic brand canned food. Cowboy hats."

Joe takes the last few ashes and places them gently in the stream that runs through the valley.

The sky is turning gray with just a few strokes of pink and gold in the sunset. A light snow has begun to fall. We three walk back across Silent Valley together, somehow feeling safely on the other side of this horror.

I begin to sing: "Amazing grace, how sweet the sound, that saved a soul like me."

"I once was deaf, but now I hear; was blind, but now I see," Joe improvises.

We hadn't expected to spend this second night here. There is a little of Elizabeth's soup left and plenty of fruit, crackers, and snacks. I am grateful to have the use of this warm and soothing cabin. Soon we are ready to sleep and ready for this day to end.

The next morning Aunt Eleanor sends my cousin Karen's family to help us move things out. She and her family live about an hour away. They have been close to their Uncle George and have visited him here many times. He frequently went to their home for holiday meals or to help with home repair jobs. Joe and Jenny know their cousins, Karen's children, from their summer visits here.

With strong arms, but heavy spirits, Karen's husband, William, and their two sons, Bruce and Paul, help us load Daddy's truck, their own truck and our rental car with boxes, tools and furniture.

As our caravan slowly gets under way, I try to comprehend the meaning of this moment.

I lost my childhood to Daddy's abuse.

I lost this land years ago when Daddy sold it in a foolish business deal.

Now, on this journey to bury Daddy, I have lost my only brother, Gary.

"Freedom's just another word for nothing left to lose," the radio sings. Joe and Jenny sit quietly looking out the windows as we drive out of Silent Valley.

Me and Joe

Chapter Two

The Journey Back

(1985-1994)

*"The silences and secrets of incest destroy
family relationships. Emotionally,
the child's whole family dies...."*

– Dr. Elisabeth Kubler-Ross

Just two days ago, my children and I drove up the back roads into Silent Valley with my brother, Gary, and encountered the bloody reality of Daddy's suicide. Just yesterday, we found Gary's lifeless body in his bed. Then we scattered Daddy's ashes in the dusk.

Driving away from Silent Valley should be a relief. Our rental car follows the pick-up truck full of Daddy's belongings to my cousins' home in Denver. As we enter the highway, I begin to recognize that we are re-entering the "real." The "normal" world. No one we encounter will know what we have experienced. We will be expected to fill up the gas tank, order and pay for lunch, smile and say, "Fine, thanks." On one level, these miniscule daily behaviors and interactions seem impossible. But a deeper part of me recognizes this duality as the familiar role-playing from my childhood.

Spreading Gary's Ashes

"What do you want for breakfast?"

I want to tell you what happened last night. "Cereal please."

"How are you feeling today?"

I'm tired. I can't sleep much, and when I do I have scary dreams. "Fine."

"What does your father do?"

He touches me and makes me touch him. "He's a mechanic."

This time, though, my relatives and friends know about what's troubling me – Daddy's and Gary's deaths. As the pick-up pulls into the driveway, we are helped and hugged by Daddy's loving and caring family. His niece, my cousin Karen, gives us beds for the children and me to spend the night. Karen, William, Bruce and Paul are quiet and gentle. They loved their Uncle George and cousin Gary, too.

Drained of hope and direction, I am grateful as Karen takes charge. She feeds us, gets the children involved in activities together, offers me a shower and a nap. I have no comfort to offer in return. After my nap, over cups of coffee, Karen reminds me that we must be at the airport early in the morning. "You'd better go look at the things you brought in the truck and decide what you want to do with them."

Most of what we brought out of Silent Valley seems to be furniture, small household items and Daddy's tools. I don't need or want these. Then, I realize and announce, "I don't want anything. Sell it or throw it away." Just let me be finished with all this. I want it to be over.

Karen agrees that she and Elizabeth and Eleanor will take care of George's belongings. George – my father, Karen's uncle, Elizabeth and Eleanor's brother – has left us just these few items – no explanation, no story. The only other legacy is our memories and our feelings. I don't want those – any more than I want his ragged assortment of belongings.

At the airport the next morning, the ticket agent gives me an address where I can send Gary's unused return ticket for a refund. He says that he's sorry my brother died and isn't returning home with us. Joe and Jenny and I have little we can say. It's as if we are in an old silent movie. We nap and read and stare out the window as the plane takes us home. Our drive back from the airport is equally silent.

The children's father, John, meets us at my house. In the ten years since our divorce, we have developed a friendly and dedicated parenting partnership. After welcoming hugs, and tears, he begins dinner preparations, does the laundry, watches television with the children. His familiar presence is a comfort for us all. I make plans for our

I think my brother died of a broken heart, of too many losses and too much sadness.

trip to North Carolina for Gary's funeral and receive consoling visits and casseroles from friends. From the phone in the kitchen, I call my work and the children's schools and tell them we will be away a few days longer – "another death in the family."

Then Mom walks up our front porch steps and I meet her at the door. After all she has been through, I wonder how she can bear it. I don't want to face her and make Gary's death real – "yes, I found him dead; yes, the coroner came; yes, his body has been sent home; yes, we will go together for his funeral." We hold each other and cry.

Joe

After a quiet and somber dinner, Mom leaves and we agree that she will return in the morning for our drive to North Carolina. John suggests that Joe and Jenny go with him and spend the night at his house so that I can have some time alone. I nod gratefully.

When the house is quiet, though, I realize that I want to see my new friend, Freeman. Once again, I call and ask him to come from his apartment. Once again he arrives, comforts my tears, and holds me close and safe through the night. I am so sorry that he will not get to know my brother. I am sure they would have been good friends.

Gary's simple funeral, a gathering of relatives and old friends, allows me finally to collapse into sadness and fatigue. Mom and Joe and Jenny are here. Dorene and Rick have flown from their home in Ohio. Mom's brother, Harold, and sister, Agnes and some of their children have come. Gary's wife, Laura, and many of their friends are here. In this safe and loving group, I share grief and stories, meals and quiet walks.

Laura and Gary lost their first baby, and now she has lost her husband. Too much loss. Too much sorrow. We all wonder at the meaning and purpose of this peaceful, gentle man's death. Mom thinks that maybe Gary realized his Daddy was gone, and he let go of trying to get his father's approval. Laura wonders if maybe he went on to be with Daddy to help him on the other side. I, myself, think my brother, Gary, died

Spreading Gary's Ashes

of a broken heart, of too many losses and too much sadness. With tender words and song, we tell him good-bye and release his ashes into the ocean.

After I return home, I burn my collection of Daddy's letters. For years I had saved every letter and card, a file drawer full of his endearments and stories about his adventures. I had guessed that someday I might read back through them and find some clues, some encoded explanation for what he had done. Now it is over – the struggle and the ambivalence – my efforts to understand and make sense of a father who could be so playful and attentive and devoted, yet at the same time inflict so much pain and damage on me and others. I feel free now from the need to explore my history and reconcile with my father. I feel healed from this past and free to move on into my future.

Daddy's and Gary's deaths gradually begin to enter and become part of life's ongoing rhythms, like woven threads of a tapestry I am continuing to weave. Thanksgiving, Christmas, New Year's Day 1986. Algebra exams, English essays, and field trips for Joe and Jenny; and, for me, practicing psychiatric nursing, shopping for groceries, attending committee meetings, sharing meals, making love and going on long walks with Freeman.

With tender words and song, we tell Gary good-bye and release his ashes into the ocean.

Why didn't you ever talk with me about the incest?

Why didn't you ask how I was feeling?

A caring friend asks, "How is all this tragedy and grief affecting your new romance?"

"I can't worry about it," I reply. "When this is over, either he will be there or he won't."

Being there, I begin to learn, is Freeman's natural style. Alongside threads of the two recent deaths, Freeman's presence and support are weaving strands of laughter and new vision into our lives. He and his two sons, Dan and Gabe, join us for meals, weekend movies and hikes. We find that all the children love Chinese food and pizza. We spend evenings together enjoying the same TV shows and board games. Dan, age eleven, displays his Lego structures and colorful drawings for our admiration, and Gabe, age four, shows his acrobatic tricks and developing reading skills. Joe and Jenny, as teenagers, are more guarded but are cautiously friendly and curious. They gradually welcome Freeman and the boys into our lives.

Freeman and I share our stories and our histories, our losses and our hopes. I tell him about my years of childhood incest, my years of therapy, my relief that Daddy is dead and it's finally over. With his shaggy, graying hair and beard, wearing casual blue jeans and sandals, Freeman's strongly held liberal politics and ideals are a welcome delight. He is an ardent and veteran feminist. He is angry and sad about my father's abuse of me and his theft of my childhood. He has other women friends who are survivors of incest and rape, and he is committed to working with men on changing this misuse of power and sexuality.

By late 1986, Freeman and I have been seeing each other for just over one year. December nineteenth is my forty-second birthday; Freeman cooks a family dinner, bakes a cake, and teases me because he is "only" forty-one. On Christmas, I meet his mother and father. On New Year's Day, he meets my Mom.

Jenny, Joe, Dan and Gabe

In February of 1987, near what would have been Daddy's seventy-first birthday, a box arrives from his sisters, Elizabeth and Eleanor. They have sent me Daddy's photo albums and their note: "You'll want these someday to show to your children and grandchildren."

Both of Daddy's sisters are collectors of family history and photos. Just touching the albums as I lift them from the box makes me recoil. I do not open them, afraid not of what I will see, but of what I will feel. I know the pictures will show only a part of the story and, just as when Daddy was alive, the rest of the story will not be visible. The albums go onto a storage shelf with other family photos and mementos. It will be seven years before I take them out again.

Throughout the spring, Freeman and I deepen our commitment to parenting and social change. In May of 1987, standing on a bridge in Rock Creek Park, we marry. We make vows of trust, respect and willingness to work through issues of pain and conflict. That summer, when the children are out of school, with two cars and a large rental truck holding all our combined possessions, our new six-person "blended family" emigrates from the intensity of Washington, D.C. city life to a small, rural house outside Charlottesville, Virginia. Here, surrounded by cows, rabbits, deer, and the majestic and protecting Blue Ridge Mountains, we establish "Mountain Magic," our new home and refuge. All six of us begin thriving in this new atmosphere of stability, respect and affection.

Freeman and I Marry

Joe and Jenny move forward confidently through high school and college and into their young adult worlds of work and travel. They volunteer with the battered women's shelter, the rescue squad, the hospice. They choose careers in health and law, both focusing on helping children and families. I feel proud to have such competent and dedicated children. "Following in their mother's footsteps," friends tell me.

My own professional work expands and, in 1989, I am able to begin a private psychotherapy practice in Charlottesville. I name my business the Child Development Resource Center. Many of my clients have a history of childhood sexual abuse and I recognize their struggles. I volunteer at our local Sexual Assault Resource Agency and serve on the community Task Force for Prevention of Child Sexual Abuse. Finally I am feeling recovered from my own abuse and able to help others with their healing.

Freeman and I share our stories and our histories, our losses and our hopes.

Not only were my children molested by my father, but I sent them to be with him.

I participated in their abuse. I betrayed my own children.

In 1992, my deaf mother, Marjorie, who is retired and living alone, moves to Charlottesville to be near our family. She had lived near me through the early years when Joe and Jenny were young, and we shared lots of meals and tasks. Now, though, without the children to focus on, we meet only for coffee or lunch. I notice my frequent irritation, criticism and sarcasm toward her. I resent what I have always experienced as a superficial niceness between us, a wall that prevents us from being real and talking about personal things. Something in me insists we can do better than this, that there is something old in the way.

At my desk, in my small office where I meet with twenty clients each week, I sit and look through the morning's mail. I have received a small, embossed, formal announcement about the arrival of a new therapist in town. The words in italics catch my eye: "proficient in sign language."

Although Mom and I have always been able to understand each other easily, because of her ability to speak and read lips and my limited ability to sign, the safe and nurturing presence of a skilled counselor who can hear, speak and sign fluently, feels like the healing opportunity she and I both need the most.

I ask Mom if she will go with me to therapy, because I want to be able to feel closer to her. Her strength and courage and abiding love come through for me, again, as they did during the years of both her, and later my own, painful divorces: "If you think it will help," she answers, "of course I will."

Mom and I finally begin to talk more deeply. With our therapist's gentle guidance, we come to the "wall," an obstacle between us that I believe is built of silence and of her refusal to talk with me about what happened with Daddy – a wall made bigger and more impenetrable by my own little-acknowledged pain and anger.

Within the safe haven of our therapy session, at last my anger pours out. "Why didn't you ever talk with me about the incest?" I shout at my mother. "Why didn't you ask how I was feeling? How could you act for forty years like nothing ever happened?"

She is stunned and bewildered. "I didn't know you wanted to talk with me," Mom says softly. "When I divorced Daddy, I talked with a social worker. She told me not to talk with you about what had happened. She said it would upset you. Maybe that was wrong. What do you want to talk with me about?"

With those simple words of acceptance, the wall disappears as my mother takes me into her arms and I cry.

We attend our therapy sessions faithfully week after week. We ask each other questions long withheld, and we tell each other our stories. Mom reveals to me that she had always felt uncomfortable and had suspicions about Daddy, about his behaviors, but she could never exactly name or identify the problem.

"He was let go from his job as a boy's dorm supervisor, just after we were first married," she says.

"Do you think he molested the boys there?" I ask.

"I wonder," she murmurs.

We wonder together. Did he molest other children in our neighborhood in those years he was molesting me? Is the rumor Mom heard true that he had molested a friend's child after he moved back to Colorado in 1958? Was it true what my cousin, Karen, told me in 1982–he was arrested because he was naked with some local children, although he had explained to her it was a "misunderstanding." "Nothing really happened," he had told her.

Mom and Me

At last we have found a place and a time to speak. Piece by piece we put together stories, questions, rumors, memories. And, piece by piece, a fuller picture emerges – Daddy molested other children, maybe many children. He molested boys as well as girls.

"What about Gary and Dorene?" Mom wonders.

What about Joe and Jenny? I can barely allow the thought.

It is as if the possibilities emerging in the conversations with Mom are preparing my psyche for the unthinkable and the unbearable.

Joe's letter arrives in October 1993, in the autumn of his twenty-fourth year. "I'm writing to arrange some time with you around Thanksgiving. I want to talk with you about Grampy. (This is also the best way for me not to back out of talking.) It has taken me a long time to get to where I want to talk with you. As I think you know, on some level or another, he sexually abused me during the six summers I was in Colorado."

My heart is split open. No. Never. I never imagined.

Then, six months later, in the spring of 1994, Jenny's letter. "I feel that it is time I told you the truth. Now that Joe has told you that Grampy did, in fact, molest us I can no longer deny it. No matter how sorry you are for sending us out there, the fact is, you did."

But Daddy promised me he wouldn't touch you!

But Daddy promised me he wouldn't touch you!

My dream of raising my children in a world of safety and protection and freedom explodes like a nuclear disaster. Not only were my children molested by my father, but I sent them to be with him. I participated in their abuse. I betrayed my own children.

I sob and scream as I face the horror of this truth. Over and over I remember the scene from the movie, Sophie's Choice, when the mother gives her child to the Nazi officer – the anguish and despair in her face. Conscious or not, intentional or not, I handed my children over and I am responsible. There is no redemption.

Me and Freeman

My heartbreak turns to numbness and dazed confusion. I try to understand and explain to Joe and Jenny, to my mother, to my husband and friends, and mostly to myself. What if…If only…How could…? Nothing is adequate. Nothing can change what I have done.

This new, agonizing truth has stunned us all. Joe feigns nonchalance in his distancing; Jenny is cold and angry. Mom tries to comfort me and practice the sharing of feelings we have learned, but the feelings are so intense that it is painful.

Freeman struggles to balance disbelief, outrage, and compassion for his wife and step-children.

I recognize the cycle of grief and guilt and shame I am in – this time not for my own childhood but for my children's. The tears come easily and frequently, especially when I look at photos of Joe and Jenny when they were little – innocent and helpless children. The rage explodes: at my father (If only he were alive so I could kill him!), at myself, at others who might have intervened and kept this from happening.

I recognize, too, that I am using my old coping patterns that helped me survive emotionally after my own abuse: working long hours to stay distracted, being preoccupied with extensive lists and details to feel a sense of control, projecting the abuse and betrayal on my husband to avoid the real story, drinking too much at bedtime to find relief from the pain.

Gradually, with the love, acceptance and compassion of Mom, Freeman, and my circle of close friends, I move through the grief and become reconciled with this horrible reality. I try to help my children do the same. They don't need to forgive me, but I realize they too must find some form of healing and reconciliation with our history.

My beloved Joe and Jenny were molested by their Grampy, by my father, by the same father who molested me when I was a little girl. My parenting skills, child psychology training, professional work with abuse victims, even my own healing have not protected my children.

How could I have been so blind and numb as to send them to be with my own abuser? Will they ever trust me again? Who can protect them now? What will become of my children?

The cancer has spread to another generation.

With the love, acceptance and compassion I move through the grief and become reconciled with this horrible reality.

Broken Rainbow

*The most deadly of all
possible sins is the mutilation
of a child's spirit.*

– Erik H. Erikson

Drawing "Broken Rainbow" by Joyce's "inner child" 1979

George.

Daddy

Chapter Three

From Ruffian to Wrestling Champ

(1916-1938)

"I'm a man of constant sorrow.
I've seen trouble all my days.
I bid farewell to Colorado,
The place where I was born
and raised."

– Traditional Song

I am deeply shaken by this earthquake of newly revealed secrets. Truth, it seems, can lie quietly buried and hidden away, but, in naming and facing my father's pedophilia and incestuous sexual abuse of my children, the fault lines deep under our family structure begin to tremble. The ground begins to open. I am drawn back to beginnings, and to why.

Who was this man? Did his friends know his secrets? Why didn't they intervene? I want and need to have answers to these questions.

I resolve to see if I can I learn from my own and my children's pain anything that can help other families. I become determined to explore and write my father's story. I ask my mother for help, and she agrees

By the summer of 1994, Mom is meeting with me regularly and offers her full assistance with my investigation. We begin the long trek back to her youth and then my childhood.

We have developed a fondness for dried cherry scones from a local bakery and each time we meet we have a ritual treat of black coffee and scones to begin our conversations. At my kitchen table, with the comforting view of the Blue Ridge Mountains in the distance, and with photos of Joe and Jenny and Gary nearby to remind us of our purpose, we study her address list.

A loyal and traditional friend, Mom has maintained contact with her deaf college classmates, as well as former neighbors, and with relatives from both her and Daddy's families. Her address list allows me access to a fifty-year social network.

With Mom's help, I create a list of my parents' relatives, their school and social friends, and their former neighbors. I send these people a letter and a questionnaire, explaining that I did not have much contact with my father during the thirty years before he died and that I am looking for information about him. I acknowledge that he is generally remembered as a friendly and responsible person, but that in his later life he developed "a problem molesting children."

I feel like a young child putting together a jigsaw puzzle.

Soon, responses begin to arrive. Each afternoon, as I walk to the black metal mailbox nailed firmly to a post at the end of our driveway, I wonder what memories and emotions will be in the day's mail. These people knew and even loved my father, but they are not angry with me for being curious about the truth. I notice my relief and my surprise.

In addition to answers to my questions about how they met my father, what activities they did together, what personality characteristics they found most memorable, I receive reassuring personal comments.

A cousin writes, "I was surprised and glad to hear from you, even if the subject was not too pleasant. I am returning your survey and adding a few memories of my own. I know it is difficult. Hang in there."

From one of my father's friends, I receive, "Your letter was a revelation and has shocked me. I never dreamed that George was involved in such behavior, especially with his own child. I feel for you and would like to do what I can to help ease what must be a long time of pain."

A former neighbor responds, "I have deep regret that this happened to you. I always

Daddy

remember you as the very quiet, nice, and grown up child. It is amazing that you have turned this experience into a positive thing by applying it to your life's work. Good luck, and may God bless you."

Comforted and encouraged by these kind and understanding responses, I find it easier to proceed with my decision to write my father's story, our family's story. With details provided by these initial letters, an outline of his world begins to emerge, and the story of my childhood and those who knew our family begins to take shape. I realize that it is time now to take out the boxes of photo albums that Daddy's sisters had sent me seven years ago, just after his suicide.

I feel like a young child putting together a jigsaw puzzle. How can I connect these new facts, people's stories and the photographs? What kind of picture will I see when I finally collect all the puzzle pieces?

First, I decide, I will gather all the pieces of the puzzle that form the outline, the edges. From interviews, letters, yearbooks, and pictures I will construct the story of George Culbertson's life that was visible to those who did not know about the secrets, the silences, the betrayals.

I want to begin at the beginning of Daddy's life, so I call his sisters in Colorado to ask if I can come to visit them. We have not seen each other since my father's suicide, and they are eager to have me visit. Within a few weeks, I have rearranged my work schedule, made plane reservations, and am on my way to Colorado. I realize that my aunt's contributions and memories will play a key role in my growing effort to understand my father.

We are sitting together on the couch, Elizabeth on my left and Eleanor on my right, with family photo albums piled on the coffee table in front of us. August in Colorado is hot but not as humid as my home in Virginia. I sip my lemonade and listen as they tell me about their childhood, their parents, and their brother George, my Daddy. Although I am somewhat guarded, seeing myself as a journalist rather than a character in the story, I want them to feel safe, open, and comfortable as they share their stories with me.

They begin with the story of their mother, Hannah. She was a first-generation American, born in 1888, the oldest child of German immigrants who had come by boat, train and covered wagon to Kansas. Hannah had three sisters and a brother, and everyone said that their father was cruel and that the family had a hard life. By age seventeen, Hannah was working to help provide for the family. She went into town – Walsenburg, Colorado – to clean houses for other families. In her time off, Hannah loved to dance. After a week of work, she enjoyed going out with her sister, Maude, on Friday evenings to the Knights and Ladies Lodge. It was at a Lodge dance that she met her husband-to-be, Samuel. They were both officers on the Lodge "drill team". Elizabeth and Eleanor want to be sure that I understand that this was a respectable club, not a bar. Their mother was an upstanding Christian lady.

Samuel worked as a smelter in Walsenburg's mining industry, was a widower, and had an eleven-year-old daughter, Lucy, who lived with him. Samuel and Hannah began as dance partners and Lodge members, but they soon decided to marry and make a life together. The daughters have a carefully framed picture of their parents on their wedding day in December of 1911.

Mother pretty much slaved away her life for us children.

Hannah and Samuel's first home was a dug-out – a home dug as a large hole in the ground with earth for floors and walls and a little doorway and window to connect with the world above ground. Samuel had homesteaded and "proved up" (Elizabeth explains this was the term for "improved") his land near Lamar, in Prowers County, Colorado, one hundred miles from Walsenburg. Here in this very simple and basic place the newlyweds lived with Lucy. Soon, in 1913, their first baby, Elizabeth, was born.

Walsenburg was a small, blue collar industrial town where most lives depended upon the ore refinery for income. Samuel stayed there through the week and came home most weekends, making the trip to and from Lamar. Hannah lived alone with Lucy and Elizabeth, cooked all their meals, sewed, washed and mended their clothes by hand, and made the dug-out into a home.

Soon the family was able to trade their rugged homestead for a little three-room house in Walsenburg, where Samuel rejoined them. Hard work and hard times were normal during these years just after World War One. Elizabeth recalls, "Mommy cleaned houses and took in laundry, but we didn't feel poor. Everyone else was working hard and didn't have much. Times were different, then." George, named for his mother's father, was born into this hard-scrabble family and this life in 1916. In 1918, his sister Eleanor arrived. Now Samuel and Hannah had four children, his daughter Lucy and their own three little ones.

There is an entire album of photos of this young frontier family. The sisters give me several to take home with me. I begin to experience surprising tenderness for my father and feel myself softening as I look at pictures of him as a little boy.

Elizabeth remembers that their father Samuel "had a temper and spanked hard." Eleanor adds that he continued his love of partying and dancing and was "always running around." Finally Hannah had enough. Eleanor said, "Mother was fed up and told him to get out." He did. In 1919, when George was three years old, Samuel left Hannah and their children and moved with his daughter Lucy to California. George never heard from his father again.

Daddy

"Although I never knew him, I have been told he was a jealous man," my father later reported to his psychiatrist. "I have been told by my uncle that my father was no good, and I believe it was all his fault that he and my mother broke up. When I was about three years old, I can clearly remember a stormy scene one night in our home. My father and mother were quarreling. We children were sent to bed and I never saw him after that. He was gone the next morning.

"Later, I felt closeness and I admired my father's brother, too. Not like a father or anything like that, but my uncle was a good family man, good to his children. He, more than the other relatives, would come over to visit us."

As he recounted these memories, my father swallowed and became emotional. "Ever since I was a child it felt that my home was always filled with women. No father, no men living in the home. During the period I was in school, it did not matter. But at home, I would have liked some greater male influence."

Hannah received no financial help from Samuel after their divorce and had to work hard to provide for the children. Eleanor recalls, "Mommy was angelic. She made so much out of everything. She sacrificed herself. We didn't know we were poor because she never talked about it."

"Yes," George also acknowledged, "Mother pretty much slaved away her life for us children. She had no education, but she did very well bringing us children up. She knew nothing about child psychology.... just brought us up as she was brought up. Our clothes were poor and threadbare, but they were neat and she kept them mended. She had a big responsibility, three children, ages one-and-a-half to six, when her husband left. All her life she had us children and never had time or money to enjoy herself. So naturally I have had feelings of admiration and devotion, a desire to emulate her. And I have done so. I've been a hard worker. In the past few years I have devoted so much time to work, in fact, that I have neglected my own family. But the motive behind that, just like my mother, was to make things better for my family."

Hannah sewed all the children's clothes, kept the little ones clean and fed, made sure the family went to church every Sunday. They lived in a tiny three-room house – kitchen, living room and bedroom. There was a toilet and coal bin in the alley and a hand-operated washing machine protected by a tin roof. Elizabeth and Eleanor shared one bed and George shared the other bed with their mother.

Mommy was a strict disciplinarian.

"My mother was always thinking of her children," George continued. "She kept a very nice home considering the money she had. She was a very good woman, an extremely hard worker, but she kept strict discipline, whipping us plenty. She would not tolerate any lying.

She used a strap.

"She was not religious, but she saw to it that we children went to Sunday School. Above all, she was a very moral person, and at times I thought perhaps she was too mean. I guess all children feel that way toward their parents sometimes. I even intended to run away, and my sisters did too, but it never came to anything.

She had to spank us an awful lot.

"Although I didn't realize it at the time, we three didn't have too much time with our mother, because she was working all the time. And we all had chores to do to help her while she was taking in washing, delivering the laundry. I believe she was kind and compassionate in her ways but because of financial worries, she could not give us what we wanted, like pets and dogs. There just wasn't the money, and no one to take care of them. It was always a marvel when we had enough to simply go on a street car for a ride, or go for a picnic."

In order to provide a livelihood for her children, Hannah lodged a female boarder in the home. When the children were all in school, she got a job in a pressing and cleaning establishment, and continued to do washing and ironing on the side. Once when she couldn't work due to surgery to remove her appendix, the Red Cross paid for the children's school lunches, a dab of potatoes with cream gravy. Other times, a friend or a neighbor would give the family a jackrabbit he had shot and they would have some rabbit stew.

Elizabeth and George and Eleanor worked to help their mother. Daddy had often told me stories about helping to pull a wagon to deliver clean and pressed laundry that his mother had washed and ironed. But Elizabeth laughs as she recalls her brother and says, "No, it was me who was pulling the wagon. I was about nine or ten. George was six and just hanging on the back slowing it down." She shows me another photo of my father, who appears at this time like one of the "little rascals" out of "Our Gang."

My aunts tell me that they and my father had adventures playing hide and seek in a nearby vacant house. They would go across town to get free miniature loaves of bread from the Rainbow Bakery. George was happy and playful but also a daredevil and a ruffian – a risk taker. He was a challenge for his mother. Eleanor recalls, "Mommy was a strict disciplinarian. She used a strap. She had to spank us an awful lot."

"She never impressed me as being happy," George added. "There was very little laughter in her home due to her hard streaks of living. She needed companionship, she needed love. She did not have love when she was married.

"I have seen her gay and laughing when she had family picnics. She enjoyed good times – trips and visits to the park – and could not have them. When you work so hard you lose sight of the leisure and family ties that mean so much. Later I was the same. In trying to make things so I would have more time with my family, I lost sight of the aim, and making money became an aim in itself."

In 1920, when George was four years old, he got "consumption" (tuberculosis). The doctor said he needed to be in the country and have fresh air and sunshine, so Hannah decided to have him spend that summer with her sister, Maude, and her husband, Ralph, at their farm near Leadville, Colorado. Because Hannah had begun working full-time to support her children, she decided to send Elizabeth and Eleanor along with George that summer. George would continue to spend summers with his Aunt Maude and Uncle Ralph until he completed high school. His first cousin, Brad, also shared these summer "vacations" on the farm. The two boys grew up to be

I was just little and I only remember the happy times. As we get older we hold the happy memories and lose the bad ones.

lifelong friends.

Ralph and Maude lived in a tiny cabin with no water. The children carried water to the house in buckets and helped with farm chores. Ralph had a horse and buggy, a sled, and a team of plow-horses. George, a competent young helper, learned to use tools for farming and carpentry, and would drive the horses while Ralph and Maude walked along beside him tossing pitchforks of hay onto the big wagon. Ralph was an important new male figure in this fatherless boy's life.

"Being sent to the farm every summer I got close to uncle Ralph, my mother's sister's husband. I admired him in a childish way, the things he could do on a farm. I thought he was pretty wonderful.

"I came to admire my aunt and uncle on the farm. They were uneducated and rough, but they were good at heart. They, too, taught me the value of hard work. Through them I have gained many experiences which I would not have gotten otherwise."

Daddy, His Mother and Sisters

But Eleanor becomes angry as she remembers, "Uncle Ralph was harsh and lazy. He loved to drink but couldn't afford it, so he got a job hauling supplies up the mountain to a mine where he could stay and drink the miners' liquor. He was such an alcoholic – no not really, because he didn't drink at home. I got so I hated him because he called Aunt Maude every filthy name."

I find myself puzzled by my aunt's definition of an alcoholic as "someone who drinks at home." It seems clear to me that this uncle was abusing alcohol regularly.

Hearing Eleanor describe her uncle's temperament, I ask if he was ever physically abusive or violent to his wife or the visiting children. "No, I don't remember Ralph hitting or hurting any of us." She pauses, takes a drink of her lemonade, and sighs. "I was just little and I only remember the happy times. As we get older we hold the happy memories and lose the bad ones."

From age four to fourteen, George spent the school years with his mother and two sisters in their tiny house in Walsenburg. He was happy and playful and a hard worker, but he began to misbehave and to be a challenge for his mother.

He disliked school and was a poor student in grade school, though he did manage to reach the seventh grade. He felt he got along well with other students and his teachers.

Elizabeth recalls that, in 1926, when he was ten, George and a friend got into "Halloween mischief" on a streetcar. She doesn't know exactly what the boys did, but the police were involved.

"Well, I had been growing up," George himself said of this period. "At that time I was associating with boys of all kinds. They were sort of a gang, and getting into trouble – petty stealing from the stores, vandalism, running around neighborhoods and alleys disturbing people just for the heck of it, playing hooky."

His mother announced, "If he can't behave I'll send him to reform school."

Hannah still loved to dance. Sometimes at night, after the children were in bed, she would lock the doors and go to the Lodge. In 1927, while she was at the Lodge, she met Jack Harris. No one knows if she loved him. Elizabeth believes Hannah married Jack "for the kids" and that she thought marrying him would help the family financially. George was now eleven years old and had a new stepfather.

Jack did help the family financially; they moved to a larger house in a better part of town, South Side Walsenburg. Elizabeth says that Jack was "good-hearted to outsiders. People liked him a lot." She also recalls that he didn't spank or hurt her and she never saw him hurt the other children.

"I think my mother was desperate," George too recalled. "We children were getting older. The house was getting smaller, we had no privacy, and we all slept in one room. So I suppose mother began to dance with the idea of finding a husband to help support us kids.

"But my stepfather was strictly no good. We children knew him very little, and mother had not known him very long herself. At the time, this new marriage didn't seem like so much. Of course, it was a different way of life. Having a father and moving to a house with a bathroom was exciting. It was not until later that it was apparent that mother and he were not happy and things became strained in the house."

And Eleanor adds, "Jack was a hateful man. He was mean to Mommy. He was an alcoholic, and when he was drunk he would beat her up. He made her beg for money. Once when Jack and Mommy went on a ride together, she came back with blood on her face. Another time, he pulled a gun on her. Another time, Mommy went down the block when he was threatening her. She must have taken candles and stayed away all night because she had to get out of the house."

Elizabeth adds, gently, "I'm not sure he was an alcoholic, but he always had a bottle

His mother announced, "If he can't behave I'll send him to reform school."

of wine up in the cupboard which he drank too much of. I don't like to talk about Jack. It makes me angry, and that's not good."

George had been the "man of the house" since he was three, when his father had left home. He had loved and helped his mother. Now Jack Harris, his new stepfather, was beating her up in front of the children. George's sisters seem sadly appreciative as they describe how George hated Jack and tried to intervene and protect his mother, even by threatening Jack and chasing him into the garage one time.

Life now was harder for this young boy. There are few photos in the albums from these years, and Elizabeth and Eleanor do not want to look at them. The years spent watching their mother suffer are still painful.

There was to be yet another hardship for George. In 1929, when he was thirteen and in the seventh grade, he went swimming in a polluted lake and contracted spinal meningitis. He was at home with a high fever and was taken to the emergency room by ambulance. He was in a coma. When he woke up in the hospital, he was deaf. Elizabeth's eyes are moist and she reaches for a tissue as she tells me about this part of her brother's life.

"Of course it was very sudden," my father remembered. "I had taken part in track, our school tryouts, in April of 1929. I had gone out the day before, ran the races and did other things in competition, to try and make the track team.

When Daddy woke up in the hospital, he was deaf.

"It must have been that night, or very shortly afterward, that I was in my bedroom shouting that I could see all sorts of little imaginary men coming through the bedroom. It was a very real sensation, I remember that; it brought my mother running and she called the doctor. The next thing I knew they were wheeling me out to the ambulance.

"The last words I remember ever hearing was on my way to the hospital in the ambulance. I asked my mother where they were taking me and she said they were taking me to the hospital. I don't recall very much of the hospital, except the pain of the spinal injections. After I became conscious, I still did not know what my sickness was or what results could be expected.

"When I asked my mother about my lack of hearing, she told me, and I think she believed it, that my hearing temporarily was stopped up. So I was content to wait for it to come back. Yet as I lay there in the hospital bed, I recall imagining the birds singing in the trees outside, or that I could hear footsteps."

"As time passed, I still believed that my hearing would clear up, but gradually I became accustomed to the world of silence. From the very beginning, my chief difficulty was in understanding other people, what it was they were saying. My mother took me to several specialists trying to get something to bolster her hopes. I

Daddy, His Aunt and Mother

think I gave up hope of ever hearing again when they took me to another hospital and gave me hearing tests.

"I saw the doctor shake his head negatively to my mother, and she started to cry. She cried almost all the way home, so finally it became clear to me what had happened. But I never cried about it, and somehow I never felt too bad about losing my hearing. I accepted it philosophically and made myself believe it was for the best. I really believe that now, and have for many years."

My father used to tell me this story of "waking up deaf." He was tied down to the hospital bed, couldn't move, and couldn't hear any of the doctors or nurses or other children in the room. The world was suddenly silent. Even though he never cried as a child, Daddy always cried when he told me this story.

When asked whether he ever felt that his loss of hearing was a form of punishment, he replied, "No. That suggestion was made to me, but I rejected the idea. Like I told you before, I thought it was fate giving me a good deal. At the time I did not believe in God; if I had, I would have attributed it to Him. Because as I see it now, God does not punish, He helps. I believe my mother felt that my loss of hearing was punishment to her. I do not know where I got the impression. I believe someone told me. I do not know why she felt she was being punished for being too severe with the children. She was a good woman and had no reason to fear punishment. She was no more severe than other children's parents, pretty much the same."

When asked to evaluate his feelings about the transition from hearing to deafness, he replied, "Well, gradually I began to accept it and it didn't seem to be too much of a catastrophe. Never seemed to effect me from the beginning, except that I lost all my friends all of a sudden, and that was a blow. I have never regretted loss of hearing; in fact it seems it was the best thing that could have happened.

"As I look back upon it now, I probably would have wound up in a reformatory or jail, or something worse. Losing my hearing cut off that kind of life completely. After staying at home for a year I was sent to a school for the deaf, a residential school. Routine and regulation did not leave much time for that sort of misbehaving."

When George came home from the hospital, he tried returning to his junior high school, but he couldn't hear or understand what the teachers were saying. His friends abandoned him because they couldn't talk to him. He would spend the rest of his life trying to teach his hearing friends and relatives to finger spell and use sign language, and he would be angry with those who refused.

A relative suggested that George begin attending school at the Colorado School for the Deaf and Blind (CSDB) in Colorado Springs, where the relative worked as a cook. Hannah didn't want her son to go to such an "institution" for high school but

The world

was

suddenly

silent.

finally accepted that it was the only way he could have an education and a social life. The arrangements were made, and in September of 1930, at age fourteen, George was admitted as a freshman to this amazingly lovely and spacious campus at the foot of Pike's Peak.

"I entered the school for the deaf at the age of fourteen," George remembered of this big change in his life. "Suddenly I seemed to learn how to study and began to like school. My grades improved; I was advanced from the eighth to the tenth grade and graduated from school with honors. When I entered college on a scholarship at the age of seventeen, I continued this trend, making good grades throughout, and graduating with a B.A. degree at the age of twenty-two."

Elizabeth and Eleanor finish showing me the albums of their early family life. I prepare to conclude our visit. I notice that Elizabeth's living room is filled with framed pictures of children and grandchildren, and the windowsills and bookshelves are display areas for handmade gifts and special treasures. Reminiscence, nostalgia, devotion – old-fashioned family values. Looking around me, I'm surprised by the sudden appreciation and affection I feel for these aunts, for their hard childhood.

We have not yet talked about my father's sexual abuse of me. Mom told them about the incest almost thirty years ago, when she was divorcing my father, but my aunts have never spoken with me about that subject. They do know, from my recent letter that part of the reason for my visit will be to ask them what they know about this aspect of George's life, and how this makes them feel.

It is late afternoon. I try to ignore the rising wave of sadness and anger that is tightening my shoulders and restricting my breathing. It's the end of our first day together, and I don't want to end it on a painful note by exploring further now.

We have been here for several hours, talking and laughing, asking questions and wiping away tears brought on by poignant memories. The lemonade glasses are empty. "Why don't we stop for today," I suggest. We carry our glasses to the kitchen sink and exchange hugs, as I get ready to drive back to the motel where I am staying.

Tomorrow morning I have an appointment to visit the History Room of the School for the Deaf where my father spent his high school years. I am both weary and confused. All these words and pictures and souvenirs represent a hard-working, strong and loving family. But also one full of sadness, anger, violence, and loneliness. My father's family. My family.

I see Elizabeth's gentle smile and Eleanor's look of concern as I depart. "Thank you for sharing so much," I tell them. "I'll be back in a few days and we can talk some more."

"We want to help you, dear – any way we can," they say. "Won't you take some of

His friends abandoned him because they couldn't talk to him.

Daddy, His Mother and Sisters

this rhubarb pie with you? The rhubarb's from the garden. You'll be glad to have a little bedtime snack later tonight."

Early the next morning, as I park my car in front of the School for the Deaf, I imagine being my grandmother, Hannah, delivering her teenage son, George, to this doorway. George's father has abandoned her and their children, she has struggled with poverty and single parenthood, George's stepfather is physically abusing her, George has lost his hearing, and now she must leave him in this residential school, an institution where he will be cared for by strangers.

I open the door with some apprehension but feel immediate relief as I encounter the high-ceiling lobby with sunlight filling the room through the large windows. Portraits of former superintendents are on the wall, and there are colorful fresh flowers on the table by the chairs. I am greeted with a warm and friendly handshake. "Welcome," says the supervisor of the school's History Room. "How can I help you?"

I explain that my father died nine years ago. When I was in eighth grade, he moved to Colorado. I had little contact with him after he moved. I want to know more about his life, and I know that he was a student here from 1930 through 1933. He was also a teacher here from 1958 through 1962. I wonder if there are any of his files or any other sources of information about his time here?

My guide is more than willing to help, and begins by giving me a tour of the campus. She indicates the older buildings, which would have been here when my father was a student – the classrooms, the gym, the boys' dormitory. As we walk around the grounds, we encounter staff and students, all of them friendly and interested in meeting me, helping me. I hope this was the kind of reception Hannah and my father received.

Then the guide takes me to the History Room, a small room lined with bookshelves and a large table at the center. All the yearbooks, school newsletters, pictures, athletic awards, state citations, and other artifacts are stored here. After a brief orientation, I find where the materials for my father's student and faculty years are located. I begin to search for my father's face and name, and become immersed in the next chapter of his life.

All that remains of George Culbertson's student file is his admission medical examination. How different this record is from what would be included in a contemporary special education evaluation. "George was not born deaf. Deafness occurred at age 13. Supposed cause spinal meningitis. Totally deaf. Can hear shrill noises. Cannot hear sound of the voice. Can understand a little from the lips of the person speaking." There is no mention of the social, emotional or intellectual impact of his deafness, his family life, or his admission to a residential school.

In the Fall 1930 issue of *The Colorado Index*, the school newsletter, I see my father's name for the first time. Just seeing it in print instantly makes his whole story more authentic and believable to me. A piece of the puzzle falls into its place.

"George Culbertson is fortunate in that his parents live in Walsenburg. They have driven up three times, since school opened, to take George home over the weekends. George enjoys these outings very much." I can imagine the hugs and laughter as Hannah and George and his sisters were reunited, but I wonder how George and his stepfather handled these visits.

Then my eyes come to rest on the front page of the December 1931 *Index*. There, under the headline 1931 Football Team, in the front row of the picture, is George Culbertson, tackle. Before my trip I had received a response to one of my letters from one of George's CSDB friends. He had written to me to let me know that he was already a student at the Colorado School when George arrived in 1930. "We became friends and played football together on the school's team, the Bulldogs. He was a very good player, big and strong, six feet tall, around 180 pounds."

Also in a 1931 newsletter, I see a short story that George wrote. He was always a good writer and seems to have made an early mark on the school's literary scene. Passing sentence on a man convicted of assaulting an Indian and stealing his horse, the judge in George's story concludes with a statement to the prisoner: "I hope that you will take this lesson to heart, and remember in the future that might does not make right."

It was a very restricted, austere social life that we students had, but in those days the social climate was much more conservative than it is now.

My father could not have known it then, but this telling passage will foreshadow his own misuses of power in years to come.

In the May 1932 newsletter, I find an essay titled "The Washington Bicentennial." My father writes about George Washington and concludes: "A study of his character leaves a definite impression that he was a man of great personal charm, of dignity, of courage, of strong religious convictions, and of tact as well as wisdom; in other words, a type worthy to commemorate as the highest type of American manhood."

I find myself wondering if these writings are true insights into the character of my father or only repetitions of values he has been taught. I have no way to know.

In the Fall 1932 and the Winter 1933 newsletters, George describes his summer and Christmas vacations, including adventures with his cousin Brad, with whom he had developed a close childhood and adolescent relationship. "We took some nice swims, a trip by auto to Leadville, Colorado to visit our Aunt Maude and Uncle Ralph, some horseback rides, and a strenuous hike to the summit of old Pikes Peak."

Brad, I'll soon come to learn, later figures large in the shadow part of Daddy's life.

There are no photos of boys and girls together in the yearbooks or newsletters. I remember the letter I received from another of my father's friends, in response to my question about whether my father had dated or had girlfriends during high school. He had clarified that there was no co-ed social life.

In his own words, my father later described his life at CSDB this way: "The boys and girls were housed in two different buildings set diagonally across from each other on the campus as far away as possible. The only time boys and girls had contact with each other was in classroom, except for occasional parties such as Halloween, and sporting events. We students all ate in a big common dining room with the girls' tables lined on one side and the boys' on the other side. Everything was designed to keep the boys and girls as far apart as possible.

"We went to classes all morning and then in the afternoon we boys were assigned to different shops to learn a trade. The girls' training was focused on home arts such as sewing, cooking, etc.

Remember that might does not make right.

"On Saturdays and Sundays, the older boys were permitted to walk to the downtown business area to go to the movies, shop, or just stroll around on their own. They were due back in time for the evening meal. If I remember correctly, the girls were required to go in groups, with a chaperone, for their weekend town visits. So it was a very restricted, austere social life that we students had, but in those days the social climate was much more conservative than it is now; we didn't think much about it, just taking such restrictions for granted naturally.

1931

Daddy and His Mother

"Near the end of high school, when I was seventeen, I had a motorcycle accident and sustained a brain concussion. Though I didn't lose consciousness upon this event, I was in bed for a day or two, and then up and around as usual."

I remember George as being very friendly and easy to get along with – a person who really impressed all who knew him as being a great guy.

George's REPORT
from *The Colorado Index*, Winter 1933
"How the Holidays were Spent"

"About two o'clock on the afternoon of December 22nd, my folks drove up to Palmer Hall. I had been waiting for them so there was no delay in getting off. I had anticipated a good time during the vacation, but I had no sooner arrived at home than I found time hanging heavily on my hands. And so it hung all through the vacation with practically no method by which I could dispose of it.

"Christmas Day offered slight diversion. One-half hour of that day I put to good account by making an enormous amount of food do the disappearing act! During the vacation I helped my sister do the dishes after nearly every meal. I washed the Christmas dinner dishes and that was some job. It was an hour and twenty minutes long!

"A couple of days after Christmas, some other boys and I hiked out to the "Big Hole" at the end of the slag dumps. The distance both ways was about four miles. I succeeded in wearing my shoe soles out, passing a few hours of time, and having some fun on that hike. I could have remained up for New Year's Eve, but, as it was, there was nothing to do so I hit the hay at 10:30 and slept until 11:30 the next morning. Nothing happened from then until two PM, Monday, when my folks drove me back to school.

"There's a long, long trail ahead of me from now till June – preparation for the entrance examinations to Gallaudet College. Time and effort will demonstrate whether or not I have the ability to pass them. Here's hopin'!"

As I finish looking through newsletters and yearbooks and return them to their shelves, I notice that on the walls of the History Room there are a few framed pictures which show my father: football teams, basketball teams, and the En Avant Literary Society, which elected him treasurer.

Among these records, I have discovered important clues revealing Daddy's lifelong enthusiasm for athletics, camping, and outdoor adventure, as well as his steady pattern of staying connected to his extended family. I find myself relieved at how ordinary my father's CSDB school years seem to have been, and yet disappointed to not find any more significant revelations.

As I make my way out, I stop by the supervisor's office to thank her for her assistance, and she invites me to "come again, anytime." Walking down the front steps to my car, I see more young students, walking across the campus to their classes or dormitories, hands dancing in animated signed conversation. As they see me get into my car and begin to drive away, they turn and wave and then resume their talking and laughing.

Leaving the Colorado School for the Deaf and Blind, I pause. Looking back over the peaceful campus, I contemplate its impact on Daddy's entire adolescence. This is where his character took shape.

After glancing at my map, I pick up a quick lunch from a convenient drive-through, and travel north to see George's good friend Gerald Bishop. He and George had been good friends since high school, throughout college, and into their adult lives.

Before coming to Colorado, in response to my questionnaire, I had received a letter from Mr. Bishop' son, who wrote to tell me that his father was now in a nursing home, following a stroke.

I had met Mr. Bishop several times during summer visits to Colorado. If George were still alive, they would be the same age, and they would probably be spending time together.

The receptionist at the entrance directs me to Mr. Bishop's room. As I enter, I see a thin, pale, aged man sleeping on the bed next to the window. I breathe deeply, hesitate, and then walk to him and touch his hand. His eyes open and look at me and I say, in sign language, "I am George Culbertson's daughter."

His eyes light up and he smiles when I name my father. With slurred speech and awkward hand gestures, he tells me "George was strong. He was my friend. He shot himself."

At the school I learned about George's academic and athletic activities, but I found no information about a social life. I realize Gerald Bishop might be my last source. I sit by his hospital bed for an hour and a half, trying to ask questions, making eye contact, offering reassuring touches on the hand and shoulder. Mr. Bishop drifts in and out of alertness, and repeats the words, "strong," "my friend," and "shot self," over and over.

I ask him if George had any girl friends, and he makes a sign language gesture, fingers of left hand in a circle sliding back and forth over the right forefinger, which suggests sexual activity, either masturbation or intercourse. I ask, again, "A girlfriend?" He

There is where his character took shape.

63

repeats the gesture, and I can only wonder if he means something George did alone, did with him, with a girl, with other boys, or with an adult?

I want to tell Mr. Bishop that I have seen the report he wrote about his Christmas holiday in *The Index* from 1932:

> "I came back to school in the afternoon about 4:30, and the first thing I did was to give George Culbertson a hearty hand shake. George is my school pal. He is sixteen and weighs 190 pounds. I am fifteen and I weigh 116 pounds. We are like Mutt and Jeff.

> "We talked about what we did during the Christmas holidays and almost before I knew it, it was suppertime. After supper George and I went to a drug store and asked for a near beer. They didn't have any, so we got root beer instead. Then we came back to school and got dressed for the show in the Chapel.

> "This morning, Tuesday, January third, we are all back in the harness again, and its only one hundred fifty-four days until the long summer vacation. Let's go!"

George was strong.

He was my friend.

He shot himself.

Gerald Bishop and George Culbertson were pals for over fifty years. I reflect that I might be visiting my father in a nursing home today, if he hadn't shot himself. Or, maybe I wouldn't.

I pull up Mr. Bishop's sheets and gently place my hand on his heart. Then I lower the shade where the afternoon sun is beginning to spread toward him. My eyes are moist with tears as I bend to kiss his cheek, say "Sweet dreams," and renew to my pursuit of my father's story.

I return to Virginia from my first exploration into Daddy's life in Colorado with a sense of excitement, feeling something like an archeologist who has uncovered important artifacts and is convinced that there is much more to learn.

I am curious about my father, who had lived in a residential school for three years and had made the adjustments to new friends and adults in his life. Now, George's hard work had paid off, and he was accepted to Gallaudet College in Washington, D.C. For the first time, he would be two thousand miles from his family, unable to see them on weekends and summer vacations. He would be in a larger and more challenging social and academic environment, where he could not be certain of being a leader in scholarship and athletics. Was he sad? Was he nervous? What was it like to be a poor country boy moving to a sophisticated city and college campus?

In 1864, President Abraham Lincoln had signed a charter authorizing the conferring of college degrees by the National Deaf-Mute College. In 1884 the school's name was

Daddy's Team

changed to Gallaudet College in honor of Thomas Hopkins Gallaudet, a minister who had devoted himself to establishing appropriate education for deaf students in America.

For many years Gallaudet College was the only academic institution accredited to provide a college education for deaf students. So, in the late summer of 1933, my father, a tall, wavy-haired, seventeen-year-old boy, traveled by train from Colorado to Washington, D.C.

My mother is the person who supplies me with the above information. And since she also attended Gallaudet College, she is able to provide me with a yearbook and with names and addresses of many of my father's classmates. These friends of his and my mother's are now in their seventies. Most are healthy, active, and articulate; and they, too, offer to help me in my search to know and understand my father's story. I do not initially tell them about my incest history because I want to know how they remember their friend, George, unaffected by this hidden part of his life.

Ed and Lois Jackson invite me to visit them at their home in suburban Maryland after receiving my letter and questions. They are friends of my parents whom I have

known since I was seven. Now, seated in a rocking chair in their living room, I see pictures of their four children who are my age – grown and married. These friends remind me that they were in the Gallaudet class of 1940 with my mother. My father was in the class of 1938, so they did not know him well during college. They remember George as a friend, hard working, and strong. Although later they would learn of the incest, they did not hear anything bad about him at college and specifically deny ever having heard anything about any sexual activity or behavior during those years.

Over coffee and cookies, we look at pictures of their grandchildren and share our delight about my mother's happiness with her new husband, whom she married just one year ago. We hug goodbye at the doorstep, and they give me cookies for my trip home.

Another of my father's friends writes to me about his memories of George at Gallaudet. He recalls that they were students together at the Colorado School for the Deaf, but that "George was several years older than I, so at the time, he was, in my eyes, one of the 'Big Boys' while I was just a little kid. I remember him as being very friendly and easy to get along with – a person who really impressed all who knew him as being a great guy." This college friend also recalls that all his friends were greatly impressed by the fact that George became a star of the Gallaudet wrestling team. He won third place in the National Collegiate Wrestling tournament.

Another classmate gives me a copy of the college yearbook, *The Buff and Blue*, June 1938, the year my father graduated. There is a picture of the Gallaudet Wrestling Team, with George Culbertson (Coach) in the center of the first row. He looks tall, broad-shouldered, strong and remarkably confident gazing into the camera, wearing dark wrestling shorts and a white tee shirt. Almost every friend from these years remarks on his being a football player and a champion wrestler.

Emotionally George was idealistic, and a lone wolf.

The other event that they all tell about is "the car accident." In 1937, George was driving several young men in his car, and he was speeding, indulging in his reputation for being a risk-taker. Perhaps alcohol was involved, although no one is sure. He lost control of the car when, coming to a fork in the road, he took the wrong one. Over-correcting on the gravel road, he skidded dangerously and the car rolled over on its side. He was the only one badly injured and was taken to the hospital with serious facial wounds and head injuries. Though the scars were hardly noticeable later in his life, he always felt disfigured by the accident.

"In 1937, at the age of 21, I was in an automobile accident," my father said later. "My skull was crushed over my right eye. I was not unconscious at first, but was later due to the loss of blood. As a result, I was badly injured about the face and head and this required plastic surgery. I had no after-effects of this accident such as headaches, but there was physical evidence of this accident, with what I've always felt was noticeable scarring of the face and head.

"I was able to return to college after six weeks in the hospital, and made up all my lost work in two weeks, graduating high in my class. In the two decades since this event in 1937, I have had no illnesses or accidents at all."

In December of 1994 my mother arranges for us to meet with Todd Benson, another of my father's Gallaudet classmates. He has been in our area to visit his son, and we meet for a brief interview at the Charlottesville Airport. Mom walks into the airport, scans the waiting area, and moves toward the three people gathered in a lively exchange of sign language. These friends, together with their grown son are waiting for the flight to begin boarding, and they must leave in just twenty minutes.

For our interview, we take seats at the back of the boarding area. Mom is here to interpret for us. Mr. Benson recalls that my father had a good personality, was popular, wrote well, played football, and wrestled. But then George was in the accident and hurt his head.

His was "different" after that; "something happened" and he was "off and on," "moody," "wary." Before the accident, he was good humored, but afterward, he withdrew.

I ask Mr. Benson if he has heard of George's problem with molesting children. He appears shocked. "What? No!"

He and my mother engage in a discussion about the possibility that George's accident and subsequent emotional changes were the origin of his "illness" which caused him to molest children. We all agree that it is sad and mysterious that this man had such a hidden life. I thank Mr. Benson for his time and willingness to talk with me and we return him to his family just as the flight begins to board.

Other letters I receive from Gallaudet classmates tell me that George is also remembered by friends from college as an active member of his fraternity. He was active in all athletics, captain of the wrestling team in the 1936-1937 school year, coach of the wrestling team from 1937-1938, and was elected president of his class for the last three years of college.

Also, here at Gallaudet, George fell in love, perhaps for the first time. Friends from both high school and college agree that George did not date or have other romances before he began courting my mother, Marjorie Forehand, a deaf student from Virginia who was two years younger. Marjorie was petite, thin, girl-like, innocent, naive.

When I talk with Mom about her college romance, she remembers that when she first met George, she thought he was nice and likeable, but shy. He didn't socialize much and had only a few close friends. She was attracted to him because of his witty

George did not date or have other romances before he began courting my mother. Marjorie was petite, thin, girl-like, innocent, naive.

conversation, his articulate writing, and his good looks.

Mom tells me about the "telegraph" system that George set up so that the boys could communicate with the girls in their well-supervised dormitory. He connected wires from his dormitory room to her room, running wires outside on the grounds between the two buildings. Using a toy telegraph set, George and Marjorie learned Morse code and then charged their friends five cents to set up dates with each other by telegraph. Since this communication between the sexes was not allowed, Mom kept her set hidden inside an orange crate draped with a cloth. "Once the housemother walked in for room inspection and she almost caught us," Mom laughs.

Mom and Daddy

In 1937, two years after meeting, George and Marjorie were engaged to be married. Marjorie's family and friends were happy for her. Her younger sister, Agnes, tells me, "Well, your mother brought him home from college and we all liked him. There was nothing in those days that would show anything was not normal about George. And Mother was so delighted because he was really such a nice person and she didn't know whether your mother, because of her deafness, would ever be able to have a normal life or anything like that. She was so delighted that Marjorie was going to be married and have a family. It just seemed so great."

A letter from her father that my mother has saved shows that he approved of George and wished them well. "Marriage is the most deadly serious thing you will ever do," he cautioned the young couple. "I am not saying this to discourage or frighten you, but to let you know that you and George must not expect everything to always be perfect. You must cultivate the virtue of patience. There is nothing that can take its place. There is no formula for happiness. People seem to learn only in the hard school of experience, and I hope your own lessons will not be too difficult."

Mom tells me, though, that even before the time George was in the hospital after the accident, she began to have doubts about marrying him. She was concerned about the fact that he could not seem to understand her ideas and point of view. She says that trying to talk with him was "like hitting a stone wall," and that good communication was very important to her.

But she believed that if she broke the engagement, friends would think it was because of George's facial wounds following his car accident. "I didn't think my real feelings could be understood and accepted by others, so I proceeded with plans for the wedding."

Daddy

My mother's sense of distress about her ability to communicate with George would continue throughout their marriage. Here was the first indicator of her wanting to speak about her reservations, but being unable to do so because of her worries about others' opinions.

Hannah and Eleanor, George's mother and sister, came east from Colorado by train for his graduation, and to meet the Virginia family of the girl whom he would marry. Eleanor has told me of the strangeness of being at Gallaudet, in a community of flying fingers where no one could hear, and about the sailor who asked her to dance when they went out on the town in Washington.

George was graduated in June of 1938 and the wedding was planned for two years later, after Marjorie was graduated and they both had jobs. In his senior yearbook, George Culbertson, B.A., is remembered as "Bravest of men. George is a big man – and at heart, too! He is a veteran and coach of the wrestling team. He will take up where others give up."

My father himself has described the process of his own development from high school and into college: "I was in seventh grade in public school, but when I got into school for the deaf they put me in tenth grade and gave me more responsibility and more confidence. I guess I realized it was up to me to handle it, and have been showing leadership ever since.

"I feel it was my loss of hearing that helped me find a place. Up until I lost my hearing I just lacked self-confidence. I had really received no guidance, and had no one to recognize the possibilities in me. So I didn't know what I had in me, nor had opportunity to use my leadership or to put my ideas across. I became idealistic, desirous of doing well in any thing I undertook. I am not conscious that I had any ideas of wanting to be a leader before, but as I entered CSDB, and later Gallaudet, I found I had the desire.

"Even so, I was somewhat shy, and found myself having difficulty with dancing and talking in mixed company. But as people eventually came to look upon me as a leader, this picture changed.

"So I knew what I could do," my father laughed, "and from then on I've had no hesitancy in trying things out.

"But although this self-confidence was recognized in my college days, I felt that I had companions, but no friends in the real meaning of the term. Emotionally I was idealistic, agnostic, and a lone wolf. Yet in the college yearbook they wrote about me taking up where others gave up. That has been true in many ways."

An essay in his class yearbook, "'38 25 Years Hence," imagined the graduating class in the future, and forecasted "I saw in the paper that George Culbertson, undefeated heavyweight wrestler of the world, was meeting a famous opponent that night." Another passage stated "George and the Missus (remember Margie) were spending a short time on the coast before leaving for their home in Hawaii."

Twenty-five years hence, in 1963, this would not be the story of George and Marjorie's life, but there was no way for any of their young and hopeful college friends to imagine the real story.

There was no way for any of their young and hopeful college friends to imagine the real story.

1943

Daddy and Mom

Chapter Four

Ahead of His Time

(1938-1944)

"Life can be so sweet
On the sunny side of the street.
This old rover has crossed over ..."

– Song by Dorothy Fields

When George graduated from Gallaudet College in June of 1938, he re-entered the public world he had left as a fourteen-year-old boy in 1930 when he had enrolled in the Colorado School for the Deaf. From age fourteen to twenty-two, he had lived in structured and somewhat sheltered residential schools for the deaf. During those same years, the United States had suffered through the worst years of the Great Depression, had experienced up to twenty-five percent unemployment, and had elected Franklin D. Roosevelt to his first and second terms of office.

With some of the policies of Roosevelt's New Deal, the economy had begun to improve, but times were still hard. George needed to find work and a place to live for the next two years until his fiancé, Marjorie, would graduate and they could marry.

Several months after our first visit, I am back at my father's sisters in Colorado. As we sit together on her couch, Elizabeth, his older sister, looks through her photo albums and finds the one with pictures from those years in the early 1930s.

She explains that while George was away at college, in 1935, Hannah, left her abusive second husband, Jack. Elizabeth had married and moved to California with her husband, Andrew, and they had bought a little lunchroom on the road up to Sequoia National Park. Hannah moved out to be near them and lived in a small cabin next to the lunchroom. She helped Elizabeth cook for customers and also helped take care of her first grandchild, who was three years old.

While he was waiting to marry and settle down with Marjorie, George traveled to California and lived with Andrew and Elizabeth and his new nephew for the next two years. He worked picking lemons and oranges and took a course in auto body repair. Elizabeth says it seemed that, after being at Gallaudet, "his deafness didn't bother him; he was happy and joking." I wonder if he also may have been relieved to be with his mother and sister without his stepfather.

Elizabeth was living just three hundred miles north of Long Beach, California, where their father, Samuel, had lived since he had left their family almost twenty years before this time. Elizabeth says George never talked about his father, but I imagine many of the issues of "fatherless boys" that are so widely discussed now also pertained to George. He may have felt confusion, guilt, anger, worthlessness, and, certainly, curiosity about the man he had not seen or heard from since he was three years old.

Mom has told me that Daddy was "not re-hired" after his first year.

Elizabeth herself expresses some of these feelings; she had been hurt by her father's abandonment and longed for a reconciliation. She then tells me that once, while George was living with her, he borrowed their car to drive the three hundred miles to their father's house. Elizabeth says that when George returned, he told her that when he got there it was dark, so he parked, got out, walked around the side of the house and looked in the window. He was able to see his father from behind, reading or listening to the radio, and he was able to get a glimpse of his father's life by seeing the furniture, the pictures on the wall. George turned and walked away. He didn't knock or go inside.

In 1956 Samuel Culbertson's son would admit that, "although my father is still living, the only contact I ever had with him after he abandoned me, my sisters and my mother, was a request for me to sign some papers for his Social Security. But when I found out that someone else could help him handle this, I just refused to provide the information he needed, and I would always vow that when I got married I would never let my children down like he did."

George and Elizabeth never talked about his thoughts or feelings, but now Elizabeth and I wonder if he was angry to see the comfortable life his father had, or if he was

KITCHEN DELUXE

Honeymoon Tent

afraid of how his father might respond to him. I think just seeing that his father actually existed may have made many things more real and possibly more painful.

"It's better that he left," George told Elizabeth when he returned from their father's house.

Samuel Culbertson died in 1972. George never talked with him.

When I am home, reviewing my notes from my talks with Elizabeth and Eleanor, I am curious about what was happening nationally during the years of my parents' young adulthood. I go to my encyclopedia and learn that in September of 1939, while George was living in California and Marjorie was completing college, Germany invaded Poland, beginning World War II. President Roosevelt, fearing that democracies everywhere were endangered, pledged "all aid short of war" to the Allies. The isolationists, those who felt the United States should stay out of the war, thought that the war was not as dangerous as Roosevelt believed.

This rift, between those drawn to intervene and help others in times of oppression and those who would rather isolate themselves from other people's conflicts, strikes me as distinctly similar to the arguments I am encountering about speaking or not speaking about problems in other people's families and lives. The challenges of confronting evil, of weighing competing loyalties, and of facing risk when called upon to act ethically, exist throughout history, politics, and cultures – not

Mom and Daddy

just in families. I wonder if the answers are the same in all of these situations. I wonder if there are any answers at all.

When Mom arrives at my house for our meeting to piece together the next part of the family story, she is wearing her light blue cotton slacks and matching sweater. Her soft white hair is cut short in the same style she has worn for years. Carefully, she places a cardboard box on my kitchen table and begins to take out numerous tiny black and white photos with curled, perforated edges. In the photos, she is twenty-two years old, dark-haired, dressed in slacks and a plaid shirt, seemingly playful and adventurous.

Sitting next to my mother, now in her late seventies, I experience a pang of sadness that I did not know her in the days when she was able to be carefree and hopeful about her future.

Mom tells me that, as Depression conditions continued to improve and World War II continued to escalate, in May of 1940 she graduated from Gallaudet College. She and George had been writing to each other regularly and making plans for their wedding. Since George had left California and was now working on his Uncle Ralph's farm, and the young couple needed this income, they decided to celebrate their wedding and honeymoon in Colorado. His bride agreed to come by train and meet him there.

Her family had little money and could not afford to travel to Colorado for their daughter's wedding, but they did pay for her train ticket as their wedding gift to the young couple.

As we talk now about her marriage, which occurred almost sixty years ago, Mom is matter-of-fact and even seems surprised that I am interested in knowing about this event. As I ask about her family, she says, "No, no one came with me. I went on the train by myself."

I express amazement about her courage; as a twenty-two-year-old deaf woman, she traveled alone for two thousand miles to meet and marry the man she had seen only once since his graduation, when he visited her in Norfolk during the summer of 1939.

She seems surprised that I think she was courageous, but she does admit, "I was disappointed that none of my family could be at my wedding with me." She also reveals that she and George had not sent any announcements to relatives or friends because of the Depression. "We didn't want to seem like we were asking for gifts," she explains.

George met his bride's train in Colorado and they were married on June 17, 1940, at the home of a deaf Episcopalian priest who officiated and pronounced them man and wife. Marjorie's dress, blue chiffon with a white lace collar, had been made for her by a classmate at Gallaudet. George's childhood friend from the Colorado School for the Deaf, Gerald Bishop, and his girlfriend were the witnesses.

The newlyweds "honeymooned" for two months in a tent house set up on Uncle Ralph's farm where George had spent his childhood summers. Mom makes no mention of romance or sexuality as she describes that they "lived in a tent house, which was a tent on a wooden floor with three-foot high walls or rails." George had built this place in preparation for his new bride.

In the manner of their times, George took care of the chores and Marjorie cooked "on a very small wood stove," cleaned, and did laundry using water from a clear creek, which ran behind the tent house. There was an outhouse a short distance away. The days were hot and the nights were cold. As Mom tells me about the pictures, she comments, "It was an interesting experience for a city girl."

I am struck with how little emotion or personal detail she reveals and, although it feels awkward, I ask my mother, "How was your wedding night?"

"Well," she says, "neither of us had any previous experience – not like couples these days – but I think everything was normal."

This is all she tells me. I am familiar with her modesty and choose to respect her privacy by not asking further questions. This information seems enough to answer my curiosity about my father's sexual experiences in high school and college, which seem to have been normal for a man of his times. I wonder where the first signs of his sexual problems might have occurred, and whether he and my mother experienced what we now call "sexual incompatibility."

Mom has all our family's photo albums and has been looking through them with me to help re-construct events. Now that we have looked through these pictures of her honeymoon, Mom suggests that I keep them to share with my sister. Along with the pictures and the story we are piecing together, I hope I can also pass on to my children my mother's strength and integrity, and her astonishing ability to continue through life with hope and optimism.

The following week I pick Mom up at her house and together we make the one-hour trip to Staunton, Virginia. As we drive through the autumn colors of the Blue Ridge Mountains, Mom recalls her journeys as a young girl, when she would leave her

I wonder if there are any allegations of child molesting.

parents' home in Norfolk each fall and come to Staunton to attend the Virginia School for the Deaf and Blind (VSDB).

Like Daddy, Mom had lived in the state residential school for deaf children since losing her hearing to ear infection at age five. Her parents traveled with her from Norfolk to Staunton by train every year, leaving their beloved eldest child in the care of strangers. Marjorie lived at VSDB year-round from age five through age eleven, coming home only at Thanksgiving and Christmas and in the summers. The teachers and other deaf children became her residential family.

Mom and Daddy

It's not the memories of my mother's childhood spent here that draw us back today, but rather the years she and my father shared living and working at VSDB, starting in September of 1940. After graduating from Gallaudet, Marjorie had obtained a position as librarian at her alma mater. Because of her subsequent marriage, George was hired by VSDB as supervisor of the boys' dormitory. The newlyweds would provide an extended family role for the young deaf children in their care.

Mom has told me that Daddy was "not re-hired" after his first year. I am curious if his personnel files will tell us why. I wonder if there are any allegations of child molesting.

As we drive onto the campus of the school, which is situated in the middle of the city, I notice that it looks surprisingly rural, with numerous tall trees and evergreens on the soft grassy hills. Mom points out her childhood dormitory, her classrooms, the gymnasium, and then shows me the entrance to the administrative building.

We park and enter the foyer of this colonial-style building, where we are met by a friendly, efficient woman who is expecting us. I called earlier for an appointment and asked if I could see my parents' personnel records, so she is prepared for our visit. We are offered a quiet office, and Mom and I sit side by side at a large mahogany table where we can spread out the forms and letters collected in the files that have been pulled out for us.

We decide to look first in George Culbertson's file, where we find the application he submitted for the job. The "experience" portion of his form reads:

I am experienced in all phases of farm work, in felling trees in a lumber camp, in automotive mechanics, in paperhanging and painting, in printing, in carpentry work, in fruit picking and packing, in oxy-acetylene welding, in auto body and fender repair work, and in auto painting, and ditch digging. My labor experiences are extremely varied, but few of them can be considered especially qualifying me for this type of work. An all around experienced man develops a practical outlook, which is of considerable advantage in any type of work, however. My primary qualifications for this work are my college record as scholar and student leader, and my personal character. I would like to teach English, Physics or Mathematics, or to act as supervisor, athletic coach or assistant printing instructor.

George was hired as a supervisor for the boys' dormitory, which involved helping the young students with their residential life – taking care of hygiene, doing laundry, dressing, bathing, getting ready for bed. In addition, he taught some shop classes for boys. In February of 1941, after six months on the job, we see that George received an "efficiency rating report" which was "below satisfactory" in areas of "classroom procedures," which included "preparation, encouragement of pupil participation, and provision for purposeful activities." Then, in another evaluation from April, the superintendent states, "I realize that it may take several years of experience to make him satisfactory in every respect, but the thing of which I complain is his apparent lack of effort and of interest." George submitted this letter of resignation a week later:

> "I shall do my work well during the time that remains to me as, of course, I do not wish it to be said that I failed at the job… I have long been planning to take specialized training in aviation instrument work, and nothing is to be gained by putting it off any longer…My resignation in no way affects Marjorie's position here. She desires to return to her work as librarian."

As Mom and I talk about Daddy not being re-hired, she remembers that he had conflicts with his supervisor. Sometimes he believed his ideas and innovations were superior and proceeded to implement them without prior approval. Twenty years later, my father would have similar problems seeking supervisor approval for his proposed improvements while working at the Colorado School for the Deaf and Blind. Mom never heard any other direct criticism of him, but in light of what we now know about his molesting of young boys later in his life, she wonders whether anything might have happened with the boys under his care in the dormitory.

We finish reviewing my father's personnel file with some disappointment because there is no explicit record of his relationships with the students or the cause of his

George was "firm and fair.

He was a fine man, a leader, ahead of his time."

dismissal. In any case, George was not rehired and the language of his personnel file gives no real clues as to why. I can't help but wonder if the vague language of criticism in his performance report hides darker truths about his molesting the boys, something which might not have been mentionable in 1940.

Next, opening Marjorie's own personnel file, we find a letter she wrote to the school superintendent in an attempt to intercede following her husband's poor evaluation. She writes, "I know George has his faults, but there is nothing hypocritical or subversive about him and you can depend on his loyalty. Sincerity is one of his strongest points." Mom and I share a moment reflecting on the irony of her faith in her husband's character.

Mom's file also indicates that she herself was responsible, competent and appreciated. She recalls how she enjoyed developing the school's library for the children. From her own childhood, she had a love of books and reading, and spent her days as a librarian organizing, cataloguing and enlarging the collection. She also remembers that, in a book series called The Little Colonel, she found a girl's name that she liked, and she decided that she would use it for her first daughter – Joyce. She tells me now, "Joyce sounded like a wonderful girl. People depended on her and if they needed help, they could always call on her."

Marjorie's record indicates that she was offered a contract for the following school year. With good jobs still scarce, and scarcer still for these deaf newlyweds, she accepted the offer to continue as librarian for the 1941-42 school year.

Before leaving the administration building, we ask for and are given a copy of the student enrollment records from the 1940 school year. Mom knows two of these students, men who are now in their sixties, who were boys under my father's care when he was dismissed from his job. She says that she will contact them and ask if they will meet with me to talk about their memories of my father.

It is difficult to feel compassion for a child molester.

Our drive back to Charlottesville goes quickly. Mom reminisces about her childhood at the Virginia School. I have a hard time listening: I am wondering about what was, perhaps, unsaid in my father's files.

True to her word, Mom soon arranges for me to meet with the two men whom she has known since they were students and she was the librarian at VSDB. My mother and these two friends are all still active in alumni activities at the school and in state organizations for the deaf.

We visit Jeffrey Martin in his home and talk about the many years he and Mom have known each other. Mom explains that I am trying to find information about my father's life and am curious about Mr. Martin's memories.

Mr. Martin tells me that he was a student at VSDB when George was a supervisor in the boys' dorm, and he recalls that George also taught shop. He describes George as "smart, macho, and masculine." Mr. Martin had heard that later in life George had been charged with molesting children, but even though George was supervising boys who were entering puberty and whom he taught about hygiene, deodorant, and other personal things, Mr. Martin never saw him behave inappropriately. He believes George would have been better suited to being a teacher than a dormitory manager. He was "firm and fair. He was a fine man, a leader, ahead of his time."

When we discuss George's sexual abuse of children, Mr. Martin appears sad and then, reminding me that the poet Lord Byron was also largely condemned by society, he quotes a poem by Joaquin Miller about Lord Byron:

> "In men whom men condemn as ill
> There is so much of goodness still.
> In men whom men pronounce divine
> There is so much of sin and blot;
> I do not dare to draw a line
> Between the two when God has not."

Pedophiles often seek out jobs that give them easy access to children.

I find it helpful to be reminded of our human tendency to label good and evil, and of our natural desire to be able to identify and separate ourselves from the "bad" person. Righteousness is so much simpler than compassion, and it is difficult to feel compassion for a child molester. Forgiveness and compassion may come, I believe, only after we admit and experience our sadness and anger about the "sin and blot."

And the larger question still remains: how can we accept and love the doer of the deed and nevertheless take strong action to limit their behavior, and to protect innocent children?

Soon after our visit with Jeffrey Martin, Mom also arranges for me to interview Sheldon Bates, who was a senior at VSDB when George was dorm supervisor. Mr. Bates and his wife are in Charlottesville to visit Mom on their way home from a trip to the beach. He remembers that all the children at the school liked George. "He was a good worker. I never heard a bad word about your father."

So, I must give up. There is no clear indication that my father was sexually involved with the VSDB boys in his care. But I still wonder.

From my own studies of psychology, I know that pedophiles often seek out jobs that give them easy access to children, something that George had at VSDB. Could he have molested a few of the boys without the others' knowledge? Or could this job have begun stimulating his pedophile fantasies? Or did he really not have any tendencies toward pedophilia at this time? I guess I will never know.

Mom and I continue to get together frequently to look at family photos and create a time line of her life with my father. She tells me that after one year together with his bride, when he was not re-hired at the Virginia School for the Deaf and Blind, George left her to live alone in a small apartment in Staunton. He moved in with Marjorie's parents in Norfolk, Virginia, where Marjorie's father worked at the Naval Air Station. George needed to find work and wanted to learn to build navigation instruments for airplane engines, and he thought his father-in-law could help him. Marjorie's brother, Harold, also lived in Norfolk, stationed there in the U.S. Coast Guard.

Uncle Harold has always been a constant and loving presence in my life. I call him and invite myself to drive to his home in North Carolina to talk with him about his memories of my father during Daddy's time in Norfolk. In 1955, when Mom first discovered Daddy's secret, her loyal brother Harold came immediately to help her.

Known for being easy-going, Harold is, as usual, sitting in his rocking chair with a cup of coffee and a book when I arrive. My uncle is two years younger than Mom and is an avid reader of U.S. history. He is friendly, casual, and always something of a tease. He offers me a pan to boil water and a jar of instant coffee. Smiling to myself, I decide that my coffee drinking habit is definitely genetic. With mug in hand, I sit in the nearby armchair and ask my uncle what he remembers about first meeting George Culbertson.

Harold recalls, "Marjorie met him in college and she brought him home before they were married. Yeah, I was favorably impressed. He was a fairly interesting conversationalist. He didn't read lips too well, but he spoke beautifully."

Harold remembers well the period when George first moved to Norfolk while Marjorie was still working at VSDB in Staunton. "George was doing odd jobs around town for anybody who wanted anything done – painting houses, repairing cabinets, fixing lawn mowers – you name it. He would take it and do it. He got a job, if I remember right, fixing dents at the Curry's Garage. He was a body and fender man. He had no trouble getting work at that. Of course that didn't pay too well, so he got a more skilled job later. People in general thought he was a very fine man, and had nothing against him."

Harold reminds me that it was in these months that the war in Europe was escalating. Hitler's armies had invaded Poland, the remainder of central Europe, and the Soviet Union. Churchill had promised the English people "blood, toil, tears, and sweat." But President Roosevelt continued to maintain the United States' neutrality and non-interventionist policy. The mood of the nation was dark, tense and uncertain as George and Marjorie entered their second year of marriage, separated by two hundred fifty miles and able to communicate only by mail and occasional weekend visits.

On December 7, 1941, Japan attacked the U.S. military base at Pearl Harbor, and the following day the United States joined the Allies in the now global war. Soon, in 1942, President Roosevelt called for the production of 60,000 new aircraft. Many believed the goal was impossible, but, in fact, U.S. facilities turned out 86,000 new planes for the Allied war effort.

George was patriotic and wanted to help the war effort, but due to his deafness he could not serve in the military. He did, however, obtain a position at the Naval Air Station in Norfolk and was given specialized training in aviation instrument work. I imagine George, twenty-six years old, frustrated that his deafness made him unable to fight overseas in the war, dedicating himself to rapid, efficient, high quality aircraft engine production. He was always proud of his mechanical skills, and they were never more valuable and more necessary than when the U.S. entered the war.

Lazy bones 1942

Daddy

Harold and I agree to take a break from talking. I am tired from my drive and want to take a nap, so he says he will just sit and read. As I pause to put the coffee mugs in the kitchen before heading for the guest room, Harold's eyes are already closed and he is sleeping in his rocking chair.

After we wake up from our naps and fix more coffee, Harold and I continue our interview, then prepare a simple supper and continue to share stories and memories until dusk.

Since I plan to make the four-hour drive back to my home tonight, Harold walks me outside to my car. I have recognized for years that this uncle provided a safe and gentle male presence that has been crucial in my life. Tonight I tell him, "Thanks for all you've done for my mother and our family. I'm so grateful. You helped me know about good men."

"I've never wanted to hurt anyone, and I'm glad I could help," he tells me. We hug good-bye, and I drive home knowing that so much of my inner strength and faith have come from my mother and her family. I am truly grateful.

A few days later, when Mom and I get together again to continue our discussions about the early years of her marriage to my father, she tells me that some friends of

George was patriotic and wanted to help the war effort, but due to his deafness he could not serve in the military.

1942

Mom and Daddy

theirs from those years will be visiting her next week on their way to a meeting of the Virginia Association for the Deaf. She wonders if I would like to talk with them. "Wonderful! What good timing!" I say, and ask her to make arrangements to bring them to my office for interviews.

Then, Mom adds, "These friends are also friends of Henry Walls, a deaf man I've met at my church. I'd really like you to meet him. Maybe we could all have lunch together after the interview meeting."

With the interviews and lunch agreed on, Mom and I begin reviewing the years after my father was not rehired at the Virginia School for the Deaf and Blind. As Daddy moved on to find work in Norfolk, Mom completed her second year as the librarian at VSDB, living alone in a small apartment and seeing her husband on occasional weekend visits.

Daddy settled into a secure, productive job as an aircraft instrument maker at the Norfolk Naval Air Station. And in June of 1942, my parents finally felt economically stable enough for Marjorie to leave her position and join her husband in Norfolk. They had been able to save money in their first two years of marriage and bought their first house, a two-bedroom, beige, stucco home on a quiet street in a middle-class neighborhood. Here, in the fall of 1942, George and Marjorie really began their domestic life together.

The young couple wanted a family and focused their life on preparing for the arrival of children. They bought a car, repaired and painted their house, planted flowers, and built a sandbox in the yard.

They also began to participate in local and state activities for the deaf. George and Marjorie were well liked and were part of all the social events. Several of their friends from VSDB lived nearby.

A week after Mom and I discuss the early years of her marriage, six of these friends meet with Mom and me in my office. They have all known me since I was born, and the room is filled with hugging and laughing as we catch up on children and grandchildren. They take seats on the couch and in several chairs arranged in a semicircle. Mom is joining us to provide her good-spirited and invaluable interpreting services. She and I tell our standard joke – that because she's so good at reading lips, it's her fault that I never learned sign language.

With photos, scrapbooks, and rapidly moving hands, the members of the group describe their friend George Culbertson. They especially remember George for starting a new club for the deaf in Norfolk, The Silent Fellowship. One friend emphasizes, "George was a leader. He knew what to do with money and formed a corporation to protect the club. The Fellowship was successful because of George, and it closed after he left Virginia because there was no leader. He was a wonderful man."

Another friend remembers that she "worked with George in the Virginia Association for the Deaf [VAD] for ten years, from 1942 until 1952. George was secretary of this state organization for two terms, 1944 through 1952, when I was treasurer," she tells me.

My father also remembered this: "Since leaving college, I have been active in the Virginia Association for the Deaf. I don't want to sound as though I am bragging, but I served as secretary for eight years. I established several ideas in Virginia that have become institutions, like organizing an Auto Club for the Deaf; and I was Editor of the Virginia Association for Deaf People newsletter. Later, when we moved to Maryland, deaf friends asked that I help remove restrictions to the deaf drivers, and I was successful in that."

He was ahead of his time, they all say, a vigorous activist for rights for the deaf. George started the first VAD bulletin and newsletter and even addressed the Virginia State Legislature, orally, to ask for separate schools for the deaf and blind.

Slowly, the group becomes quiet and the mood becomes more serious. I ask Mom to explain that we know my father had some problematic behaviors and we wonder if they have any information about other parts of his life.

Hesitantly, one man in the group mentions that one time when they were visiting, George gave Marjorie a sleeping medicine. Then, when she got drowsy and went to her bedroom, George wanted him to go outside and look through the window to watch Marjorie undress. This man knows that George asked the same thing of another friend of theirs at another time. "I'm sorry," he says. "I don't want to say bad things about your Dad."

"I'm sorry," he says. "I don't want to say bad things about your Dad."

Mom reassures her friends that she already knew about these two incidents, because George himself had told her, and they seem relieved that they have not hurt her with this revelation.

Many times people say they were molested and other people say, "No. That can't be true. He's such a nice man."

I ask her to sign to them, "I wonder if you ever heard anything about George molesting children?" We explain the intention of my book.

No, they had not heard about his child molesting. One of the women says she thinks it is awful, and hard to believe. They had no idea. "He must have been born that way and couldn't change," she says. "I'm so glad you are writing a book. It will be very helpful, because many times people say they were molested and other people say, 'No. That can't be true. He's such a nice man.'"

I am gratified that these friends of my father and mother, these people who have known me all my life, believe and accept my story, and, even more importantly, that they are so aware of the importance and difficulty of speaking out about "good people" who do "bad things."

After several further anecdotes, the conversation turns to plans for lunch and Mom says Henry will meet us at one of our favorite restaurants, the Blue Bird Café. I thank her friends for sharing their memories with me, and tell them I look forward to our upcoming lunch.

An hour later, when I arrive at the Café, I look inside the dining room and see that Mom and her friends have not yet arrived. As I turn back to the waiting area, I see a bear-like man with curly white hair and lively, friendly eyes, sitting alone in a chair, seemingly waiting for someone. Approaching him, I begin simultaneously to speak and finger spell, "Are you Henry Walls?"

His surprise turns to laughter as I explain that I am Marjorie's daughter. Henry stands up, large and solid and gentle, and gives me a warm hug. "Your Mom is very special," he tells me.

I have no way to know how very special Henry himself will soon become in my life.

Chapter Five

Rollercoaster at Ocean View

(1944-1951)

"You are my sunshine, my only sunshine.
You make me happy when skies are gray.
You'll never know, dear,
how much I love you.
Please don't take my sunshine away."

– Song by Jimmie Davis

Daddy and Me

In the months after I first met Henry, Freeman and I join him and Mom several times for dinner, and we learn he is a widower with no children. At Christmas, we are invited to his unusual antebellum home in Scottsville, Virginia, and find ourselves captivated by this engaging, energetic gentleman. Like my mother, Henry grew up in a residential school for deaf children, then pursued a career as a machinist and, in later years, worked at the Pennsylvania School for the Deaf. He and my mother have become very close, sharing church activities and other common interests.

The next time Mom and I get together, she tells me she has some wonderful news. During a romantic supper at the Boar's Head Inn, seventy-three-year-old Henry proposed marriage to my seventy-seven-year-old mother, and she accepted. She is both surprised and delighted, and says they plan to have the wedding in May.

Joyce

Me

Giving my mother an enthusiastic hug, I tell her how happy I'll be to have a new stepfather. We talk excitedly about her guest list and other arrangements. She asks if I would read one of her favorite Bible verses, "To everything there is a season…" at the ceremony. She hopes Dorene will read the passage from Corinthians that says: "The greatest of these is Love…." I look forward to helping my long-lost, new-found mother celebrate.

In spite of this excitement, we soon get back to work and begin unfolding our time line, preparing to discuss 1944, the year I was born. Again Mom has brought photos, as well as my baby book, some letters, and her own special memories. She reminds me that during the time she and Daddy were awaiting the arrival of their first child, World War II was ravaging Europe and was the main focus of attention in the U.S. news. My father was still making aviation instruments for the Navy planes being used in the war.

Mom was three months pregnant on "D-Day," June 6, 1944. The Allied troops, with the largest sea-borne invasion in history, landed on the beaches of Normandy in northern France and took the Germans by surprise. By the end of June, one million Allied troops had reached France.

What a happy and good-natured baby Joyce is.

I realize that if my father had not been deaf, he would have been enlisted in this "war to make the world safe for democracy." Had that occurred, I ask myself, "Would I have been conceived? Would my father have returned from the war? Would he have been present for his wife's labor and delivery?"

Mom remembers that she had such a hard labor that at one point the doctor considered performing a Caesarian section. But her baby daughter finally arrived naturally after thirty-six long hours. She opens my baby book with its faded pink satin cover and shows me the tiny red-inked footprints of her new baby. Under "Days to Remember," Mom dated my "first smile" at two weeks. I "laugh aloud" at three months. In her careful script, Mom has written with a blue fountain pen, "What a happy and good-natured baby Joyce is."

There are entries about my first visit to the doctor, my first visit to Santa, my first lost tooth, my first sentence.

There is no record of the first time my father molested me.

Mom has also brought some letters that she has saved inside the cover of the baby book. The letters were exchanged between my parents and two of Mom's Gallaudet College classmates, Jane and Charles, who had also married after graduation. Charles had a job at Gallaudet teaching mathematics. These friends visited back and forth with my parents and, because Mom and Jane had been roommates and were especially close, I would grow up calling them "Aunt Jane" and "Uncle Charles."

The first letter mom shows me is dated December 20, 1944, the day after my birth. The letter is from Daddy to Jane and Charles. "Just a line in a heck of a hurry—Joyce Lynn arrived Tuesday afternoon at 3:11 o'clock. Weighed 8 lbs. 3 oz. Marjorie is feeling fine and didn't have a very hard time of it."

Then, dated Christmas Day, 1944, I received my own first letter. Mom has saved it for me in its old faded envelope. The 3-cent postage stamp has a purple background with a white eagle surrounded by thirteen stars and emblazoned with a banner saying "Win the War." In the letter, Jane wrote:

> Dear Joyce,
>
> This is our first letter to you....
>
> You are only 6 days old now and much too young to understand what we are trying to say. We hope, though, that in some mysterious way, you do know how much love and welcome this letter contains for our "little niece." You have a grand mom and pop and a nice, cozy place to come home to, but we wanted to extend our Welcome, too, and to send a wish for all the years to come, for you, dear Joyce.
>
> Affectionately, Charles and Jane

There is no record of the first time my father molested me.

Sitting at the table with my mother, I find myself crying at the tender wishes and deep devotion that welcomed me to the world, and for the innocent prayer that this new little baby girl would live a life without shadows.

I slowly fold the letter and the poem and replace them inside their envelope. Mom had told me before that I was a "wanted child," that she and Daddy had been ready to start their family from the time he moved to Norfolk. I cannot imagine a better beginning for a baby than being welcomed into a family and friendship circle full of such love.

Mom explains to me that she had been instructed by the doctor not to "spoil" her baby by picking me up or feeding me when I cried. She would sit next to my cradle, weeping, as she watched me begin to cry three hours after a feeding. She and I would both cry together until the four-hour mark when she was allowed to pick me up and nurse me. She wanted so badly to be a "good mother," to do the right things for her baby.

This same determination – to be a good mother and follow the rules –influenced her, for over forty years, to avoid addressing with me the facts of my father's incest. This is a rule I wish that she had broken.

My baby book mentions that, in March of 1945, Jane came to Norfolk for a week to help Marjorie with the new baby. I ask Mom if she remembers this visit. She recalls it well and tells me how appreciative she was for the company and for the help.

I hesitate, and then, knowing that I can trust my mother to deal with truth and feelings, I tell her about a letter I recently received from Jane, in response to the questionnaire I sent her a few months ago. In the letter, Jane describes this trip to visit her friend and new "niece." She tells me:

"For the first time, I saw an aspect of George that had never surfaced before! He started 'coming on' to me and one morning actually crawled into my bed in the room next to your mother's! Nothing happened, really, but I was wary thereafter and left before I had planned."

Jane has never told her friend, Marjorie, this story and leaves it to my discretion about whether to share it with Mom. "They say it's better to tell the truth," she writes, leaving it up to me to decide.

To my surprise, as I cautiously reveal this "secret," Mom laughs and says, "Oh, I've known about that for years! Daddy got up to 'fix breakfast' and crawled in bed with Jane. Several years later, after I learned what he was really like and was thinking of divorcing him, he was trying to hurt me, so he told me about all his "escapades" – his having friends look at me through windows, his approaching my friends and sister, his affairs."

Mom wanted so badly to be a "good mother," to do the right things for her baby.

At the time these unsettling events occurred, my mother went through a deep depression. She was learning that Daddy was not the knight in shining armor she had hoped her new husband would be. "I cried most days for a whole year," she tells me.

As we speak, she is oddly matter-of-fact about these once painful events. I know that, through the years, my mother has cultivated the gift of letting go of anger and not becoming bitter or vengeful about her life.

Mom and I talk about the years of silence between her and Jane regarding Daddy. It will be up to them, I realize, to decide if they want to discuss it with each other. Mom thinks it happened too long ago and is not worth bringing up. But I know the distance that can be created by unspoken secrets, and I am a little bewildered at why she would just shake her head about the strange, perplexing ideas and behaviors of her husband.

We return to our focus on the first year of my life. Mom notes that I was just eight months old when, on August 6, 1945, the United States Air Force dropped the first atomic bomb on the city of Hiroshima, Japan.

I know that between 70,000 and 100,000 people were killed by that bomb, and that the devastation and ongoing damage were immeasurable and indescribable. The huge mushroom-shaped cloud that lingered after the explosion became my generation's symbol of danger and destruction. Ten years after this bombing, this frightening cloud would appear in my dream. It became the image of the devastation of my family by incest.

The bombing did, however, lead to a quick and definitive end to the War. Japan surrendered on August fourteenth and, in October, the fifty-member United Nations was established to promote world peace.

Mom and I notice that in both national and personal history, the questions of proper use of force, moral justification for inflicting pain, and responsibility for repairing damages seem to persist.

Returning to the baby book, I read that for Christmas 1945, when I was one year old, my parents and I went to spend the holidays with Mom's younger sister, Agnes. She and her husband, Brett, had a daughter, Susan, who was just twelve days older than I was. This was the first time the sisters saw each other's babies and it was my first time to play with my cousin. Susan's name is entered in the baby book beside the words "first playmate."

By now, Mom and I have spent several hours sharing questions and stories about her first year of motherhood, my first year of life. I see in her mementos the evidence for what I have always known – that I was welcomed and cherished from birth and throughout my life. Often, when I am asked what helped me survive and heal from incest, I mention the importance of my mother's love, the deep trust and hope she instilled in me from the beginning, and the complete acceptance and sense of her parental responsibility that she always communicated.

"You are so important and special," I tell her as we hug and say good-bye.

"I'm just your mother," she says.

Mom's simple statement understates the value she places on motherhood. It is, in fact, a profound summary of her recognition of the depth of commitment and responsibility that she believes and accepts as right and natural for a mother. My mother's inability to protect me from my father, or even to talk with me about it for so many years, in no way diminishes the fact of her deep love for me and my brother and sister.

In the best of worlds, every child would be born into the essential simplicity of this deep maternal love.

Mom was learning that Daddy was not the knight in shining armor she had hoped her new husband would be.

"I cried most days for a whole year," she tells me.

Reading in my baby book about our family's early visit to my Aunt Agnes and Uncle Brett's house, opens another interview possibility for me. I wonder if Agnes, like Jane, will share memories of my father acting inappropriately; and if Susan, my "first playmate," has early memories of spending time with my father.

In the spring of 1995, after a round of phone calls, Agnes and Susan agree to meet with me to talk about my request for family information and stories about my father. We have not been together since a family reunion almost ten years ago. I tell each of them about the research I am doing about my father and find out that, although my aunt has known about the incest ever since my mother discovered it, she never told her daughter. Susan is sad for me, compassionate about the years of struggle, and willing to talk. I have not seen my cousin in years and am touched by her concern and interest in my project.

Susan and I each drive four hours to meet at Agnes's house on Maryland's Eastern Shore on the Chesapeake Bay. We take a short walk in the fading afternoon light. Aunt Agnes expresses her delight about her elder sister's approaching marriage, and looks forward to attending the wedding.

After our stroll, we gather in Agnes's living room. There are also family photos and mementos honoring Agnes's life as a mother and now grandmother.

Discussing the values that have always been a part of my family, Agnes says passionately, "When you have a child, you've made a commitment! You do whatever you need to do to take care of your child!"

When you have a child, you've made a commitment!

Susan has brought a childhood photo album her mother prepared years ago for her as a gift. In the album, Agnes has arranged and added captions to pictures of Susan's childhood. Some of the pictures include my family and me.

As I ask about the first Christmas visit, which Mom had described in the baby book, Agnes says, "George's behavior just wasn't quite right. I knew there was something wrong. When you were a baby, he would change your diapers, and sometimes I thought he was overly attentive to cleaning your private parts." She adds, though, that she did not observe any inappropriate behavior. The black and white photos of this time show two little girls wearing freshly ironed dresses, wide-brimmed hats, and hair bows.

The following summer, in June of 1946, when my mother was seven months pregnant and waiting for her second child to arrive, Agnes and Susan came to Norfolk to visit. Agnes's husband, Brett, was stationed overseas. Susan and I look at photos in her album of two chubby eighteen-month-old toddlers in sun suits. A handsome, dark-haired man, wearing shorts and no shirt, is standing behind them pushing them in a swing. Susan recalls, "Uncle George played with us a lot."

Agnes tells another story. "During our visit, George came into my bedroom and gave me some lacy lingerie. I was shocked and embarrassed and told him to get out."

"Later on, though," Agnes says, "there was a time when George wrote me a letter about how attracted he was to me. It scared me and I tore it right up. I never told your mother. I never told my mother. I never told anybody but my husband. But after that, I would never let Susan visit your house unless there were a lot of adults there." Agnes decided that she herself would never visit her own sister unless her husband was with her.

Through the evening and on into the next morning, Agnes and Susan and I share stories and laughs. It is good to be reminded that my family shares other memories besides the painful ones brought on by our discussion of my father. After breakfast, when I am ready to leave, Susan suggests that I take her photo album with me so that I can spend time looking again at the family pictures.

Mom and Me

As I drive home, I wish that, in addition to photos, I could somehow borrow my friends' and relatives' memories. As I begin to interview people about stories that include me, more than ever before I am confronted emotionally by my own lack of conscious recollection of my childhood. Confusion, sadness and a certain detachment and bemusement become my companions on this part of the journey.

I lost contact with so many of my friends and relatives during my years of healing from incest. I assumed they did not know the secrets that I was struggling with, and since I was neither ready to tell them my story nor able to continue hiding it, I stayed away from them. The incest, I see today, caused me to lose all the Susans of my childhood.

I am also beginning to recognize another piece of the jigsaw puzzle. Like more overtly abusive husbands, my father was, deliberately or not, beginning to create a home where his wife was being isolated from her close friends and family. Her best friend, Jane, and even her sister, Agnes, no longer felt safe visiting her. Mom's circle of relatives and friends who might have helped her judge and discuss what is "normal" and what is "not quite right" was being eliminated, dropping away.

As I began writing this book, I felt grateful for the loving and accepting responses I received. Now, seven years later, I am more aware of the gaps in my own memory that extend far beyond my molestation, that creep into all the nooks and crannies and even wide sunny days of my childhood.

Back at home, reflecting on my visit with my aunt and cousin and on our family's life during those early years, I look at the photos and time line that Mom and I are assembling. Our family was still living in the little beige stucco house in Norfolk when my brother Gary was born on August 18, 1946. I was just twenty months old. Marjorie and George were settled into family life now and were doing well in the post-war boom.

I had mailed one of my questionnaire letters to two people on Mom's Christmas card list who were among her friends and neighbors from these years, and I receive responses from both of them. I go to Norfolk to meet with them and to look at two of the first homes in which I lived.

Marian Morse invites me to join her for dinner at her condominium in Virginia Beach, not far from the home on Randolph Street where she raised her seven girls. "We kept trying for a boy," she laughs. Mrs. Morse moved here to this retirement residence several years ago after her husband, Steve, died. The children are all grown, and her small, cheerful living room is full of pictures of her daughters and their families.

I lost contact with so many of my friends and relatives during my years of healing from incest.

Mrs. Morse says her family moved to Randolph Street in 1947, when their oldest daughter, Theresa, was five and their next child, Diane, was three. "Your parents and you and Gary were already living there. Steve enjoyed George, and they both worked at the Naval Air Station. At first we didn't have a car, and Steve rode to work with George and another rider. Your mother used to take me shopping to the A&P store on Friday afternoons, but we did buy a car in 1948 – a green Streamline Pontiac."

Mrs. Morse tells me that my father was well liked. George and Steve did construction projects together – they built a cabinet and they cut up some ammunition boxes into pickets and made a picket fence. George helped Steve build a dollhouse in the back yard for his girls.

She also recalls meeting my grandmother, Hannah, when she came to Virginia to visit her son's family. "After meeting his mother, I always felt like George had to come from good stock. To me, she was what I would like a mother to be. She was very comforting and consoling and reassuring. She just made me feel like things were going to work out."

Mrs. Morse's daughter, Diane, who is my own age, also responded to my questionnaire. In her letter, she recalls that her family moved down the block from us when she and I were three years old. She remembers that my parents were deaf, that our families were friends, and that our fathers car-pooled to work. "I remember your dad had thick curly hair and strong features," she writes. "And I also remember that you were one of my first friends."

I remember nothing of her, or her family.

Diane tells me, "My mom kept a close handle on us. She didn't let us run and play, and she would always be with us supervising. I wasn't allowed to go to other houses until I was ten or eleven years old. Mom told us later that she was strict because she was sexually abused when she was a little girl."

Diane's sister Theresa tells me she doesn't remember my father at all, even though she was older.

This feels significant to me because of my own lack of memories about my father. With sad irony, I see that even though Mrs. Morse herself had been sexually abused as a child, she was no more capable of being able to detect Daddy's pedophilia than were others completely unfamiliar with abuse.

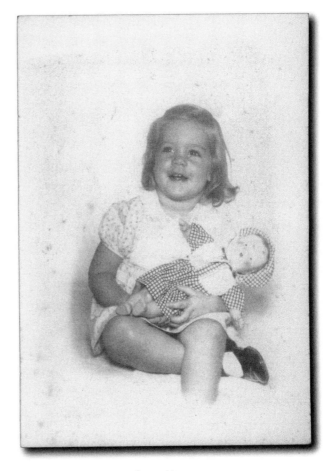

Me

The other person I am able to interview during this trip to Norfolk is Bonnie North, who lived next door to us after we moved to a three-bedroom, white shingled house on Ocean Avenue in 1950. I was six, Gary was four, and Mom was pregnant with her third child.

Bonnie North's three children became our playmates. Mom and Mrs. North have been exchanging Christmas cards for over forty years. When I arrive at the home Mrs. North now shares with her second husband, she has prepared photographs and albums for me to look through with her.

Although we lived next door to this family when I was six and seven years old, I do not remember any of the children or activities that Mrs. North shows me in the pictures. The photos show five kids sitting on the porch steps sharing watermelon, showing our neighbors my new dachshund puppy 'Flippy', and hanging by my knees from the trapeze on the backyard gym set that my father built for all us children to enjoy. I tell her that Mom says it was Mrs. North's oldest son, Robbie, who told me there was no Santa Claus, and that I cried and didn't believe him. When I demanded the truth, Mom and Daddy told me that Santa Claus is love and the spirit of giving.

"Your mother was always such a sweet person," Mrs. North says. "I was so sorry to hear about her divorce from your father. Your mother and I have always kept in touch, but after the divorce I only saw your father once. He visited me after being released from the hospital where he was treated for a nervous breakdown he had due to your mother divorcing him. He just seemed to want to see an old friend, and he told me he had found God and was a new man now. We didn't really have much to say to each other and I never saw him again."

What this former neighbor does not choose to mention is the day my mother went over to her house in search of my father, who had gone there to borrow a tool and who had been gone a long time. Mom didn't see them, and since she couldn't call out and hear a response, she went upstairs looking, where she found George in bed with Mrs. North.

Mom has told me that, even though she and Mrs. North managed to remain friends, this was the first time she had really known about any of my father's secret sexual behaviors, and that she was devastated. Mom describes this moment in her marriage by saying, "My world fell apart."

My father was beginning to create a home where his wife was being isolated from her close friends and family.

As we sit looking through her album, I realize this neighbor's affair with my father is not central to my search for information about his sexual abuse of children. I decide there is no need to pursue this topic further. Leaving this weight of unspoken stories and questions, I thank Mrs. North for her time and assure her I will pass on her good wishes to my mother.

I pull away in my car and stop a block or two down to study my map of Norfolk, which Mom and I highlighted together before I left Charlottesville. I then proceed to search for my first homes and school.

I find the house on Randolph Street, still a small, beige, well-cared-for stucco home. I am also able to see which house belonged to the Morses. I recognize these houses from pictures I have seen, but I have absolutely no memories of any activities either inside or outside them.

Mom has told me that from his birth until 1955, Gary and I shared a bedroom. It was in this house that my father began offering to take care of the children at bedtime while Mom would finish up in the kitchen. Daddy instituted a regular ritual: sitting in his lap to read a story, kneeling for prayers by our beds, and bestowing a good night kiss and tuck-in.

In my late twenties, when I began to experience physical and emotional flashbacks, I recognized that the incest began when I was three or four years old. Today I am in my car looking at the house where my father began molesting me. I feel a huge, empty place inside my heart where childhood innocence and joy belong.

From here it is just a few minutes' drive to the location of our second house on Ocean Avenue, where we lived next door to the Norths. But it is gone. In its place is a parking lot for the expanded air base.

Another family with five children had lived down the block. Their house is also gone. Their daughter, Sharon, was my friend. I remember her name, but not our activities. Mom has shown me pictures of our outings with Sharon's family on Sunday mornings to the nearby beach, Ocean View, where Sharon's father, a Navy

Daddy

cook, made breakfast for all of us over an open fire. I have pictures of Gary and me playing with these children, but they feel like strangers to me.

Our family also used to go to the nearby Ocean View Amusement Park, and although I don't remember being there, in Mom's albums there is a picture of me standing in front of one of the rides and eating pink cotton candy. Mom says Daddy called me a "scaredy cat" because I didn't like the roller coaster. During my years of healing, I wrote a poem about being on the roller coaster with my father. Today I see it as a metaphor for his abuse of me. I still have a copy:

> I been on a roller coaster once when I was just a kid.
> My Daddy bought the ticket and took my hand,
> Me draggin' my feet behind
> 'Cause I get scared of things that's high and fast....
>
> He lifts me into the roller coaster car
> An' he's all happy 'cause this is gonna be fun.
>
> But...I know this ain't gonna be fun
> 'Cause I might die.

I drive now to look at the emptiness where the roller coaster used to be. The park was demolished for an explosion scene in Death at Ocean View Park, a movie made for television in 1978, when I was thirty-three years old. I remember feeling a strange happiness when I saw pictures in the newspaper of the explosion and debris.

I feel a huge, empty place inside my heart where childhood innocence and joy belong.

From these years on Ocean Avenue, when I was between the ages of five and seven, a time from which adults can often recall their earliest memories, I know only what I have seen in photographs. Driving today to see those places, any hopes of finally recovering memories of my girlhood by seeing its locations are now also demolished. The absence of the amusement park and my childhood home feels particularly congruent with my inner world.

As I drive home from Norfolk, my body feels heavy and my insides feel empty. So much of me is missing. Now my quest to understand my father is having other unexpected effects. I am beginning to fill in the gaps of my own past, to see in person some of the people and places I previously knew only through photographs and other people's stories. But my gratitude for those who are sharing their memories of me and my childhood is caught in an undertow of sadness that I can never truly possess my memories – the bits and pieces of my own life. I live a life of hearsay.

I don't remember being molested by my father. I don't remember bedtime stories, family dinners, birthday parties, my first day of school, being sick with chickenpox, taking tap dancing lessons, playing with my brother Gary, or the birth of my sister, Dorene. I don't remember being loved and cared for by my mother.

But I know all these events took place. There are pictures of everything except the fondling and the oral sex that my father forced me to perform for him.

As a psychiatric nurse, I know that the term "dissociation" refers to "a disruption in the usually integrated functions of consciousness, memory, identity, or perception of the environment."

"Dissociative amnesia" is a form of dissociation involving impairment in memory in which "memories of a personal experience cannot be retrieved in a verbal form." This type of amnesia is "usually related to traumatic or extremely stressful events."

Not remembering my abuse may be a particular kind of blessing, but the price has been to lose the "integrated" memory of my entire childhood. I lost the story of who I am, what I've done and, most of all, the deep feelings and connections with people who love me.

The other form of dissociation that helped me survive was "depersonalization" – feeling detached from my self. Depersonalization is the "sensation of being an outside observer of one's mental processes, one's body, or parts of one's body."

This blessing kept me from being conscious of both the physical and the emotional feelings of my abuse experience. From age twelve, although I have some memories, I usually observed myself from above and behind my right shoulder. I watched myself talk with my brother and sister, roller skate with friends, bite my fingernails, and stand in front of the class to give my report on lions and tigers.

I have come to describe my memories as pieces of a jigsaw puzzle. I have some left-brain, verbal memory pieces – memories stored as words. These include stories, songs, and random phrases. Mom has told me about things I used to do, such as, "You used to like to jump over the heat grate in the hall." I remember songs I used to sing in Sunday School and Brownies, such as, "Make good friends, but keep the old. One is silver and the other, gold." I also remember words Daddy said, like "Don't wear underpants to bed. It's not healthy."

I have some pieces stored as body memory. When I am hungry, I begin to feel anxious and frantic, the way an infant might feel while waiting to be fed. When I wash dishes, drive my car, or fold the laundry, my body "knows" what it was taught to do. For many years, when I began to feel tired and sleepy in the evening, my body moved into "hyper-vigilant" behaviors – organizing stuff in drawers and closets, playing loud music, making lists and charts – trying to stay awake and keep from being alone in my bed. My body remembered and wanted to avoid the incest.

I have sensory memory pieces, stimulated by smell, sound, touch, sight, even taste. The smell of corn bread calls up the memory of summers at my grandparents' house. The smell of the after-shave lotion my father used makes me nauseated. Pink mimosa

So much of me is missing.

blossoms bring back the loneliness of my adolescence. Having my mouth touched unexpectedly makes me gag.

My dream or image memory pieces include dreams of being rocked in my mother's arms and of playing beside a creek with my friend JoAnn. In a "guided imagery" session, I was once instructed to "see my childhood home and go to my safe place." In my imagination, I had to leave my house and go outside and down the block to find a 'safe place' alone under a tree. Ten years ago in an art class I drew a picture of myself as a little girl. I had no hands and no mouth.

My emotional memories often arise unexpectedly, usually in response to some experience. When I see reruns of "Lassie," feelings of affection for my long-lost collie, Honey, well up. During intimacy, if someone says "I need you," I usually feel frightened. Crying during sex, which occurred during the first fifteen years of my adult life, is an example of sorrow associated with abuse.

Daddy and Gary

I do have some fragments of these varied types of memory experiences. What I lack is the connections that turn pieces into what people usually call a "memory," an actual whole recall of a moment with picture image, words, sounds, and other parts to complete the story. My experience is that I am missing my "self," the wholeness that might be "me," my "story," my "integrity."

However, I do have three clear "integrated" memories of the first seven years of my life. The first is of a boy in my first grade classroom giving me an "Indian burn" by twisting the skin on my arms in opposite directions. I cried, put my head on my desk and refused to go out to recess. The teacher wanted to know what was wrong, but I wouldn't tell her. I was already used to being silent about what was hurting me.

Another memory I have is of being on a swing in my friend Sharon's back yard. As I went up in the air and came down, the air went up under my dress and I suddenly realized I was not wearing any underpants. I was frightened, crying and trying to get home to find some underwear before anyone found out.

My third memory is of jumping in the waves in the ocean at Virginia Beach. We lived nearby and could go frequently in the summer to spend the day picnicking and playing in the sand. As I splashed and jumped, a big wave came and knocked me over. I could feel the heaviness and power as it surged above me and held me down. I was frightened and thought I was going to drown. Daddy was laughing as he lifted me up after I surfaced. "You got caught in the undertow," he said cheerfully. It didn't seem funny to me.

I notice that these three memories each involve some extreme of physical or emotional difficulty. Maybe pain and fear were the only ways to break through the dissociation.

I examine the question, "If I can't 'remember' the simple events of my girlhood, how do I 'know' that my father sexually abused me?"

I 'know' with a certainty that most incest survivors do not have. The first way I know is through my mother's account of finding Daddy molesting me in the bathroom when I was ten years old.

Second is my father's own admission to me, when I was eighteen, that he needed to have sex with me since my mother was "not affectionate enough."

Third is the stark fact of my father's sixteen month commitment at Spring Grove State Hospital, my review of over fifty pages of his psychiatric record there, and his explicit, repeated admissions, while there, of the incest.

Fourth, my research and interviews about my father's life have uncovered a consistent pattern of his engaging in fondling and oral sex with children from three through fifteen years of age. Part of the pattern is his telling the child that "I'm doing this because I love you," and instructing them that it be kept a secret "because other people won't understand." I know that many survivors of childhood sexual abuse do not have these forms of external verification of their secret, isolated experiences. However, I have studied research data indicating that, even without this validation by others, most survivors remember at least portions of their abuse.

However, for those adult survivors like me, who do not have the "normal" integrated picture, sensory, and story memories of what happened to them in childhood, the process of "remembering" can be overwhelming and confusing. Without this validation by others, which I have been fortunate to have, I would have only the memories which emerged in my body, my emotions, my dreams and my art during a ten year period of intense flashbacks, depression and psychotherapy.

When these pieces emerge, in no order and often with no warning, it can be like

Daddy said, "Don't wear underpants to bed. It's not healthy."

having piles of loose jigsaw puzzle pieces, without a picture to show how they will fit together – or even if they belong to the same puzzle.

I have friends and clients who live with these unconnected, confusing memory "pieces." Often, they must come to accept that they may never have a "whole picture." My blessing, I realize, is that even if I do not have the memories available inside my own mind, I do have enough other information to complete and tell my story.

Turning on the radio, I listen to tragedies reported on the evening news: war, earthquake, train wreck. The survivors of these events are both overwhelmed by pain and loss, yet grateful to be alive. Some are hysterical, some are angry, some are numb. But at least they have the opportunity to speak about what happened to them.

The pain felt by survivors of child sexual abuse is not necessarily greater than that experienced by survivors of natural disasters. The difference is that abuse victims often cannot clearly remember trauma that occurred in private and silenced by secrecy, nor – all too often – can they even find anyone willing to listen to their grief, to give it the essential validity which simple acknowledgment conveys.

CULBY & GENE'S PLANE al,

Daddy

After this trip to Norfolk, my investigation into the mystery of my father's life feels even more important. Reading these pieces of my father's story may be the closest that some survivors, and some of their families and friends, can come to making their own abuse seem whole, coherent and true.

When I get closer to home, I am ready for a change in mood and I switch the radio to a familiar local station. I sing along to country music tunes as I turn off the interstate and head toward the mountains. Although it is evening, the sky is still light and the spring air is warm. I finally pull the car into our driveway.

When I walk up our steps, I see Freeman sitting outside on the front porch. He is holding the book he is reading with one hand and petting Slide, the cat, in his lap with the other. When he sees me, he stands and spreads his arms into a welcoming embrace. I rest my head on his shoulder and take in the warmth and steadiness of his love.

I am tired and glad to be back in my safe and comforting home. Freeman gets us each a glass of water and puts aside his novel to listen to my update.

I tell him how photos, family stories, other people's memories, and even driving the streets of the town where I spent those years have helped me see that my young girlhood is like the stereotype of the 1950's suburban, nuclear family. The picture shows Mommy, Daddy, three children, a dog, a white picket fence, mothers exchanging recipes, fathers carpooling to work, playmates building sandcastles at the beach.

Nothing is visible about the nighttime secrets and nightmares. No one can give me any photographs or stories to confirm what I know, or describe what I don't remember. Only my brother Gary might have been able to share his memories, if he had some, but he is no longer here.

Freeman listens attentively and gently, as always. He is a person who is able to clearly remember his brothers, his parents, his houses, his friends and his schools from his childhood. It is hard for him to imagine not having those memories. As an avid reader of fiction, he likens my experience to that of a character without a setting.

Tomorrow morning, Mom will be coming over to hear about my trip and to look through more pictures from our years in Norfolk. I will write down more of her stories and memories and ask her more questions.

But tonight, I let it go – the pieces, the empty spaces, the questions, the confusion, the mystery, the tiredness. I accept the things I cannot change. In this peaceful silence, Freeman and I sit together and watch the fireflies come out as the sun goes down.

I'm doing this because I love you.

When Mom and I get together next morning, we first finalize details for her and Henry's wedding ceremony, to be held at their church the coming week. My little sister, Dorene and her husband Rick will be coming from Ohio. Mom's brother Harold, her sister Agnes, and most of her grandchildren also plan to attend. She seems so happy.

I tell her about seeing our first home during my trip to Norfolk. She hands me a battered gray composition book, which she says is the only other family record from this period. In the summer of 1948, when we still lived on Randolph Street in Norfolk, my mother and father took Gary and me on a cross-country automobile trip, and Daddy kept a logbook:

> "NOTES on a trip from NORFOLK, VA to WALSENBURG, COLORADO, and return – July 24 to September 5, 1948 – by THE CULBERTSON FAMILY: Joyce Lynn (age 3 yrs. 7 mo.), Gary Richard (age 23 mo.), Mother Marjorie, and Daddy George R.
>
> CAR – 1947 NASH '600' – speedometer reading at Norfolk 15153."

That's the way the front page reads, neatly written in Daddy's methodical, cursive, blue-ink handwriting. And for the next 70 pages, he describes the journey from his own point of view. "Getting eight weeks leave with full pay from my work at the U.S. Naval Air Station, Norfolk, Va., we're headed for a family reunion in Walsenburg, Colo. Who has extra pincushions? We're all on pins and needles 'cause we leave tomorrow," his narrative begins.

He has written meticulously and daily about our route (Smokey Mountains, then into Tennessee, Mississippi, Arkansas and on westward)... but has included almost nothing about his own family and how they interacted on the trip. However, Daddy has recorded the Burma Shave signs: "The man who wins his girl's applause must act – not look – like Santa Claus."

Finally in Colorado, he recounts how I meet my Grandmother Hannah, as well as so many aunts, uncles and cousins, for the first time.

His narrative continues with accounts of our visit to Pike's Peak, and campouts in the Rockies. He records when we toddlers sit astride our "first horses." Daddy apparently led us all on "strenuous hikes."

And then, "Rocky Mountains are fading from view. They were wonderful. How long before we see them again?" Little can my father know that he will live out his last three decades – alone – in the wilds of these mountains we are leaving.

We drive homeward via Chicago, where Daddy has to see the famous "Tucker car" manufacturing plant. More and more map and route details.

Gary and I are mentioned less than a dozen times in seventy pages of this journal.

Next, my mother shows me a picture of me at the age of five, standing in the back yard of the house on Ocean Avenue and wearing a white nurse's uniform and cap. Mom says I wanted to be a nurse from the time I was five years old.

She also has my report card from Ocean View Elementary School, where I began first grade in 1950. With a blue fountain pen, in perfect script, the teacher has written, "Joyce is a good pupil. She has a splendid attitude toward her work and classroom activities." Mom hands me a photo of me in the school Christmas play. I was the bedraggled "poor little rich girl" with only a rose to give to the baby Jesus.

Mom tells me that for my sixth birthday, in December of 1950, she and Daddy planned a party with the neighborhood children and some of my new first grade classmates. She says I cried and wouldn't play any of the games Daddy was leading for the children.

She points out our first television in another picture. She and Daddy couldn't hear, but she says they still were fascinated by being able to see the pictures, and she remembers the first show they watched. It was "Your Show of Shows," starring Sid Caesar and Imogene Coca. "You didn't have to hear to enjoy that show," she tells me. "It was so funny just to watch their faces and the things they did." She remembers the shows that Gary and I first watched – "Roy Rogers," "I Love Lucy," and "The Lone Ranger." I have, tucked into my verbal memory, the theme song from another show, "Howdy Doody." But I don't know when or where I heard it.

There is a picture of Gary and me sitting in Daddy's lap for story time, and Mom reminds me that two of my favorite books were The Pokey Little Puppy and The Little Engine that Could.

There are also pictures of me standing by our big green Nash car, hanging from my knees on our climbing gym that Daddy built in the back yard, and sitting with several friends in a circle while Daddy tried to teach us the manual alphabet.

My father decided he wanted to learn how to fly a small airplane. Maybe all the years working at the Naval Air Station had inspired him. Maybe it was his adventurous, risk-taking nature that motivated him. Perhaps he wanted to defy his deafness. There are tiny black and white photographs of Daddy standing in front of the small two-passenger airplane he was learning to pilot. He had always been a leader. Now the local newspaper did a feature article noting that he had successfully become one of the first deaf pilots in the United States. The story noted that, when the nurses told Daddy his third child was on the way, he took his plane up to 7200 feet, twice as high as he'd ever been before, just to celebrate her arrival.

My new baby sister, Dorene, was born in March of 1951. I was six-and-a-half years old. Although there is a photo of me holding her in front of the house right after Mom came home from the hospital, I don't remember this or any other part of the early years of my sister's life. Dorene says she has always felt like an outsider in our relationship. Maybe that's because emotionally I wasn't really present there with her.

My mother tells me that her marriage was in a crisis by the time Dorene was born.

My father had begun insisting on being nude inside his home, and that his children be naked also.

Daddy and His Children

By then, she had discovered the affair with Bonnie North. My father, she says, encouraged her to have affairs of her own, and invited her to engage in group sex. She refused.

In addition, George had begun insisting on being nude inside his home, and that his children be naked also. He had unrealistic dreams about marketing inventions he was working on, and was making risky financial and business plans. He was harsh with his son, Gary. Both Gary and I were sucking our thumbs regularly, and wetting our beds almost nightly. Our father mocked and belittled all of our mother's concerns.

However, with three young children to care for now, Mom could see no options but to make the best of it.

I remind Mom that this perception was accurate during the fifties. There were few good options for raising children as a single parent, and very little social acceptance of divorce. She did not know yet about the incest. My mother replies, with a look of remorse, "How I wish I had known. I should have known."

As I carry the legacy of lost childhood, my mother carries the legacy of "not knowing." She no longer feels weighted with guilt, but she will always feel regret and remorse. She wanted to be a good mother. She would have protected her children if she had known what was going on.

The change in our relationship over the past few years has become very noticeable to both of us. Now we can tell each other our feelings without fear or blame. As our afternoon together comes to a close, I reflect, within myself, on Mom's coming marriage to Henry. As we hug good-bye, I tell her how sorry I am for what she went through with Daddy, and yet how joyful I feel in seeing her present happiness.

Within a few days, I receive two more letters from people who knew me and my father during those years in Norfolk – one from Betsy Rogers, a friend, and another from one of my cousins.

I phone Betsy. She is several years older than I am, but because her parents were also politically and socially active in the Virginia Association for the Deaf, Betsy and I used to see each other a few times a year when our parents visited each other. I had not realized just how close our families were.

Betsy tells me, "Your family always was real important in my life. Your Dad was my godfather. When I was baptized at the Episcopal Church, your parents came. My parents thought so much of George.

"I visited your home in Norfolk when I was eight or nine years old. It was extremely hot, and we had been to the beach. George was walking around in underwear; you and Gary were walking around nude. George wanted me to get naked, too. I said, 'No,' but he tried to convince me it was okay. I was very uncomfortable."

I explain that this pattern of watching naked children appears frequently in stories about my father's later life. Betsy also tells me that once when she was alone with George in the car he made her sit in his lap. "I think it was a sexual thing, but nothing real overt. He wanted me to drive, and I protested."

Another time, George took her up alone in an airplane. He wanted her to look over the side and he took her picture in the plane. "Did anything else happen?" she asks herself, wondering out loud. "I don't know."

She also tells me, "He was so different – cavalier, very handsome, mysterious, powerful. My parents said he had a nervous breakdown in Maryland; that he had problems. My mother told me later on that he had molested kids in Colorado. I feel very sad for him – he was such a creative person.

"I wonder about the airplane. I was uneasy about everything I ever did with him. Something wasn't right about this – to be all alone, far away from everyone, with

I carry the legacy of lost childhood, my mother carries the legacy of "not knowing."

*Your dad
was so
different –
cavalier,
very
handsome,
mysterious,
powerful.*

him. I was afraid of the plane and afraid to drive the car. I didn't want to. He kept egging me on. I never met a man like that. He was always acting like a child."

The other letter I receive around this time is from my cousin, Matt, the son of Mom's brother, Harold. His family lived nearby when our family was in Norfolk. In response to my questionnaire, he writes, "Only a few things come to mind when I think of your family. I remember the lights over the doors that connected to the doorbell, so they would flash and your parents would know someone was at the door. I thought that was really neat! I remember a Nash auto. I was impressed by the rear window wiper. I also recall it had a long flowing hood ornament – strange things impress small boys!

"As for George personally, I really only remember him as very large and sort of boisterous – not necessarily in a bad way. I do not recall any inappropriate sexual behavior toward me, but I do recall Mom saying something about she and Aunt Agnes having to keep away from him, because he was always 'coming on' to them. So his inclinations were not all directed at children."

My cousin's mention of his mother, my Aunt June, reminds me of the earlier information I learned about my father approaching Mom's sister, Agnes, and her friend, Jane. Although June and Uncle Harold have been divorced for many years, I decide to contact this aunt, whom I remember from Thanksgiving dinners that were held in her home when I was a teenager.

I mail a short note to June, asking her if she would be willing to have me visit and talk with her about my father. I do not tell her about the incest, deciding that is better left for when we meet in person. Within a few days I receive a friendly phone call and an invitation to come and meet with her in her home in Richmond, where she provides foster care for infants who are waiting to be adopted.

I am curious as I make the two-hour drive to her home. We haven't seen each other for over twenty-five years. June is now in her seventies, lives alone, and answers the door with a happy, chubby baby in her arms. I am immediately relaxed by her friendliness, warmth and openness.

She invites me to join her and six-month-old Buddy in her living room. This husky, active little boy plays with toys on the floor near June's feet while she and I talk. I tell her about my childhood incest, my own children's abuse, and about the book I am planning to write.

She gives me a sympathetic look and says, "I guess I should have known about your father, but I didn't. There was something not right about the way he played and showed affection with children, but I told myself, 'Everybody hugs kids.'

"I despised your father," June continues with refreshing frankness and humor. She tells me that George would often pat her on her bottom when she visited my family.

Then, when he became more and more insistent and began to show up on her doorstep, it wasn't funny any more. She told him to "forget it," but that didn't stop him from just walking into her house and making advances, so she began keeping her door locked. At the time, she knew he was having two other affairs.

"He was an open, friendly guy. The way he was treating me was like he was doing me a big favor, being generous, that it wasn't for him. How conceited can you be?

"George was gifted, talented, and he could fix things. He overcame deafness like it didn't exist. He had four thousand good qualities. But his intrusive behavior and personality were totally impossible. I despised him."

June didn't want to say anything to Mom, so she chose to be nice to George during family visits, but she made sure never to be alone with him.

My aunt has not known until now about the incest and my father's abusive behavior with other children. "Thank God I was avoiding him, so he never got near my kids. It never occurred to me to protect the kids from him. I feel guilty that I didn't know."

I take away a sense of appreciation for June's dedication to the children in her care. I also come away knowing that this aunt understands and cares about me. I have had a number of encouraging notes from her since then, telling me that she is proud of me. I feel like I have another family member back after the long silence.

These interviews with family and friends who knew my father when I was a little girl have helped me know my own childhood more fully.

As for my father, this is my first clear information about his sexual behavior, both with adults and with children. People who knew him in high school and in college reported that he did not even date or have girlfriends until he became engaged to my mother. Friends and students from his first job at the Virginia School for the Deaf and Blind did not know about any sexual behaviors with the children there.

Later in my investigations, I will locate my father's psychiatric hospital record and learn much more about my father's life, including his sexual inclinations. His revelations in these records help me understand the explosion of sexual interest and impulsive, inappropriate advances that came during the second five years of his married life.

"I became aware of myself sexually at around age thirteen," reported George. "It was only daydreams at first, imaginary incidents that were sexually stimulating. Gradually I began exposing myself, having the warped notion that the girls enjoyed seeing me exposed. Now I feel this was the time when there began to be something wrong with me mentally, so I do recognize I am in need of hospitalization.

There was something not right about the way your dad played and showed affection with children.

"About the first thing I ever heard about sex – I must have been 9 or 10 at that time, I'm not sure – really made an impression on me. I was talking with an older boy, who asserted that all girls wanted sex, and to succeed it was all a question of approaching them in the right way. But it seems to me that any boy or girl learns or hears this at that age. I was never in any trouble as a child, and had nothing further, sexually, on my mind until the time I lost my hearing.

"After I lost my hearing, I withdrew into myself because I lost my friends. I spent more time around home than an average boy did. During that time I started to read a lot. Some of this reading was good, but I also got hold of some sex magazines, and I read several of these at a time.

Gary, Dorene and Me

"That put ideas in my head, and it was not long before I consciously began exposing myself to my sisters around home. It was a very bold approach, but I managed to make it accidental, since there was little privacy in our small house. Exposing myself, ever since age thirteen, I have always done that way; never bold outright exposure.

"I was not at home after I started school at CSDB. I was away nine months of the year, then in the summers I went off to my uncle's ranch. That kept me away from home. Up until I went to college I never had any tendencies to expose myself outside of home. I was always shy with women until I met my wife, and I never did make approaches or make advances to a woman, except for exposures, until after I was married.

"Thereafter, I found many times to make what looked like an 'accidental' exposure. It began with my wife's sister Agnes. Lest you get the wrong idea, there have only been seven or eight women to whom I have exposed myself. It wasn't widespread, just personal friends and relatives.

"These behaviors might suggest that I lived it up, but I had been told, as well as read, that a man had to have sex release or he would go crazy. I know these behaviors are finished now.

"Before, sex used to predominate in my mind; it was a constant feeling, it seemed. But such exposures were always with my friends, or my sisters, and, in later years, my wife's and my friends. I made them with a pretty firm belief that I was, in a way, giving other women pleasure. I felt that they enjoyed it.

"I would make plans how I could expose myself to those women, both before and after our marriage. I see now this was improper thinking, especially after I began to imagine situations that were exciting. My fantasies encouraged the behavior.

"There were times that I felt such remorse that I decided to change, but I did not have anything to use except will power. I could not stop those thoughts.

"I never had physically known any woman before my marriage. I had wrong ideas of what to expect from sex and marriage and was disappointed – dissatisfied.

"After our marriage, I developed the feeling that my wife and I were not sexually compatible; our sexual relations were very unsatisfactory. Nine years later, I met a woman who had similar ideas to my own, and I had my first extra-marital intercourse. She was married, and we had an affair. Soon after, I had an affair with another woman… both affairs at the same time. I also had a very satisfying sexual experience with a neighbor, and about this time I gave up caring for my wife.

"But when my wife found out about these affairs – they came to light and caused trouble in my home – I promised her I would not have anything to do with other women. I have kept my word on that to this day, and since then, I have not touched any other woman."

I see that by 1951, even though George is married and has three children, he is encouraging friends to engage in shared voyeurism by watching his wife undress. He is making unwanted advances to Marjorie's sister, sister-in-law, and best friend. He has engaged in three adulterous affairs. He is having his children play naked in the house when his wife is absent, and he is coercing his young goddaughter to undress and sit on his lap.

From his earlier sexual shyness and inhibition before becoming a husband and a father, afterward George seems to have developed a number of diverse sexual behaviors – most of them distressing to others. His tendencies toward exhibitionism have given way to bold advances toward adult women and coercion of children. I wonder, but cannot know, what happened to cause this change. In his hospital records, my father himself explained his extra-marital affairs as results of sexual dissatisfaction in his marriage.

But his sexual interest in children cannot be explained as simply.

I have known that I lack memory for my own childhood abuse, but Betsy Rogers remembered clearly my father's requests for her nudity in our house, as well as her uneasiness, as a young child, about times spent alone with him. I am curious how

George's sexual interest in children cannot be explained as simply.

many other children, like Betsy, remember his advances, and how many others, like me, do not.

Daddy didn't tell Mom about molesting his own daughter.

In the past few months, I have received several letters from cousins and childhood neighbors who say they are glad to hear from me, but they are sorry they cannot help. They don't remember my father. So, although I have pictures of my father playing with these children, their lack of memories about him will be some of the missing pieces in this story. Again, I wonder, but cannot know, were they just too young to remember Daddy? Did they not have significant contact with him? Or did they too, lose memories of frightening and confusing experiences?

My mother has said that Daddy once told her about his "escapades" to provoke and hurt her. But he didn't tell Mom about molesting his own daughter, or about his efforts to seduce other children. His deceit and manipulations in these early days were but the first stages in a pattern of victimization and betrayal of trust that my father would visit on his sisters, nephews, nieces, grandchildren, and friends and their children, over three decades to come.

Daddy

Daddy, Gary, Dorene, Me and Mom

Chapter Six

Father Knows Best

(1951-1955)

"Oh yes, I'm the great pretender,
Pretending I'm doing well.
My need is such I pretend too much.
I'm lonely, but no one can tell.

Oh yes, I'm the great pretender.
I seem to be what I'm not, you see."

– Song by Buck Ram

My father had worked at the Norfolk Naval Air Station through the war and into peacetime, but my mother says he began to realize there was no further possibility for him to advance. He heard from friends about a job as an instrument maker for a small engineering research company in the newly developing Maryland suburbs of Washington, D.C. This move north would also allow George and Marjorie to be closer to their deaf friends from Gallaudet College. Many of their college classmates now lived in the area, and several of the men were now professors at their alma mater; their wives were mothers and homemakers.

When our family moved to Langley Park, Maryland, in the summer of 1952, I was seven and a half, Gary was six, and Dorene was one and a half. We moved into a one-story, three-bedroom brick house with a basement and a yard. The house was on a cul-de-sac, and the neighborhood children played safely in the street and could follow a nearby stream into a local park. Like the family on the new television show, "Ozzie and Harriet," we lived in suburbia at its best. We walked to school and came home for lunch. Mothers were home after school. The neighbors all knew each other and kept an eye on each other's children. We were all supervised and protected.

Another popular television show, one that my deaf parents could enjoy because there was a written message they could read on the screen, was "I've Got a Secret." A guest

Mom, Me, Gary and Daddy with Dorene

contestant would have a "secret," written out so the audience could read it, and the panel members would ask questions in an effort to guess the secret before the time ran out.

Today I think back to the secrets my own family had by this time.

I remember one more TV show our whole family watched together. It was called "This is Your Life," and brought together guests who revealed stories from a person's past. Now, all my interviews seem to join with one voice to say, "This is your life, George Culbertson."

Again I am aided on my journey by Mom's Christmas card list. She has stayed in touch with Myrna Carter, our next-door neighbor from Langley Park. Mrs. Carter replied to my initial questionnaire in 1994, and in 1995 I call and ask if I can visit her. Now she lives in a larger house about five miles from Langley Park. She and her husband moved here as their two sons grew older, but her husband died some years ago, and now the children are grown and married.

Although I do not really know or remember this neighbor, when she opens her door to welcome me, her face and voice seem very familiar. Mrs. Carter invites me into a lovely sitting area in her living room, offers a pillow for my back as I take a seat on her brocade wing back chair, and serves me a cup of tea. She tells me she regrets not being able to attend Mom and Henry's wedding, and we celebrate my mother's new happiness.

Our conversation turns to Mrs. Carter's memories of my childhood and family, and she describes fairly ordinary, but warm and personal, events. She remembers meeting her new deaf neighbors and being surprised at how easy it was to talk to Marjorie, "because she read lips so well."

Mrs. Carter and Mom would visit each other over coffee several mornings each week, taking a break from their housework and sharing recipes and child-raising stories. When I ask, this friend says Mom never talked with her about marriage or family problems.

The Carters had two boys who were somewhat younger than Gary and I, so "you all never really played together too much," she tells me. She knows about my book interviews and has asked her sons if they remember Mr. Culbertson. They tell her that they don't remember him, but they do remember playing with Gary in our back yard.

Mrs. Carter herself says she doesn't remember much about my father. She recalls that he was a "large, very muscular sort of a man, more of a loner than your mother." She also remembers that my parents "entertained and they seemed to have a lot of friends." I tell Mrs. Carter these friends were my parents' "Potluck Group," who still continue to meet monthly almost fifty years later.

Before leaving, I ask this neighbor and friend of my mother's if she knows how to contact any of the other families from our cul-de-sac. She tells me who moved and who died. As far as she knows, none of the families from our time are still living there. The only ones she is in touch with are the Poultons.

I am delighted to learn this and to get their telephone number, because Dana Poulton was my best friend from Langley Park. I thank Mrs. Carter for her time and she apologizes for having so little information. I reassure her that her view of my family as ordinary and unremarkable is exactly the kind of information that is valuable in this story. Incest most often occurs in ordinary, unremarkable families. Child molesters and pedophiles often seem ordinary and unremarkable to their relatives and friends.

I drive fifteen minutes through the Maryland suburbs, through places that were "in the country" when I used to live there, and finally return to Langley Park. When our family moved to this suburb in 1952 this was a newly built housing development, not far from a modern shopping center. Now there is a shopping center on each corner of the major intersection, along with four-lane highways, fast food restaurants, and discount stores.

I know how to get to our street because, for most of my childhood and early adult life, I lived within thirty minutes of this place. I have driven by several times in previous years, never with much focus, just tracing the route of my life – alone, with Gary, with Mom, with each of my two husbands – taking the "where I lived during my childhood" tour. On each trip, I talked about the ages we were, the schools we attended, and other mundane things that I knew as facts. Only with Freeman did I talk about what happened inside the house.

On the way to our house I pass my elementary school. One of my few clear memories is of my teacher, who had the whole class buy "tonettes" – little plastic flutes – and who taught us to play music together. During these years, each morning my mother would give me French braids. Recalling this brings back one other memory.

Once a week we had a singing class, and the teacher was able to hear the monotone in which I sang. One day she stopped the class and said, "Don't sing way down there, Joyce! Sing up here." She grabbed my braids, yanking them painfully and humiliatingly upwards as she said, "Here." For the next thirty years, I never sang again, choosing to stay safe and just mouth the words. My father had already ordered me not to speak, and now I couldn't sing.

Incest most often occurs in ordinary, unremarkable families.

Past the school, at the top of the hill, I turn right, drive down to the bottom of our cul-de-sac and stop my car in front of the aging brick house so I can write some notes about my memories. From this time in my life, third and fourth grade, I have photographs of bike riding and roller-skating with my best friend Dana, of using crayons to color the designs on paper napkins, and cutting out clothes for paper dolls.

I do remember one time when Dana and I secretly packed a doll trunk with graham crackers, apples, and some clean clothes, so we could run away from home. We left boldly, two eight-year-olds walking up the street in broad daylight, each holding one end of the small trunk. But after we had walked three blocks we became tired and worried. We had no place to go. We decided that maybe we shouldn't run away after all. We turned around, walked back into the welcoming cul-de-sac, sat down in my back yard, opened the trunk and ate our graham crackers and apples.

Dorene was sucking her thumb. I was biting my nails to the quick, and all of us were wetting our beds.

Still, though, I don't remember family life or the inside of my home here. I am sure we had meals, baths, holidays and birthday parties there. I do remember Joan, my first friend at my new school. When I interviewed her, she told me, "When I first met you, Joyce, you were already talking about being a nurse at Children's Hospital. A Washington Post columnist regularly solicited contributions for the hospital, and for several years I remember that you asked to get all your birthday presents as checks, which you then mailed in to the newspaper. You were so thrilled when your name was printed in the paper as a contributor."

I would share classes with Joan through third and fourth grade, and then again from seventh through twelfth grades. After that, we would live together for three years in our nursing school dormitory. "I remember your parents because they were deaf, and you came to my house after school," Joan tells me. When I tell her about my father's pedophilia, she pauses to reflect. "Oh, Joyce, I'm so sorry," she says. "I remember you were always so serious and quiet, so I see how you would never have told."

During the two years we lived at Langley Park, I have only two memories from inside the house. The first is a memory of lying in my bed at night. Daddy walks in and sits on the edge of the bed, and I pretend to be asleep. He calls my name and shakes me gently to try to wake me, but I lie stiff, unmoving, my eyes closed. Finally he gives up and goes away. My guess is that my child's psyche could hold this memory because it was an experience of power, of saying, "No," of getting him to go away.

The other memory that I have from inside the house is of a group of children – maybe five or six of us – lying in a row on the basement floor. We all have our underpants off – that is all I see. We are "playing doctor" – that is all I know.

Now, though, I wonder, why would such a large group of young children "play doctor" by lying in a row naked? I wonder if my father was "playing doctor" with us? I also wonder why I would retain this particular memory. Could this be the first time Daddy had a group get together inside our house? Or maybe the last? Maybe somebody told, maybe someone walked in and saw.

When I look up from my note-writing and turn to glance again at my old home, I see two little children, who have paused in their play to look at me and wonder what I am doing parked in front of their house. I smile and wave and drive away.

The next morning, after a quiet return trip and a good night's sleep, I call the phone number Mrs. Carter gave me to contact our other neighbors, Dana's parents, the Poultons. I leave a message and in the evening am surprised when I answer the phone and a woman's voice says, "Joyce? Hi. This is Dana."

This is the voice of someone I am seeing as a nine-year old girl.

We have not talked with each other for forty years. I feel young and awkward, but we soon make some adult connections. Dana's parents are not well and she is at their home in Florida to help them with some tasks. She is married, has children and works full-time.

"Me, too," I say. "I work as a nurse."

When I share the focus of my research with Dana, she says that she never had any idea I was being molested and that my father never approached her. Specifically, she does not remember anything about being naked or "playing doctor" in my basement. She says that she has heard a lot about pedophiles in the news, and is sad about what happened to me.

Aug. 20, 1953

"The gang"

Neighborhood Kids

Dana reminds me that we went on lots of bike rides. "The main time I remember about you, Joyce, is one day when my mother called me into the house and told me my grandmother had passed away. When I came out you asked, 'What did your Mom want?'

"I didn't want to be a baby, so I just said, 'My grandmother died.' You said something nice and then I got back on my bike and we rode to Langley Park School. I had tears rolling down my cheeks. Joyce, you were so sweet. You didn't say anything. I will always remember. You were just a good friend."

Us Kids and Honey

My eyes are moist now as I listen to Dana's memory. For forty years she has remembered a friend who "didn't say anything" – a friend who just listened and stayed with her in silence while she cried. So many times in my life I too, was blessed to have someone who was "just a good friend."

I thank Dana for being such a friend to me tonight and for sharing her memories of my family and me. Although we probably won't meet again, this forty-year-old childhood friendship feels important in my story.

My cousin Pam, Uncle Harold's daughter, who was Gary's age, writes, "The only things I'm able to remember are that Uncle George had very dark hair and deep set dark eyes, and we came to your house on Sunday afternoons to play with a little dog that looked like Lassie!"

I have talked about my years in Norfolk with my cousin Susan, and my "best friend," Diane, two children who spent time with my father and who don't remember him. Now, I have talked about the years in Langley Park with another cousin, Pam, and another "best friend," Dana, who also spent time with my father and do not remember him.

Daddy himself understood that molesting children was wrong

These missing pieces of my puzzle seem curious. I know for certain that my father was molesting me during these years. I wonder if he was molesting any of these cousins and friends of mine as well?

When Mom comes to my house again to help me put together this part of the story, I tell her about the recent interviews and my two memories. She is sad, as she always is each time she learns additional details of what happened to her daughter. Surprisingly, though, she offers immediate validation for my memory. My mother says she remembers a time when Daddy came up the basement steps into the living room and he was wearing only his bathrobe. She asked him why he was in the basement with the children in his bathrobe, and he got angry with her for having a "dirty mind."

In Langley Park, however, even before she had any real evidence of this sort of behavior, Mom was becoming more and more uncomfortable and suspicious that there was something wrong. She couldn't see it or name it. What she did know was that now Dorene, too, was sucking her thumb. I was biting my nails to the quick, and all of us were wetting our beds almost nightly. She could tell we were "not as carefree as other children."

She also tells me that my father often went to the basement. "I have to play with the children. They keep wanting to wrestle with me," he would tell her.

"There was something in the way he said it," she remembers. "He looked guilty, not happy like he would if he was having fun with children."

Another time, when my friend Liza came to spend the night and she and I were sharing a bed together, Mom says she saw Daddy standing in front of my bedroom door with his bathrobe open in front.

She said to him, "Why are you standing like that? Are you molesting the children?"

Her husband's response was, "Do you think that low of me?"

Despite this denial, in later years, during hospitalization, George admitted "frequent exposure to my children and their playmates" throughout this period.

This was the first time my mother had put her worries into words, but even then she couldn't really believe her feelings of unease. Mom tells me she had trusted her husband completely, because her own father had been so trustworthy. She continued to struggle with her doubts and concerns, but thought that maybe George was right, that she "was being suspicious and had an unhealthy mind."

Mom tells me she now believes that "You have to trust your gut!" Her recollection causes me to notice. Here is early and distinct evidence that Daddy himself understood that molesting children was wrong – a 'low' form of behavior.

My father took too long tucking us into bed, walked around naked, and wanted his children to be naked.

My father took too long tucking us into bed, walked around naked, wanted his children to be naked, and seemed to spend an unusual amount of time playing with the neighborhood children.

In addition, my father continued to pressure my mother about sexual activities that were unacceptable to her – to allow him to have extramarital affairs, and even to involve a third person in their sexual activities. He said she was "a prude," "narrow-minded," and "old fashioned" for refusing.

As Mom and I talk, I notice how angry these revelations about this man who was my father are making me.

George would later, in the hospital, refer broadly to these marital intimacy issues.

"Myself, though I never had had intercourse, I had no sexual abnormalities prior to marriage," he asserted. "I started masturbating while in college – not too frequently – but after marriage I stopped this for awhile.

"When we were first married we were sexually innocent. To me, our intimate relations soon felt very unsatisfactory. I came to feel that my wife, while a neat, frugal, and intelligent woman, was somewhat inhibited.

"I do feel I always tried to please her, and I, of course, never forced her to have intercourse, but our relations became such an ordeal that I began to dread it. For this reason I had several affairs with other women, began masturbating frequently, and found myself preoccupied with sexual thoughts.

"I guess I hoped for nothing more or less than the kind of sexual activities I understood that most married couples have. We talked it over, she and I, and looked at our general sexual attitudes. At the time I never felt I had any abnormal or pervert ideas."

I reflect on the irony of my father's not choosing to acknowledge that his history of exhibitionism and voyeurism might have been considered "abnormal or pervert ideas."

I am

ten years

old,

and he has

had me

remove my

underpants.

Mom was still determined to save her marriage, and she finally decided to seek outside help. My father went with her to see a social worker for marriage counseling, but he only attended two sessions and then refused to return, convincing the counselor that all the problems in the marriage and family were his wife's fault. My mother believes that Daddy charmed and manipulated the social worker. He wanted to start his own business, but Mom was concerned that this would harm the family's financial stability. The social worker, who advised her that George needed his wife to make him feel more successful, more masculine, urged her to agree to let Daddy quit his job and open the lawn mower repair shop he wanted to start. Since she wanted to be a good wife, she tried not to doubt her husband. Over the coming two years, however, she continued to see the social worker by herself whenever she felt disturbed by her husband's behavior.

In August of 1954, Marjorie and George sold their idyllic family dwelling in suburbia and moved their three children, now nine and a half, eight, and three and a half years old, to a weathered old house "across the tracks" in an industrial zone in College Park, Maryland. Here the family could live adjacent to George's new business, "Culco Enterprises."

"I began my own company, which grew from my mechanical abilities and interests," George recalled. "I built a cinder block shop next to our house, laying all the blocks and doing the construction myself. I took care of general repairs, cabinet making,

120

electrical appliance repair, as well as saw and lawn mower sharpening."

Living here was economical for my family, but we were also removed from the two years of friendships and childhood culture in which I had finally found some sense of normalcy and happiness. In this new house in an industrial neighborhood, there was little opportunity to find escape from the abuse that, by this time, was going on regularly inside my home.

In September, Gary and I started as new students at College Park Elementary School. My verbal memory knows that Mrs. Cooper was my fifth grade teacher and that I had a friend named Barbie. But now, once again, I find an absence of visual and sensory memory at school as well as at home.

In Mom's album, though, there are photos of me in a Girl Scout uniform, next to Gary in his Cub Scout blues; of Dorene playing in the yard with our dog Honey; and of Daddy flying small airplanes out of a nearby airport. I know from the pictures that I flew in these planes with him, but I don't remember the trips.

Gary, Me and Dorene

In this home, just as in our last one, I have only three memories that break through the fog. One is of my sitting on the front seat of the car as Daddy is driving. I am ten years old, and he has had me remove my underpants. Now he wants me to turn and sit facing him with my dress pulled up so he can see me and touch me down below. I am upset, crying, afraid someone in another car will see me. But he insists.

Another is what Daddy always told me to do during the card games he played with me, Gary, and Dorene while Mom was cooking supper. "Joyce, be sure to leave your underpants off and sit across from me as we play. Keep your legs apart so that I can look at you."

My third memory is of Larry, a boy about two years older than me, whose family lived above the store next door. My father was friendly to Larry and often invited him to play in our yard and work in his tool shop. As a ten-year-old girl, I remember being advised by my father to undress and walk naked in front of the open window in my second floor bedroom. In his house, Larry's

Me and Honey

bedroom was opposite mine, and my father had instructed him to go upstairs and watch me from his bedroom. Daddy said I should let Larry see me naked so he would want to be my boyfriend. Although I cried and resisted, my father stood in the room, calm but insistent, until I disrobed and paraded in front of the open window.

Unsuccessful at locating him in my search for former neighbors, I wonder if Daddy molested Larry, too?

My sister Dorene, who was three years old when we moved to College Park, has more memories of our house and family from this time than I do. When I visit her at her home in Ohio, she talks freely while the tape recorder is running.

"I don't remember anything in Langley Park," she begins, "but I remember College Park. Daddy had started his repair business in the shop that he built on one side of the house.

"I remember Larry, the boy who lived next door. I have a picture of you together. I think you were in your Girl Scout uniform." She also remembers a "bunch of girls, maybe Girl Scouts," sleeping in the back yard in a tent.

Then Dorene tells me, "I fell into the creek behind the house, and Daddy pulled me out. I was all wet and I was crying. I was afraid he would get mad, but he was just laughing and laughing. It seems like the more miserable you were, the more he laughed. Did you ever notice that?"

This surprising observation from my sister reminds me of the time I was caught in the undertow at the ocean. Yes, I had experienced how he would tease and laugh when we were frightened or hurt.

"I remember the bathroom at the College Park house, too," Dorene continues. "It was big and very white. White tile and white tub, white sink and maybe even white walls. Mother took me in for something and when we went in Daddy was in the tub. I don't know if I needed a band-aid or what. I remember it struck me as strange, seeing him sitting naked in the bathtub."

I notice I am holding my breath and closing my eyes. I don't remember this "big, white bathroom," but I know it is the place my father sometimes took me for our "secret." Sighing deeply, I decide not to mention this to Dorene right now. I want to hear the rest of her memories.

"I always thought Daddy looked just like the actor who played in "Superman." That was one of our favorite afternoon TV shows, remember? I thought he looked like James Garner in "Maverick," too," says my sister with a far-away sigh. "I guess he wasn't, though."

"My favorite memory is when we used to play cowboys in our bunk beds after bedtime," continues Dorene, reminding me that we all three shared a bedroom. Gary had an upper bunk, Dorene the lower bunk, and I had a nearby twin bed. For our game, Gary would sit on his top bunk, pretending to be his favorite television cowboy, Roy Rogers. He would drive our stagecoach-bed through Indian territory.

My sister tells me that I pretended to be Roy's wife, Dale Evans, and that she was Roy and Dale's daughter, to whom we gave the name "Kathy." Dorene and I would ride together inside the stagecoach, being frightened and asking "Roy" to reassure and protect us.

Dorene says, "After we would play awhile, I remember Daddy coming up the steps. We would all jump back into our beds and act like we were sleeping. I don't remember more than that. I don't have all those bad memories of him like you do."

Sadly, I must wonder what happened after Daddy came into our bedroom and ended our cowboy game. Dorene doesn't have those memories and neither do I.

Most readers of this book who are middle-aged can recall the loveable television situation-comedy, "Father Knows Best." Its competent, good-humored mother, Margaret, and warm, all-knowing father, Jim, became weekly evening fixtures in my girlhood living room. Dorene and I still marvel at how the Anderson children, quiet, bookish eldest daughter Betty, irrepressible adolescent son James, and funny young sister Kathy mirrored exactly the personalities and makeup of our own family. However, the father's pet names, "Princess," "Bud" and "Kitten," conveyed clearly to viewers his love for them. Our own father had no such affectionate names for us.

Dorene also remembers the Potluck Group, all of whom I had interviewed in 1995. None had new information about our father. All of these families got together with our family several times a year for holidays and special occasions. Now I decide to contact their children. From three of them come other stories about our family in 1954 and 1955.

One friend was Liza Jackson, the girl my mother remembers spending the night at our house. Lisa wrote to say, "Our family moved to Maryland in 1952, the year our parents started getting together. I can picture the house you grew up in with the front yard and the three kids. I do remember going to your home to visit you, but I cannot

My father advised me to undress and walk naked in front of the open window in my bedroom.

The Potluck Kids

remember what we did. I always liked your mom, and recall she was smiling all the time, but I really cannot picture what your dad looked like."

Here is another absent memory from a girl who is one year older than I and even spent nights at my house.

The daughter of another Potluck family tells me, "The only direct memories I have of your Dad is that he was a good-looking man, and one other memory that is very clear. We had gone to your home or your Dad's shop in College Park. It was near the airport and very exciting for a mechanically-minded little girl. You kids and your Dad had set up a 'haunted house' in the garage. It was full of bowls of peeled grapes for 'eye-balls,' spaghetti or macaroni for 'veins or brain stuff,' and other items to amaze and horrify us. We put on blindfolds and were led through the maze. I was in awe.

"I remember maybe a year later my mother telling me not to pay much attention to your Dad, because he and your Mom were having some problems. I was not supposed to be with him without your Mom. But she didn't give me any reason for this, and I thought it was very silly and promptly forgot all about it."

A third Potluck child, Evelyn, who was a bit older than I, had a disturbing memory: "Your dad was visiting our family, and came out where I was playing alone in the backyard. He showed his sexual parts to me, and tried to kiss me. I was shocked, and later told my parents, but my father said, 'It was just bad judgment on George's part, and nothing harmful occurred.' My parents chose not to tell your mom about this, because they didn't want to unnecessarily upset her."

The other letter I receive about Daddy during these years in College Park comes from another of his friends.

"My memories of George are simply those of a tall, husky, rather brooding man who introduced me to the joys of flying. We never got close and our personal contacts were short lived. I was much younger, so we never really 'clicked.'

"I had always wanted to learn to fly, but never really knew how to go about it. George encouraged me to go up with him and I grabbed the chance. He had a Piper Cub, old, slow and reliable. We flew out of College Park Airport and flew around the area for about an hour; and he let me try the controls for a little while. It was enough to whet my appetite, and I began looking for an instructor. I believe we flew together once more and that was pretty much it.

"I recall that George tried to start a small business making wood things. He sought financial support and I gave him some money. I recall that the business never got going and soon closed. I associated that with George's hospitalization and divorce.

"I had no idea of the real reason for your parents' separation and divorce. I confess to being rather dense about family tensions. I can only remember having heard that George had been hospitalized and that after that there had been a divorce. I don't believe I ever saw him again.

"I never had any inkling, let alone knowledge, of his having molested children. I'm really disturbed to learn that now. Had I known, our brief acquaintance would have been much briefer. I never knew that he sexually molested you and am saddened to learn that. I do not recall ever having heard about his molesting children anywhere, here or in Colorado. Matter of fact, I do not recall having heard that he committed suicide, only that he had died.

"Your letter was a revelation and has shocked me. I never dreamed that George was involved in such behavior, especially with his own child. I cannot understand that sort of thing and certainly would not have condoned it. I feel for you and would like to do what I can to help ease what must be a long time of pain."

Again, I receive compassionate and generous words from a family friend who knew nothing of the secrets in our home. I am moved and grateful.

My parents chose not to tell your mom, because they didn't want to upset her.

These most recent letters do refer to my father's psychiatric hospitalization and my parents' divorce, but I realize that my informants could never have imagined the secret my father had been concealing for years. Even my friend who had been told not to be around him did not take this warning seriously.

I was beginning the sixth grade, dissociated and struggling to blend into the background, when the event occurred that would finally tear my family apart. After years of exposing himself, pushing himself at women, and having extra-marital affairs, my father would at last prove my mother's worst fears correct when she discovered that his increasingly predatory sexual focus had turned toward a more vulnerable target – children.

Gary and Daddy

Me

Chapter Seven

The Atomic Bomb

(October 1955)

*"It is such a secret place,
the land of tears."*

The Little Prince,
by Antoine de Saint-Exupéry

I am dreaming that an atomic bomb is exploding over our house. It is just like we have been learning in school. A huge mushroom-shaped cloud hovers in the sky, fires burn orange and yellow and black, and only cinder blocks and debris remain. Mom and Daddy and four-year-old Dorene are dead. All of the Potluck friends are dead. Aunts and uncles and grandparents are not to be seen. Just Gary and I are here, alone, pajama-clad and walking hand in hand through the smoldering devastation.

This is the only childhood dream I remember. I can still see it vividly. The house that was bombed is the white, shingled, two-story house in College Park, with Daddy's shop next door, where we lived when I was nine and ten.

Our elementary school under-desk bomb drills prepared us for the possibility of an atomic bomb attack. In my dream, at this house, it finally happened.

When Mom talks with me about what caused the explosion, she remembers I had been gone to the bathroom for a long time. She came upstairs to see if I was all right. When she opened the bathroom door, she saw me on my knees before my naked father, holding his penis in my hand. She can still recall that I had a shocked look on my face as she walked in. What she and Daddy said to each other remains a complete blank to her.

The only memory I have of this event, a clear visual memory I can still see today, is of a tiny rust-spot on the bathroom window screen. I don't remember the house, the bathroom, or the event at all. Just that spot.

Daddy's Shop

Today I am sure that this discovery by my mother set off my vivid atomic bomb dream. They both occurred in the same house when I was the same age.

At my school, my teacher had prepared us for the bomb. She repeatedly told us, "Take cover and protect your head. Crawl under the desk or get in the hall on your knees, put your arms over your head, and take any shelter you can find from fire and falling debris."

Daddy had prepared me for the bomb, too. "Don't tell anyone. They won't understand. Act normal. Keep our secret. Be a good girl. If they find out, Mommy will get angry with us. They might send me away. You won't have a family any more." Losing family is the childhood emotional equivalent of an atomic bomb.

In September of 1955, I had begun sixth grade, my second year at the school near my father's shop. During the summer before, I had discovered atomic fireballs – a round red candy that was fiery sweet on the tongue. I saw possibilities in atomic fireballs and bought a large, full display box of one hundred cellophane-wrapped red candy balls from the little country store where I first found them. A cartoon atomic bomb mushroom cloud was drawn on the box.

With my box of candies in the space under my desktop where my books and pencils belonged, I sat quietly at my wooden desk, trading one fireball for two pennies. Classmates passed fireballs and pennies from hand to hand under the desks as the teacher talked about Columbus discovering America.

Our principal walked into the midst of this educational endeavor. She spoke briefly to the teacher and then walked straight toward me. How, I wondered, had she heard about the atomic fireballs? "Joyce, come to the office with me," she said.

In the principal's office, instead of the candy police, I saw my Uncle Harold, my mother's brother.

Gary was brought in from his fourth grade classroom. "Your father has to go away to a hospital," Uncle Harold said gently. "I am here to help your mother. All three of you children will be going to New York to stay with Aunt Agnes until your mother can take care of you again. Let's go now."

Carrying my history book with the story about Columbus and my box of atomic fireballs, I walked home with Gary and Uncle Harold. I didn't yet know that Columbus didn't really discover America, that kneeling under a desk won't really protect a child from an atomic bomb, and that keeping secrets couldn't keep our family together.

The day after my mother opened the bathroom door and discovered the incest, she met with the social worker she and my father had been seeing intermittently for marriage counseling. This advisor counseled her wisely that she must call her parents and ask them to come and help. Two days later, she also took me out in the car and told me, "Joyce, Daddy is very sick, and has to go to a hospital where they can help him. He won't ever live with us again." Mom tells me that both of us cried together during this drive.

When called, her family came at once. Her parents and two siblings traveled from Florida, Virginia, and New York to converge on our house like the Red Cross, United Nations or National Guard. When I interview my Uncle Harold, he remembers this moment as "one of my more disturbing memories, but if it will be of any help to you, I'll be glad to tell you whatever I can recall."

Harold tells me that "Marjorie had a friend call our father, and Dad called me – he wanted someone to back him up. I was quite surprised, because this was the first I had heard of any problems."

I ask my uncle if he or anyone ever said during this time, "This can't be true."

"Absolutely nobody ever doubted your mother. Whatever she said you could take to the bank. It has always been that way. Our father told me that Marjorie had more character than any other woman he ever knew in his life, and I think he had good reason to say that."

Harold continues the story by telling me that he and my grandfather were sitting on our front porch on a swing when my father came home from his shop for lunch. "I told George what we were there for and his face sort of fell. He didn't deny anything. We explained to him that he could either go to jail or to a psychiatric hospital, and he chose the hospital.

"Then I went to the elementary school to pick up you and Gary. I remember how young and pitiful you and your siblings were. It was terrible. All of you were so small and none of you cried, but obviously you were all terribly upset."

Keeping secrets couldn't keep our family together.

When Harold brought me and Gary home from school, we joined Dorene, who tells me she remembers nothing about this event except that she was sitting on Daddy's lap holding her special "comfort blanket," and Mom was crying. "Daddy was there and then later he wasn't there," is all she knows.

Harold says that "the biggest thing I remember was that George had some candy for you children and he wanted to give it to you. Then your Granddaddy and I took your father to two doctors to get a certified psychiatric commitment for him. After that, two of your mother's male friends and I took him to the hospital and turned him in."

In his certificate of entry to Spring Grove Hospital, my father said, "I have masturbated in front of my young daughter and encouraged her to touch my penis, and was discovered by my wife exposing my genitals to her. She is ten years old. I have been exposing myself to her, had her handle my penis, and I also touched her genitals, extending over the past six years.

"My wife and I were in agreement that we should teach our children about sex and not hide anything. The lot fell on me to tell our children because my wife was too embarrassed. When Joyce showed interest and began to ask questions, as a little girl, I may have gone into too much detail, explaining too much to her in the first sitting. My tendency was to talk to my daughter, to show her more about the subject of sex than was necessary under any circumstances. I exposed myself and explained my own genitals to her. Anyway, it grew out of that.

"After moving to Maryland, this intensified, and I began molesting my daughter physically.

"Through the course of normal play with my children, wrestling and carrying them around, I got to brushing my hand against Joyce more than should have been accidental. It got so I had begun openly fondling Joyce, and rubbing my hands over her. I never violated her, only manipulation of my hands.

"As I think of it now, the sex with Joyce began as a suppression of my activities with women. After this developed, I began exposing myself frequently to her playmates, four or five other little girls.

"My wife became suspicious about me and asked if I was doing anything with Joyce, but I felt I was not in too deep, and I denied it. From that time on, I was living a lie all the time. She still had her suspicions and was not happy at all.

"We moved to College Park, a little less than two years ago, so I could start my business enterprise. Things kept on like this with Joyce until my wife caught me one day in the bathroom. I had induced my daughter to put her hand on my penis. How could I have done a thing like that?" Medical notes indicate that my father was crying at these last words.

My wife asked if I was doing anything with my daughter, but I denied it. From that time on, I was living a lie all the time.

"I never at any time injured my daughter," he continued. "I never attempted intercourse. It was entirely manual touch and visual stimulation."

My father concluded these admissions saying, "Joyce is a very bright girl; she will understand that I am sick and that was the reason for my behaviors toward her. I don't have delusional thinking or hallucinatory experiences or strange dreams. I'm sure she will love me, and will not be afraid of me."

My father also claimed, "I have in no wise bothered my two younger children. I have not been, and cannot be, a bad influence on them. All my children love me as their Daddy, and they need me."

My father's comments confirm my body, emotional and dream pieces of my memory puzzle. I reflect on all my years of healing – intense depression, nightmares, and flashbacks, including repeated body memories of choking on my father's penis, and am enraged at my father's claim never to have injured his daughter.

After Harold and Granddaddy took our father away, Mom recalls only that we three children stood still and uncomprehending while Grandma and Agnes helped Mom get food, clothes, school supplies and toys together for me and my siblings to take with us to our new home. Holding back tears, our mother hugged us and told us she would come and get us as soon as she could. We climbed into the back seat of Agnes's car and we turned to wave good-bye to our mother as Agnes drove off, talking cheerfully to us of the fun we would have in New York – new friends, new schools, sharing rooms with our cousins.

Suddenly, things had changed for us, and nothing would ever be the same. We huddled in the back seat, still and quiet – shell-shocked. Aunt Agnes took us on that long car ride and into her home, with her husband and her own two children, willing to provide and care for us for an indefinite time until her sister was ready to have her children back.

I can barely imagine the circumstances my mother faced. She had just discovered that her husband had been molesting their daughter for an indefinite number of years. Her marriage was over. She would have to raise and support three children alone. To do that she must get job credentials, sell a house, and move her children to a smaller place. Meanwhile, she must complete legal and medical processes to have her husband confined and psychologically evaluated.

Now, as an adult, I feel deep gratitude for my mother's family and recognize that their unequivocal help and support made the difference in our survival. This is how families and friends, neighbors and nations help each other during disaster and tragedy. I know this now.

But children do not think this logically. They know only what they can see and

Suddenly, things had changed for us, and nothing would ever be the same.

Me and Susan

touch and feel. My child's mind had blocked out traumatic memories of the incest and now, also, it blocked the memory of the discovery. It was as though all this "knowing" was in a separate compartment of my mind. I couldn't touch or feel anything about this terrible upheaval. Years later, I would realize that I had believed it was somehow my fault. I let Mommy learn about the secret. Now she was angry. She had sent Daddy away. Our family and house were gone and I had caused the bomb to explode.

"Your Daddy is sick. He had a nervous breakdown. He is in a hospital." That's what we were told. That's what we said to people who asked.

Gary didn't know about the secret Mommy had discovered in the bathroom. Gary only knew that his father had disappeared in an instant. As a teenager, when Mom took him to a psychiatrist, he would ask, "Do you know why my parents got divorced?"

"Something to do with sex," the doctor said evasively.

At the time, Gary was a nine- year-old boy wondering why his father had abandoned him.

Lost in the explosion, Dorene was just four years old. She didn't know what had happened. I realize now that she could only comprehend as a normal four-year-old. Maybe her Daddy disappeared due to the magic and power of her own thoughts and behaviors – maybe because of something she did or didn't do, because of something she felt or wished. She was at an age when the bomb would damage her young development of trust and confidence.

Mom stayed in Maryland to deal with the overwhelming and, at times, unfathomable complexities of her situation. She was a "displaced homemaker" before there was such a term. She found a realtor, sold our house, packed all our belongings, and moved into the home of her friends, Jane and Charles. She stayed with them until she could earn a credential in library science to supplement her bachelor's degree and enable her to obtain employment. This would allow her to buy a small new home and reunite her family.

Her marriage counselor discussed with her the best way to meet the needs of her children, the morality of divorce, and her emotional and spiritual obligations to her husband. She met regularly with the social worker and psychiatrist at her husband's hospital.

We children meanwhile were kept safe in Aunt Agnes's home on Long Island, New York. We shared bedrooms with our cousins, Susan and Curt, and had our meals and clothes provided. Homework was supervised, TV monitored, special outings arranged. We were there for about five months, from October of 1955 until April of 1956.

When I visit with my cousin, Susan, who is now an optician, she begins our visit by saying, "What can I do to help you? I'll do anything." I notice how surprised I feel that she seems so concerned and close.

I ask her what she knows about my family, and she says she thought my parents got divorced because my father couldn't deal with being deaf – had too much anger – but she doesn't know how she got that idea. When I describe the incest and discovery that led to our coming to live with her, she is sad and says, "I have pictures of George. I vaguely remember him. Nothing threatening." Then she comments, "Most people do inappropriate hurtful things for reasons they don't understand."

I tell Susan that I remember being shy and anxious in my new sixth grade class and worrying that the boys who laughed and flirted with her would talk to me. "Why are you here?" my new classmates would ask. "That was The $64,000 Question," I laugh, referring to one of our favorite television shows. At the time, multiple answers came to mind:

My father had a nervous breakdown.

There was a big explosion when the secret was discovered.

My family all died.

I would say instead, "My parents are selling our house and we're moving to a new place."

Susan says she didn't know anything about why we had moved into her home. She says it was like we "just happened" to her family.

"Do you remember when we went to Coney Island?" she asks me. "We had the best time.

Susan tells me that one day we went to New York City and did a lot of sightseeing – the ice skaters at Rockefeller Center, the Empire State Building, the Statue of Liberty. She has pictures in her album of us posing in front of the New York skyline on that outing, and she gives me one to take home with me.

I tell Susan that, in the five months I lived with her, I remember only a few things: drinking eggnog made with chocolate milk for breakfast; learning how to wash dishes

Our family and house were gone and I had caused the bomb to explode.

– first the glasses, then the silverware, then the plates; having a fierce fight with Gary on the sidewalk as we walked home from school; and crying myself to sleep each night after the lights were turned out.

Susan remembers the first three events but says she didn't hear me crying at bedtime. Perhaps it was silent grief that only I could hear.

The hospital, where my father was committed for psychiatric care in October of 1955, is an hour's drive from our old home in College Park. Freeman is with me today, forty-five years later, as we drive through the gates and onto the grounds of this state-run facility. A sign at the entrance says, "Spring Grove Hospital, established 1797."

Immediately, our eyes are drawn to the old, dark stone building on our right, with large stone columns guarding its entrance. Most all of the glass windows are broken, but there are bars and wire still in place as evidence of the prison-like security. The sign, "Psychopathic Building, erected in 1914" suggests that more seriously disturbed patients were housed in this location. It is now a dilapidated, museum-like relic of an old hospital, which looks curiously like a combined prison and courthouse.

Newer buildings on the hospital campus are brick with white wood trim, looking more like college dormitories spaced on the neatly mowed and landscaped grounds. I am curious about where my father might have stayed when he was a patient here.

We follow signs directing us to the Health Information Services offices, the location of patient medical records, where I have an appointment this morning. I have talked with the director of this office and, as "executor of George Culbertson's estate," have obtained permission to review my father's hospital records. The records from 1955 and 1956 are on old microfilm tapes and, the director explains, are only required to be retained for twenty-five years, so we are fortunate that Mr. Culbertson's records are still available for review.

Medical records may not be removed from the premises and a staff member must be present while I read them, the director explains, to make sure there are no alterations or damage to the documents. She places the microfilm of my father's records on the viewing machine and offers me a chair in front of the screen so I can read the notes.

This moment feels eerily like the times in my nursing career when I have attended an autopsy on a dead body, waiting to discover exactly what happened – the cause of death. I am calm, matter-of-fact, and detached, prepared to know whatever is or is not discovered.

Freeman sits in a nearby chair with pen and paper poised to make notes, while the Health Information Services director positions herself discretely at a table, where she can work on a task while supervising our use of the microfilm.

Thankfully, I have brought my small tape recorder along and when I see that the document we will be able to view is more than thirty pages, I decide that, in order to obtain the full contents, I will read it verbatim into the tape recorder and transcribe it later.

In my most professional and well-modulated nursing voice, I begin reading out loud.

> George Culbertson: Case #22949A
> Admission Date: 10/19/1955
> Age: 39
> Education: College Graduate
> Occupation: Instrument mechanic
> Civil condition: Married
>
> **Patient was admitted to the hospital on the authority of two medical commitment certificates…According to the commitment certificate this patient has derived great pleasure from exposing himself and has felt he has given pleasure to others by exposing himself. For the past five years he has been exposing himself to his young daughter and has had her handle his penis. He has masturbated in front of her on at least one occasion. He states he would like to stop this behavior but is unable to control himself. Patient's wife and children left him after he was discovered exposing himself to their ten-year-old daughter."**

My story is true. I already believed this, but seeing official entries, on official letterhead documents, verified by official signatures, creates a startling and surprising validation, a "reality." My heart is pounding and I take a deep breath.

> **Patient is the informant. As the patient is totally deaf, it was necessary to conduct this examination with the examiner writing questions and the patient writing his answers.**

Two hours later, when I finish reading the entire record onto two tape cassettes, I thank the director for her gracious assistance, reach for Freeman's hand, and walk silently and somberly outside. Once again I see the residential buildings where my father was confined, evaluated and treated for what would be called, when he was released on February 7, 1957, sixteen months later, "sexual perversion."

I have been searching for Daddy's life story for six years now and it has been here in this record the whole time. Often I had thought of contacting Spring Grove Hospital, but then I would put it off, following other interview leads, talking to more relatives and friends and neighbors. Now, comparing what I have constructed from my interviews with what I have read here today in my father's own words, I am both

Sometimes others believed him, sometimes they suspected he was lying.

ecstatic and sickened by the recognition that the stories are nearly identical. If anything, my father's words add to and elaborate on some of the interviews, but there are no real contradictions.

My father's hospital diagnosis upon entry certified him as "not psychotic, but displaying sexual perversion and exhibitionism," and, during his stay, records would note that "his religious feelings border on the delusional." Approaching discharge sixteen months later, a final summary described him as displaying "mixed Neurosis with Anxiety and Obsessive Compulsive Features."

That clinical report continued: "He shows passivity, and dependency and a passive homo-erotic flavor is also suggested. His feelings towards sex present a problem. He has such very strong sexual impulses, with frustration at not finding adequate release; this leads to preoccupation with these impulses, and to the use of religion as a means of denying and covering up these feelings.

"This is an individual who is presently functioning at a very superior level with respect to his intelligence, who has very excellent language fluency and fund of vocabulary, very good organizing and integrative ability, and who seems to have the potentials for creativity.

"While showing interest and sensitivity toward interpersonal situations, as a result of his disability, he tends to isolate himself, using fantasy to compensate for his handicap. He also has a very good capacity for achievement.

Spring Grove Hospital

"A lot of tension and anxiety is present in this individual, and some lack of inhibitory mechanism, but he seems to be able to channelize it, and uses various mechanisms to handle it without any marked impairment of his reality content.

"In his attempts to handle his sexual impulses, he shows some weakening of his defenses, although no gross pathology is evident. No evidence of psychosis is obtained. For the most part, this patient has adequate reality contact and ego functioning."

Daddy wanted to do good, tried so hard to earn respect and admiration, needed so much to be loved, and did so much damage in the process. Sometimes he believed himself, sometimes he knew he was lying. Sometimes others believed him, sometimes they suspected he was lying.

Love, power, betrayal, grief – the elements of every drama and tragedy are the more complicated when they are intertwined with human sexuality and family intimacies.

Chapter Eight

Rebuilding from the Rubble

(1956 – 1958)

Dorene

"Twirl me about and twirl me around
Let me grow dizzy and fall to the ground
And when I look up at you looking down
Say it was only a dream."

– Song by Mary Chapin Carpenter

Even though Mom had discovered the incest and Daddy had been removed from our home, I would remain mostly unconscious and numb through the next few years. From 1956 through 1958, ages eleven through thirteen, I went through the motions. Looking back today, though, I can remember few specifics of my life during sixth through ninth grades.

I knew somewhere deep inside that my father had done sexual things to me and that the discovery of this secret had caused him to go away and our family life to radically change. But I did not know any words for what had happened. The incest was never mentioned to me by the adults who knew, not even my mother, and I never told anyone.

"Where is your father?" people would ask me.

"In a hospital," I'd respond.

"Why?"

"He had a nervous breakdown."

"What's that?"

"I don't know."

"Oh."

While Gary and I stayed in New York with our cousins, our mother remained in Maryland. Because Dorene was so young, Mom soon brought her back to stay with her, but she did not yet have the time or money to care for me and Gary. Mom was still taking courses in library science full-time at Gallaudet, and Jane took care of Dorene during the day. With help from her parents and brother, she sold the house in College Park, found a smaller, more affordable house, and in April of 1956 – five months after we had gone to live with our cousins – she brought her children back to live together with her again.

My grandparents provided financial assistance so that mother could complete her librarian credentials. In June, she graduated and was hired by a government office in Washington, D.C.

The overwhelming confusion and numbness persisted.

In our small cinder block house, Dorene and I shared a room with pink and white dogwood flowers on a gray background. Mom had a room, Gary had a room, and there was a kitchen, a living room and one bathroom. It was enough. We were together again, but we had moved to a location in another school district and had to begin at new schools – my third sixth grade classroom. In this school, I remember being made a member of the Safety Patrol, probably by a teacher, to increase my self-confidence. I wore a white belt, and scanned my intersection carefully each morning and afternoon. I took it very seriously. In a symbolic way, this was the beginning of my career, my determination to make the world safe for children.

That summer of 1956, as our mother began her new job schedule, we three children went by Greyhound bus to spend the summer with Mom's parents, our Granddaddy and Grandma, in St. Petersburg, Florida. Again, I have photos of this two-month vacation, and Dorene has been able to tell me some of her vacation memories, but I was not psychologically present.

In September, I began seventh grade. Gary was in fifth grade, Dorene started first grade, and Mom had to cope with our needs on top of her new work schedule. She left at 7 a.m. each morning and returned at 6 p.m. each evening. I guess there have always been single-parent families, but in 1956 I didn't know any others. All the families I knew had two parents and lived in the suburbs, like those in the situation comedies on television, "Father Knows Best," "Leave It to Beaver," "Ozzie and Harriet." Our family tried to fit into this idealized model. It was all we knew to do.

In our script, Mom was the father because she went away each day to her office, so by default I became the mother. This "parentified child" role is classic for an oldest daughter. It was the perfect role for me. I could move directly from childhood to adulthood, entirely skipping all of the emotional ups and downs of adolescence, which my own past would have made even more difficult.

Me, Dorene and Gary

In the mornings, I got Gary and Dorene out the door to school. In the afternoons I told friends, "No, I can't come to your house, join a club, attend a meeting. I need to go home and take care of my brother and sister. I have to iron, cook dinner, clean, and do homework – everything."

I have almost no memories from sixth to ninth grade at home or in school. The overwhelming confusion and numbness persisted.

Only the terror of junior-high gym locker rooms remains. How could I get undressed and change into my gym suit, undress again and shower without anyone seeing my body?

My father had always wanted me to be naked, not wear underpants, to be readily visible to him. At school, the thought of being naked and visible made me shake and feel nauseated. Every day as I changed, I tried to hide behind the locker door. How fast can I get the dark blue gym suit on? How can I be last into the shower with my towel pulled tightly around me, or dress with my back turned to others so even if they see me I won't see them?

From the fall of 1956, I have photos of the house, of Mom and Gary and Dorene and me and our miniature collie. Mom says that we went to Sunday school and church each Sunday. I was nearly thirteen, still biting my fingernails and wetting the bed.

I also have photos of our father visiting with us on weekend visits from the psychiatric hospital, accompanied by a minister, Reverend Foster. This hearing minister, who knew sign language, had been put in touch with him at SGH. I know one time that Daddy and Rev. Foster took all three

Me, Daddy, Dorene and Gary

of us children to an amusement park, but I can remember nothing else about those visits to us.

My father may have been using a new-found interest in religion to fool himself, or to manipulate his doctors. "I realize the terribly warped way I had been thinking, my lack of respect for moral ideals," he had told them. "Before, I shrugged off my guilty conscience, but now I understand what religion is. I have truly found God since coming here and my whole way of thinking is changed. Ideals suddenly have great importance to me; whereas I formerly scoffed at them, now I realize that my wife's ideas were near perfect. Now that I have this new understanding of Christianity, now that I know what love of fellow man means, I know that what I did before can never happen again. I know, and God knows, that I am cured of my foregoing trouble."

His hyper-religiosity did not fully convince the clinicians. "Our staff initially was impressed with this man's insight and desire to be helped," they noted. "He assured us that by being here he was able to figure out many things and has found support by finding God. However, later on we began to suspect his religious preoccupations were somewhat superficial. Together with other paranoid thoughts, they led us to feel that he was borderline psychotic, and may be delusional.

"We also received a Social Service history reporting this patient's receiving prior counseling, together with his wife, in Washington, DC, to address extra-marital affairs he had initiated. He also engaged in manipulations then to convince his therapist and family that he was okay. But as soon as patient discontinued therapy he became involved with the same kinds of affairs."

Despite these reservations, in late January of 1957, George's doctors debated the possibility of his release. "Our problem has been whether to release this patient on parole or to request a sanity hearing and to allow a jury to decide whether or not he is ready to go. Since his admission to this hospital on medical certificate, he has cooperated with the program we have recommended, and no longer exhibits symptoms of psychosis. He has returned to work while still a patient here and has entered into psychotherapy with a private psychiatrist. During his hospitalization and during the time he has spent outside the hospital, he has not gotten into any difficulties.

"Based on this, and my review of the records, it is my decision to release Mr. Culbertson on a parole status. At this point, I cannot definitely state this man would get into trouble, or that he is harmful to the community," wrote the supervising psychiatrist. "I also feel that subjecting him to a court hearing is potentially traumatic to him, and may undo what psychotherapy he has already had, and his continued use of it."

In February of 1957, after he was released from the hospital, my father found work and rented a room in a boarding house. We continued having weekend visits, with Daddy and Reverend Foster coming to pick us up at Mom's house and take us out for the day.

I have a photo from that summer. We had gone on an outing to the local swimming pool with our father. "Gary is getting huskier, isn't he?" Daddy has written on the back. "Remember how thin he used to be?" He has listed our ages: Joyce 13; Gary 11; and Dorene 7.

September of 1957 through June of 1958 was my eighth grade year in school. As I close my eyes to try to recall this time, I see only the outside of my school building and the outside of our little concrete house. Inside the house, I can see myself lying in a contorted position on my bed in order to bite my toenails. They are bleeding and it hurts a lot. Today I know from a clinical perspective that a child who feels complicity or guilt may engage in acts of self-mutilation. Then, it was as though only the sensation of physical pain could seep through and stay distinct in my mind.

After more than two years of living apart, my parents divorced; Daddy moved back to Colorado. I have no memory of any discussions or of being informed about what was happening. Dorene remembers some conversation with our parents and remembers asking, "Does this mean Daddy has to go away again?"

"My home situation is very upset," my father told his doctors. "I know my behavior has been wrong, and I realize my wife's leaving me is my own fault. I must accept the fact that she no longer loves me and can no longer live with me. This means separation and perhaps divorce. While I love her and do not want a divorce, I too want separation for a while, until she can once again see me as a new man and love me and trust me. I sincerely believe this will come about eventually because I will be a model man henceforth.

"After she has had time to think things over, she will come back to me."

Daddy did go away again. He left the East Coast, where he had first come in order to attend Gallaudet College, and also left his marriage, his wife, his children, and his friends behind. He returned to his childhood home, Colorado Springs, where he had obtained a position as a teacher at his own boyhood alma mater, the Colorado School for the Deaf and Blind.

After she has had time to think things over, she will come back to me.

While my childhood mind was baffled by the changes in my family and I was still unable to hold in memory the details of my day-to-day life, my mother was doing her best to hide from us children the psychological, legal, financial and moral dilemmas that were consuming her life. In my mind this had been one single series of events – hospital, divorce, move – happening in an emotional instant while I was frozen in time.

Mom meets with me to talk about her memories of this time. She comes up the steps to my porch and into our dining room carrying only one faded manila envelope. After hugging me, she hands me the envelope and says, "I saved all this in case you might need it someday."

The envelope is frayed around the edges and the paper feels brittle and fragile, so I am very cautious as I turn it over. On the front, in my mother's handwriting, the package is labeled: "Papers re: Daddy." The weight is solid but not heavy, and the envelope is fastened only with the flimsy metal clasp folded through the hole in the tab.

This slender sheaf of documents, the gift she had been saving for me since 1958, has become the most moving evidence of my mother's love, ultimately revealing the breadth of her wisdom and integrity. This time we do not sit for small talk and coffee, but move directly to the living room and sit side-by-side on the couch. I remove the papers from the large envelope and find a collection of typewritten letters, each one dated and stapled carefully together. These are copies of correspondence between my mother and our minister, Dr. Stuart, whom she had consulted for advice and assistance during this difficult time.

On the top of the pile is a handwritten letter that Mom wrote out as a bequest for her children, ten pages of carefully worded information and explanations. She tells me that when she divorced Daddy, she knew we children were too young to understand what had happened, and she wanted to create a record that she could give to us if we ever wanted to know.

I cannot begin to describe the pain.

For me, this moment is reminiscent of reading George Culbertson's statements in his hospital records. Here are my mother's own words from long ago, written intentionally for me to read one day:

"I grew up sheltered from the seamy side of life," begins her account. "I had high ideals of having a happy marriage, happy, well-adjusted children who would grow up to have happy marriages too, and live happily ever after. I enjoyed being a housewife and mother, and in spite of problems of living with Daddy, I was still able to be happy. I was probably living in a dream world. Then when I discovered what Daddy was doing, first in his affairs and then with you, my world came crashing down and I had to rebuild my life and my children's from the rubble. It was very, very painful – I cannot begin to describe the pain…"

It was professional helpers, I learn, who advised Mom not to discuss with her children what had happened – the incest, the discovery, the hospitalization – because "talking about it might upset them." She wanted to be a good mother and so she followed the advice. She kept silent.

"Even though I was now in school full-time," Mom wrote, "I went up to New York most week-ends to see you all. I wanted to get you all back with me under one roof. I was staying with Aunt Jane, which put me under an unwanted obligation, but seemed to be the best arrangement at that time. A house a few doors down from Jane was up for sale and seemed to be the most suitable place to move to. The price was low enough so that if we sold the house in College Park, the share I would get would be sufficient for a down payment for this house. It was near our friends, who could help me look after the children.

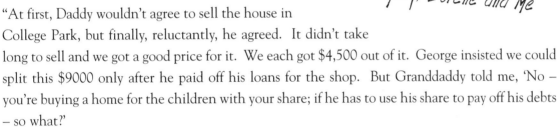

Gary, Dorene and Me

"At first, Daddy wouldn't agree to sell the house in College Park, but finally, reluctantly, he agreed. It didn't take long to sell and we got a good price for it. We each got $4,500 out of it. George insisted we could split this $9000 only after he paid off his loans for the shop. But Granddaddy told me, 'No – you're buying a home for the children with your share; if he has to use his share to pay off his debts – so what?'

"George had also said I wasn't entitled to the unemployment or sickness pay his company paid me for the support of the children because I had left him. He never seemed to consider that whatever I got from him would be for the children, not me alone. I don't know what he thought the children would do if I had no money, but he couldn't see allowing me extra for the children."

As I read my mother's account, I reflect how, in the hospital record, Daddy had cried and professed tremendous concern for us children, describing how much he loved and needed us.

"At first we all showed concern for George," Mom's narrative continues. "Uncle Harold visited him. My father wrote a nice letter expressing concern over his illness and offering to pay for full private psychiatric treatment, but pointed out that it didn't necessarily mean a return to the family. George's response was a vitriolic letter accusing Grand Daddy of all kinds of meanness and selfishness. Finally, my family decided it would be best to have nothing further to do with him.

"I kept going out to visit him at least once a week because I felt that a sick man shouldn't be abandoned, and that as a Christian I should visit him and show that I was concerned. I explained we could not resume life together and that it would be best for him to begin to plan a life for

Gary, Me and Dorene

himself. He insisted he was a changed man, had had a religious conversion, and would be entirely different now. The way he talked was all too familiar. The only thing I could say was that when he was really well, he was bound to see things differently and to understand why we couldn't live together again.

"My main problem was what to tell you children. If I told the complete story I felt it might destroy your love and respect for your father and, regardless of what he had done, I felt it was very important that children should love and respect both parents. I was trying to avoid undermining your love for him, and thus felt paralyzed in how to communicate with you. George, on the other hand, had no qualms in undermining your feelings for me. The best I was able to say to you three was that Daddy was sick and had to go to the hospital for treatments to help him get well.

"George also told anyone who came to see him all the things I had done wrong to cause him to go to the hospital. That made it hard to face people. It is so hard to know how to describe this pre-divorce year. It seemed as if life continued to be an endless ordeal.

"At the hospital, I had to go see a social worker, who asked about you and whether or not I thought you should see her too; she felt you might be carrying a deep burden of guilt. I agreed. I didn't see how an experience like you'd been through could help but distort your thoughts and feelings and your relationships with your family. I worried that many ideas you picked up from Daddy needed to be discussed and cleared up, especially your ideas about me, which were colored by his viewpoint.

"Later, the social workers insisted that, since you were doing well in school and had social contacts there, it was best just to let things work themselves out. I never felt comfortable with this decision, but they felt that it could only make things worse if we made anything of it. So I assumed they knew best.

"These social workers helped me in my resolve to divorce your father. They were explicit that I was not responsible for anything Daddy did – he was responsible for his own behavior. They also said although Daddy could do well with adults in activity or task-based relationships, he was unable to emotionally function on an adult level, and therefore turned to children for his emotional needs. They could not guarantee he could be "cured" – only hoped that he might understand himself and his problems and try to control his behavior.

"They also asked me about my feelings about you, Joyce, asking if I held you responsible for what had happened. I said, 'Of course not!' You were a child, and in no way could be responsible for anything he did. George didn't know how to be a real father or husband; it was as the result of that there were problems.

"They told me George was diagnosed as a severe neurotic with paranoid tendencies, who did not face reality, as shown by his delusions of grandeur and unrealistic business plans. They also revealed to me that Daddy's abuse of you had not just begun recently, as he had said, but began when you were five or earlier. After asking me numerous questions about my feelings towards the children, these social workers told me I was doing very well.

"It was a book that helped me make my final decision. One chapter described instances when the church considered divorce justified, and concluded that a person who failed to initiate divorce after trying in every way to save the marriage was showing lack of courage. That was it! I was still afraid of divorce, but I knew I had tried all I could, and there was only one thing left to do – but how?

"Inevitably, the ministers who visited George all came to see me to try to persuade me he was a changed man. It had always been humiliating to be held responsible for his deeds. I tried to explain to them the things I had learned from the social worker; but when they all talked with me, they sounded just like Daddy – repeating almost all he had said.

"Rev. Foster even claimed he had talked with the doctor and social worker in the hospital, that they said Daddy was going to be well, but would need lots of help in starting a new life, and that it was my Christian duty to continue to help him. When I asked the social worker at the hospital about this, she reported neither she nor the doctor had ever talked with anyone by that name.

"When Daddy got out of the hospital, Rev. Foster insisted on us all going on picnics together a couple of times and still insisted the people at the hospital had told him we should remain together and I should help him. He browbeat me, saying I had deserted my husband. I replied by asking, 'Was I supposed to continue to live under the conditions I had been enduring?'

"Some of the other things this Christian minister asserted or accused me of were: my husband wanted a home while I didn't; I had no right to prevent my husband from seeing the children since they were his as much as mine; if I took the case to court, the court would favor him rather than me; he had known children to turn against the parent who prevented them from seeing the other parent.

"When I tried to tell him what the social workers had said, he said social workers were a cold-hearted lot and would think nothing of breaking up a family. He said

Was I supposed to continue to live under the conditions I had been enduring?

when a person is sick, you do not leave him to die. Finally, he persuaded me to let my husband visit the children every two weeks beginning on Easter of 1957.

"I did try this. But, after the third visit, I decided I could not let Rev. Foster run things for us, and that the only way I could deal with him was through another minister. By this time, I had seen Rev. Foster tell his son to do something dishonest – to get tickets for a circus by cheating. So, I realized I couldn't really trust him."

In July of 1957, my mother wrote Dr. William E. Stuart, my minister from Sunday School, a long letter explaining her worries and asking for his help. Again, I reflect on mom's dedication. Although she was deaf, she had wanted her hearing children to have religious training; for years she had driven us to weekly worship and Sunday school.

And now, since she was deaf, she must write rather than call on the phone, or have an appointment where words, both spoken and heard, would occur. Dr. Stuart had responded that before advising my mother, he wanted to talk with George's doctors at the hospital. This was exactly what Mom wanted, too.

"My observation of my husband during his visits to the children convinced me that he has not changed at all," my mother wrote to our minister. "If he were back in the family, the whole pattern would be repeated. If I do not take precautions about his visiting, he will barge in and take over, doing whatever he likes and, in general, upset all of us. It may be that legal steps will be necessary in order to assure restrictions over which he may not step.

"The social worker at the hospital told me they could not hold George legally except through court order, and suggested that I discuss with my lawyer the possibility of bringing charges against him, presenting the chance that he might be sent back until he was really cured. But my husband's lawyer wants to settle out of court in order that his offenses should not be written in the records.

"Before my husband went to the hospital," the letter continued, "the children sensed the strain in the home; the relationship between Joyce and myself was not as good then – she'd get very angry with me every time she couldn't have her way; Gary was sullen and felt that nobody liked him.

"Now we have begun a new life for ourselves, and have made a complete adjustment. All the children have stopped sucking their thumbs and wetting beds, and there is a much better feeling in the home. Joyce and I get along very well, while Gary has a much happier expression. Naturally I am anxious all these changes should not be upset, and I am afraid they will be if my husband is not restricted.

"Also, since my husband has been out of the hospital I have been living under constant dread that he would try to get in touch with the children without my

I have been living under constant dread that he would try to get in touch with the children.

146

knowing about it. Sometimes it seems that there is just no possible solution to these problems, but I am hoping your talks with the psychiatrists at Spring Grove Hospital will prove helpful and that we can begin to work out something."

These precious documents my mother saved feel like a treasure trove. As I continue to peruse them, I am relieved on her behalf that finally, in Dr. Stuart, she has found a solid ally.

Mom

Chapter Nine

"Queen for a Day"

(April 1958)

"She gets up every morning
Gets the kids out the door
Then it's carpool and shop
Vacuum and mop
Until they're back home at four
Then it's supper and homework
Until they're all tucked away..."

"...She's only doing her job
like folks everywhere.
Where she comes from
It's just how things are done
Doing her share."

– Song by John McCutcheon

Mom

In the aftermath of a divorce, new family dynamics are created. Awkward and unformed at first, these gradually coalesce into a pattern that not only the children but also the parents can use to make new sense of a fractured marriage. In successful divorces, each of the adults, as well as the children, adapt to these patterns and, in the process, achieve growth and new bearings of stability.

But many divorces fail to achieve this success, and such would become the case for my own parents. My father, who for sixteen months had asserted he was a totally changed man, showed his true colors almost immediately upon discharge from Spring Grove Hospital.

148

While there, he had asserted that his wife was "totally good." Now he commenced a manipulative battle with her to resume his marriage and return to a full parental role with his children. Where once he claimed he had found God, now he enlisted his minister's alliance with him in a selfish battle.

Perhaps most damaging of all, where he previously had claimed his primary concern for the well-being of his children, now he began writing to me, Gary, and Dorene, telling us how much he needed our help. He even urged us during custody visits to change our mother's mind about the divorce.

And as to caring for his family financially, he laid first claim on his and Mother's financial assets, and showed little regard for her monetary welfare or contributing to child support.

The obstacles facing my mother in her crusade to become sole provider for a family of four in 1958 were nearly insurmountable.

In the first place, she had no professional livelihood, having worked as a homemaker for most of the eighteen years of her marriage to George. In addition, the concept of equal pay for equal work was nearly unheard of in this era.

How could she take care of us children and still work a forty-hour week? Where would we live? With regard to overseeing my own, Gary's and Dorene's relationship with Daddy, how could she insure our father had truly been "cured" of his pedophilia?

And while my mother, through her remarkable character, education, intelligence, and determination had already overcome many cultural obstacles to her hearing disability, her new role as breadwinner would be seriously challenged by her deafness.

In 1958, deaf people could not use standard telephones. They couldn't attend staff meetings, supervise hearing subordinates, do work involving sound or film presentations, or do direct work with the hearing public. It was hard for them to find white-collar jobs. Many members of America's deaf community worked as machinists, printers, mechanics and other jobs where manual skill and immunity from the noise distractions of industry were assets. But at age thirty-eight, my mother possessed neither industrial skills nor much work experience.

Reviewing Mom's written notes of what she went through, I compare her mental and emotional struggles with those I myself would later face as I, too, became a single mother. To sort through and make sense of the many dilemmas she was facing, I reconstruct the following communications (which occurred over many months by letter) between my mother, my father, Dr. Stuart, and the divorce lawyer.

"I talked by phone with your husband's present psychiatrist, who said his hospital interviews with Mr. Culbertson were not highly satisfactory," wrote Dr. Stuart to Mom. "Mr. Culbertson spent very little time discussing his own problems. Instead, he concentrated largely upon insisting that he was all right, denying that he had done anything wrong. I believe that your husband is definitely in need of further psychiatric help, which he very likely will not accept."

"Yes, the hospital social workers helped me see that, too," replied my mother. "They made me see that my feelings for my husband were rooted in my feelings for my father, who is an entirely different kind of person from my husband. I couldn't grasp this until you also made the remark that George was unable to give or receive love.

"Now I see that, indeed, this is what I did. I transferred the feelings I had for my father to my husband, to whom I attributed the same qualities my father had, even though I was not sure I wanted to marry him. Perhaps the fact that my husband was not able to receive the trust, respect, and confidence I tried to show him accounts for much of our difficulties in adjusting, and the frustration I felt in trying to deal with him in our day to day living. It hadn't been hard to please my parents, but it was extremely hard to please my husband."

"You know, desertion is not always physical," Dr. Stuart replied. "It can also be mental, emotional and spiritual. By his actions, it appears to me that George has definitely abandoned his responsibility as husband and father.

Her new role as breadwinner would be seriously challenged by her deafness.

"Therefore," continued the minister, "I think I am at the point where I am ready to say that if you were to decide to obtain a divorce, thereby relinquishing any future responsibility for your husband's welfare, you could not be blamed. His condition is too serious to hope for a sudden or easy recovery.

"Although I have not talked with him or Reverend Foster, I am dubious as to the depth of his religious experience. All too often people in George's emotional condition are inclined to use religion as a front. For your own peace of mind and welfare, to say nothing of the welfare of your children, I think it is best to take the necessary steps toward divorce, which apparently are already in your thinking."

"Not wanting to hurt either of our families has been the primary feeling which kept me from leaving George for so long," replied my mother. "Now, ironically, it has become the main factor in my not wanting to take him back."

"I shall do everything possible to help you explain to the children why such steps are necessary," said Dr. Stuart. "They are going to be hurt either way. If there is a choice between exposing them to the highly unstable influences of their father while waiting for his improvement, or denying them a father, I choose the latter, even with all the disadvantages that not having a father involves."

"I know it's inevitable that the children should be affected by all that has happened," Mom responded, "and I discussed ways of helping them with the social worker at the Child Center. She told me that I do better with the children than anyone else who comes to see them, that I had good feelings toward them, good judgment in handling them and that she did not feel that I needed advice on the children. She feels I need help for myself, because their sense of security and balance would come from my own sense of security and balance.

"Her remark that, 'because he was that kind of person, a pedophile,' and that even after his sessions with the psychiatric social worker they could not guarantee that my husband would not repeat his behavior, gave me nothing to hope for from George.

Dorene

"It seems to me now," she continued to Dr. Stuart, "that instead of worrying about my husband's influence on the children, perhaps I should trust their drive to do right, to grow in spirit, which I believe is inherent in every one of us. My goal should be to keep them on the right course and to help them grow into the fine people they are intended to be, letting them know that whenever they are confronted with problems which they cannot solve, there is help available to them from many sources – and particularly their minister."

Mom told her minister, "I believe, from the way we have worked together through all of this difficulty, that my children know that I have tried to do the best I could for them; and they will know it even more when they are older. If this outlook is right, then the big question left to settle concerning them is what visiting arrangements with their father would be best for them."

Having clarified her resolve, Mom then wrote to Daddy. "Nobody can know better than you how much reason you have given me to distrust you. This cannot just be wiped out by your say-so. What I need to know is that you finally have found a sense of personal responsibility toward our children, whereby you will neither take advantage of any leniency on my part, nor attack me personally in front of them if I should set rules I feel are best for their welfare. When I know you can accept restrictions from without, I will more likely be able to believe that you can impose restrictions from within."

Daddy, it seems, had written a number of letters to me and to Gary, urging us to be his ally against our mother. "There will be no more discussion of visiting until you stop writing the kind of letters you wrote the last two times," mother wrote him angrily. "Telling Joyce and Gary that I was destroying their love for you, and that you need their help, is ridiculous! An eleven-year-old child is not equipped to handle a problem of this kind. It puts too heavy a burden on a child. Your daughter is so confused and worried that she can't sleep.

"Whose welfare are you really considering?" mother concluded. "If you don't like my decisions regarding the children, I am sorry, but the final responsibility is now mine."

In a more certain frame of mind, she now wrote to Dr. Stuart, "I feel that marriage is more a spiritual bond than a legal bond. When the spiritual bond is broken or never existed, the only reason for keeping the legal bond is whether or not it serves its purpose for the family. I am convinced that ours does not."

You know, desertion is not always physical.

It can also be mental, emotional and spiritual.

The minister put my mother in touch with a well-regarded attorney who was a member of his congregation, who began assisting her in filing for divorce. Between them, they decided to use desertion, on George's part, as grounds for divorce, rather than specifying the true reasons. This was to spare us children an ugly court battle and to make it easier for my father to start a new life without any scandal or smirch on his name.

Dr. Stuart also informed both the attorney and my mother of further consultations regarding George that he had undertaken. "I have had a telephone consultation with a prominent Washington psychiatrist, who in the past has been very helpful to me when I needed to give psychiatric advice.

"He confirmed the opinion of the psychiatrists at Spring Grove Hospital that Mr. Culbertson was not psychotic. Having had a great deal of experience with this type of mental disturbance, he understood what was at stake here. I asked him under what conditions your husband might best recover – being restored to his family, or living outside the family?

"His reply was that obviously Mr. Culbertson would be happier at home but this was not necessarily essential to his improvement and that he might just as well adjust outside the family as within.

"I then asked him if he felt there was a chance of recovery. His reply, and I am quoting him as accurately as I can possibly recall, was, 'We do not speak of recovery in cases like this. What we hope is that a person who has had this background can keep his activities under control.'"

"In view of these circumstances," her lawyer told her, "you are entirely justified in limiting visitation of the children to a very minimum amount of time. In fact, the more you limit it may make it possible for us to bring this matter to a conclusion at the earliest date."

Mom's lawyer also wrote, in frustration, to my father's attorney: "I understand Mr.

Culbertson has threatened to involve and ruin the reputation of several members of her family if my client does not do exactly what he demands. I quote to you something that disturbs me greatly, from a letter he wrote her recently: 'You can settle this whole thing immediately by consenting to my one request. You can save your mother's happiness, and perhaps her life, as well as the happiness of your sister and brother and friends.'

"The one request that he seems to refer to is a matter of the summer vacation, having the children with him. However, you must realize that all of these violent threats and demands by your client only add to my conviction that he should not have them."

On September 30, 1957, my mother received a letter from her lawyer discussing the divorce issue she was most concerned about." If we got an order giving you exclusive custody of the children, with the right of visitation by Mr. Culbertson only at such times as are reasonable and proper, we could well control his visits while he is in the East," said the lawyer. "If he goes to Colorado, we of course would not let the children go except upon such conditions and terms as may be agreeable after conference with you.

Gary

"It is really my feeling that if we get him in Colorado, we probably won't have any more trouble because we would simply not allow the children to go there, and he probably would not go to the expense of coming back here to Maryland. Once the court has decreed permanent custody and guardianship, I think you will have the matter under control."

In April of 1958, my mother achieved a Final Decree of Divorce with the following conditions:

"Marjorie Forehand Culbertson is awarded permanent custody and guardianship of the minor children of the parties hereto, namely: Joyce Lynn Culbertson, Gary Richard Culbertson, and Dorene Sue Culbertson, with the right to the defendant to visit said children at such times as are reasonable and proper. In the event the parties are unable to agree as to reasonable and proper visitation, then the same shall be determined by the parties hereunto in conference with attorneys and clergy."

"This makes me feel as if I can now close the door on the past," my mother wrote to

Joyce

Dr. Stuart. "Although I had been deeply disappointed that my marriage failed, now I feel that I have worked through this problem, and can look towards the future with confidence and optimism.

"I still don't feel that I can trust George's moral judgement," mother continued. "He is an example to me of how a person can lose everything by taking, holding, demanding; he needs to be held in line by some means such as the law. Now that this has been accomplished, I find myself feeling much less apprehensive.

"I cannot keep from saying again how happy I am about the way the children have been doing," she concluded, more optimistically. "If I need proof that I have taken the right step, I see it every day in them – their happy and relaxed attitude, their complete acceptance of their life as it is now."

I feel that marriage is more a spiritual bond than a legal bond.

With anger and frustration, I reflect on all the ways Daddy had browbeaten my mother. He encouraged a minister to use spiritual coercion against her. He undermined her resolve, saying, "You can't make it on your own; you need me." He raged at her and at her family. He manipulated his children's emotions, and created terror in Mom that he might see the kids without authority and supervision. He stopped seeing his psychiatrist. He lied to all their mutual friends, blaming mother for the divorce. He then hired a lawyer to argue for maximum possible visitation.

Yet, somehow, Mom completed school, bought a house, and found a full time job. With the assistance of her children, she re-organized our family's life. And with the support of a few close friends, two admiring social workers, and her minister, she withstood all of my father's emotional assaults.

In 1958, Gary, Dorene and I would watch "Queen for a Day" virtually every afternoon. Women who overcame great odds, holding families together through illness and hard times, were crowned each day. I sent in a lengthy letter about my hero mother, nominating her to be the Queen for a Day. In the face of amazing odds, Mom's abiding love and steady determination had allowed our family to establish a new, and much healthier, foundation.

Unexpectedly however, when my father reestablished himself in Colorado, he wrote to my mother demanding that his children come to visit him during their summer vacation. In distress, Mom consulted her advisors. Both Dr. Stuart and Mom's lawyer pointed out that, after all, her ex-husband was still the children's father.

These experts told her that since he had promised not to molest Joyce again, and that his sister Eleanor had agreed that the children would stay at her home, not George's, during the vacation, my father's request should be granted. Believing her minister and lawyer were trained to know what was best, my mother reluctantly surrendered.

"I should have trusted myself," my mother says today, her voice tinged with remorse at the memory. "But in those days they wouldn't let me. I had to agree to the summer visits although I was strongly opposed."

In our family, a belief had now emerged that essentially said, "Under the right circumstances, it can be safe for children of a pedophile to have visitation with their father, and that adults untrained in the nature of this illness are competent to supervise such visits." This pattern would have devastating future effects.

In return for choosing not to seek a court order for George's return to the hospital, my mother obtained custody of her children, as well as indications that George intended to depart the East Coast and return to Colorado. But she had been compelled to compromise. By promising mother that his own two sisters in Colorado would carefully oversee these visits, George managed to obtain extended, annual summer visitation with his children.

A new shadow had been cast.

I can now close the door on the past.

Chapter Ten

Hiding Out in High School

(1958-1962)

"The place she remains to hide her pain
Is somewhere dark and deep.
In a world where he can't find her
There are no ghosts behind her
And there are no secrets left to keep."

– Song by Terri Allard

In 1995, ten years after my father's death and one year into my journey to learn about his life, Freeman and I visit my sister at her home in Ohio. Dorene had not come to Colorado when our father died. She felt that she didn't really know him. Now, as we talk at the dining room table in her small rural home, I learn that she has always felt outside of the family.

Earlier, I had sensed a wall between my mother and me that hindered our closeness. But now, with Dorene, instead of a barrier, I have more of a sense of distance between us, perhaps a wide, deep moat. It surrounds a small island where, forty years ago, Mom and I became isolated from others in our family by unspoken secrets. Sadly, those secrets could not allow Dorene, or even Gary, to join us on the island. Today, on a cold but sunny spring morning, my sister and I finally begin to build a bridge to connect our separate worlds.

Dorene, Daddy, Me and Gary

Like Freeman, Dorene and her husband, Rick, love gardening. The two brothers-in-law have gone outdoors to inspect Rick's greenhouse and spring seedlings. Early blooming shrubs and bulbs, I notice, are making purple, yellow and pink offerings to this bright April day. Dorene and Rick also enjoy

creating hand-made crafts; Rick carves wood sculptures, and my sister is currently developing an assortment of decorated gifts – bird feeders, clocks, and Christmas ornaments – made from her homegrown gourds. I am astonished and deeply pleased to meet this artistic, intelligent, sensitive forty-four-year-old woman, whom I last lived with when she was a sullen and rebellious fourteen-year-old.

Six and a half years younger than I, Dorene was four when Daddy was taken to the psychiatric hospital. She was eleven when I left for nursing school, and fourteen when I got married. We had limited contact as our worlds diverged and, by the time she was sixteen, she had dropped out of high school to join the Air Force, where she met and married her first husband. After leaving the military, they moved to Ohio near his family and had two sons. Although they subsequently divorced, Dorene remained in that area so the boys could grow up close to their father.

Living at such a distance, with very little mutual emotional history to connect us, we have seen each other only a handful of times in the last thirty years – at Gary's funeral, at the birth of Dorene's second child, and for a few holiday visits. We will not be able to talk today about everything that's been left unspoken between us for so long, but we are both excited and a little nervous about starting to get to know each other.

Mom and I became isolated from others in our family by unspoken secrets.

JUN · 61 ·

Dorene

I have told Dorene about my plans to write a book about our father's life and have asked permission to interview her and tape record our conversation. We start with our brother, Gary, who was the connection, the bridge between Mom and Dorene and me.

"You and Gary were always so close," Dorene begins. "It was like you were probably the most important person in Gary's life, and I envy that, because I loved him very much too. You talked a lot more with Gary about Daddy, the incest and our parents' divorce, than you did with me. I never got in on those discussions. Also, you and Gary were always interested in psychology and philosophy. I never shared those deep meaningful things with him."

"Did Gary ever talk with you about Daddy?" I ask.

"No. Gary never mentioned Daddy at all," she shrugs.

I think how peculiar it is that, over the course of forty years, neither Gary nor I spoke even once about our father with her, nor did our younger sister ever ask. What could keep a family that much out of touch?

It was just too awful and too unexpected.

Dorene also tells me that she doesn't remember anything about the time when Daddy lived with us. I ask her about the time after Mom discovered the incest, when we kids were taken to Aunt Agnes's in New York. After we came home to live with Mom again, she can recall only one time that Daddy came to see us. "He and Mom were talking. I don't remember what they said but I remember asking if it meant that Daddy had to go away again?" She admits sadly that she never knew why our parents got divorced. "When I was seventeen, I finally asked about it. The way Mom phrased it, I got the idea Daddy was paranoid or something, that he was mentally ill."

Neither of us remembers clearly, but we both agree it was from me that Dorene first heard about the incest within our own family. She recalls, "It was fairly recently and it was so appalling that I didn't want to think about it. It was just too awful and too unexpected. I'm still not used to the idea and, because it didn't happen to me, I still don't think about it much. I'm only talking about it now because you are here, but it's so sad I feel like telling you, 'Go home, so I don't have to think about it.'"

I am so moved by my sister's openness. She has tears in her eyes. So do I. Just as silence blocked my relationship with my mother, the secrets in our family have separated me from my sister all these years. "Why didn't you ever ask about the reason for our parents' divorce?" I say. "Then I would have told you about Daddy molesting me."

"It never would have crossed my mind. Why didn't I ever ask? Because it never occurred to me he would do such a thing. Why would I think to ask? Even today I am still learning things I wasn't aware of. I never knew he was physically abusive to Gary, sexually abusive to you, that their friends in the Potluck Group knew why they split up, that Mom had to go back to school to be able to go to work and support us. How come I didn't know about this? Your life was so different from mine, yet we lived under the same roof."

We take a break – have coffee and cookies, play with her animals, and plan a supper menu. My inner radar flashes a signal for "avoidance." Neither of us really wants to talk about our father, but we are both committed to completing this conversation. This time, when we sit down, we bring a box of tissues to the table and place it next to the tape recorder.

"How about Colorado?" I ask. "Do you have memories of visiting Daddy after he moved?"

"Yes, I remember a small trailer that had an entryway built onto the front. Our two cousins, Wendy and Karen, and you and I were there. There was no shower in the trailer. There was a separate shower area with stalls like in a park. All four of us girls had gone to take showers and then we were in a bedroom where there was a big bed. We were all drying off and changing. We were undressed, and Daddy walked in. All of us were shy and embarrassed that he was in the room, but he said, 'This is nothing. I have seen this lots of times.' Finally he left, but he sort of imposed his prying adult eyes on us young girls."

Then, almost as an afterthought, Dorene says, "There was another incident. It was on one of our summer trips, when I was about seven. You and Gary were in the back of the pickup truck and I was in the front seat next to Daddy. Daddy had an erection and he reached over and put my hand on his penis, through his clothes, saying that it felt good. I took my hand away and he reached for it and put it back."

Dorene doesn't remember if molestation incidents like this happened more times than that. She didn't tell anyone because "it was about sex. Sex was embarrassing and shameful." She says she doesn't recall any other sexual incidents with Daddy.

My sister's secret is one that, even now, I had not anticipated. I am sad and enraged. After a year of hospital treatment, after the painful divorce because he had molested

Just as silence blocked my relationship with my mother, the secrets in our family have separated me from my sister all these years.

me, our father had repeated his behavior as soon as he had access to his younger daughter – just as he would later do as soon as he had access to his first-born grandchildren.

Dorene has kept this secret all these years, part of the dark water separating us. Even more poignant, though, is the way her psyche has kept this secret from her own awareness, as she told herself, "I didn't know him. He wasn't important in my life. It never happened to me."

I have scraps of memories, like torn pieces of fabric that might be made into a quilt, but I can't quite stitch them together.

Suddenly, I understand that I have been separated from my sister for forty long years, not because of our age differences, not because of our distinct personalities and interests, but because of the long-term destruction caused by our family's secrets about incest. Today, with tears on our cheeks and late afternoon sun shining on the spring flowers on the table, we embrace and say "I love you" with new meaning. In these few hours, we have had more real sharing than in all the years since we were little girls together.

This conversation has been therapeutic for both of us, but at last we head for bed. The next morning, after breakfast, Dorene gives me a special little "treasure box" made from a small round gourd with the top sliced off and then carefully reattached with small strips of soft brown leather. Maybe, now that we are both adults, I can practice the easy give-and-take of friendship rather than the caretaker role of our earlier years. I have realized that my sister has so much to give me, if I can just learn to appreciate and receive her gifts.

After a warm goodbye, Freeman and I leave for Virginia. Over this three-day weekend, we made the eight-hour drive to my sister's home in Ohio in one day, visited with Dorene for one day, and now have to return on this third day. This long automobile trip and short stay are physically challenging, but we couldn't have had this conversation by phone or letter.

When we get home, I unearth from our basement a battered box. "Joyce – High School" reads the label in thick black pen. Here I find pictures from the summer visit to Colorado in 1958, the summer after Daddy moved out there, the summer Dorene remembers him putting her hand on his erect penis. Gary and Dorene and I, for the next six summers, are smiling in pictures taken while we are spending our school vacations with our father – camping, learning to drive, riding horses, touring scenic mountain spots, target-shooting, visiting with Aunt Eleanor and her family.

I remember none of these events.

As I entered adolescence, I no longer faced the constant physical and emotional threat of Daddy's presence. I was no longer being violated weekly – or nightly – by molestation and his continual needs for emotional companionship. Nevertheless,

160

Dorene and Gary

the patterns of amnesia and dissociation, so helpful for surviving the years of incest, continued to dominate my life and keep me isolated. I have scraps of memories, like torn pieces of fabric that might be made into a quilt, but I can't quite stitch them together.

In 1958, my friends were trying cigarettes, using make-up, telling dirty jokes, kissing boyfriends, and defying their parents. Elvis was on the radio. I met my first black acquaintances, as our ninth grade class became integrated during this year.

In school I had four "safe" friends to sit with at lunch – Diane, Lynda, Norma and Barbara. They talked about boys and parents and beauty tips. On weekends we might go roller-skating or bowling or have a sleepover. They didn't ask why my father was absent and I didn't tell them.

Also that year, I remember that our Social Studies teacher told the class something so strange I could not forget it. "I love my wife so much, that if she didn't want to

I am doing this to you, against your will, because I love you.

have sex with me, I'd have to rape her," he said. Today, I understand this was the same kind of thought process at work when my father, by his actions, said to me so often, "I am doing this to you, against your will, because I love you."

Around this time, my "vocational aptitudes" test scores revealed that I should be a nurse or a social worker. And in home economics class, my final project was a demonstration: "How to Iron Your Husband's White Business Shirt."

My life script, similar to the one shared by my entire generation, was becoming very explicit. I would finish high school, go to nursing school, and marry a man with whom I would have sex and for whom I would iron shirts.

Hi.

My name is

Joyless.

My father

had sex

with me

because

he loved me

so much.

One weekend, when my friends were at my house for a slumber party, we were outdoors in the morning and my three-year-old neighbor came into the yard. She had a lisp and, as she gave me a hug, she said, "Hi, Joyless."

My friends laughed and the name stuck. Looking back, it seems ironically appropriate.

Hi. My name is Joyless. My father had sex with me because he loved me so much.

Adolescent sexuality and rebellion were my friends' preoccupations at school. I began to retreat to the safety of the grown-up role I had taken on at home since the divorce. I went directly home each day to my cooking and ironing tasks, and worked until late at night on my homework. On Friday and Saturday evenings, I baby-sat for neighbors' children. In order to avoid being with the other teenagers in my Sunday School class, I started supervising the three-year-old children in the church nursery.

The rest of high school was a blurred, repetitious pattern. Watching myself, from above and behind, I saw my own body. I watched other people's bodies and faces to see what they were thinking and feeling. I tried to say and do the right things to make them happy, make them go away.

Watch – the man is looking at you.

Watch – don't move your hips when you walk.

Watch – she wants you to laugh.

Watch – you laughed too loud. Quieter next time.

My life was observed from just above my right shoulder. I was not in my body or aware of my emotions. I watched others and told my body to move or hold still, when to smile or laugh. I was safe because I was removed; I felt nothing, and other people only saw me as a nice, normal girl.

162

I made mostly A's in eleventh grade, dropping out of advanced chemistry and trigonometry because they might be too hard. I might have gotten a B, and I couldn't risk being imperfect.

As my World History teacher walked up and down the room, she tapped girls whose knees were apart. "You must keep your knees together so boys can't see up your skirt," she would say. She never had to tap me.

One of my mementos from high school is a notebook from biology class. Our Advanced Biology teacher's enthusiasm and humor made this class come to life. I was frightened of the activity and interaction he encouraged – the only class where we moved around the room and talked to each other, even to the boys. One boy called me at home to ask about homework. He sounded friendly.

Gary, Dorene and Me

Would I like to go out on Friday? "No." Never. I baby-sit every weekend and clean house and will always be busy – forever. He didn't call again.

I could avoid boys, but not biochemistry. I was smitten. Carbon chains, photosynthesis, Kreb's cycle – finally a world that made sense, was rational and predictable and yet alive, spontaneous, creative. I had found an intellectual playground.

But in our "Problems of Democracy" class I didn't fare as well. The teacher was interested in class discussion and graded us on our voluntary participation. I was afraid to speak in front of others and had never done it without being called on. His ultimatum – that our grade would be based on participation – gave me my first opportunity for resistance. For the entire semester, I refused to speak or make any comment. Resisting his power felt so good. You can't make me. I won't. No! I made A's on all my papers and tests, but the teacher gave me a D for the semester – the only one I ever received. I was so proud of my refusal to cooperate. This was the first time I had ever refused to do what a man expected me to!

My life was observed from just above my right shoulder.

My high school yearbook from twelfth grade shows a serious, mature girl with glasses, wearing a black sweater and a single string of pearls. It says I participated and held offices in Advanced Biology Club, Interfaith Club, Latin Club, and Future Nurses Club; that I won second place in my eleventh grade science fair; and that I was a National Merit Scholarship Runner-up. I have no memories of these events. As I look at this yearbook, I feel like I am reading about a stranger. Inside the front and back cover, there are dozens of messages telling me what fun my friends had being in classes and clubs with me. There is no evidence that they saw anything wrong with me. They couldn't tell that I wasn't really there, that I was just observing. I feel sad, empty and confused as I put the yearbook back into the box.

The last souvenirs I find in my old box are from a trip that my friends Diane, Norma, Barbara and I took by bus after our high school graduation in June of 1962. We traveled together to Florida and stayed at my grandparents' home for a week. Most of our time was spent sunning ourselves at the nearby beach. I remember this incident from that time.

Our legal system had no requirement mandating required public identification of child molesters or pedophiles.

"Will you hold my glasses while we go in swimming?" a man's voice asked.

I looked up from my beach towel, where I was lying in my vertically striped bathing suit, watching myself from above to be sure I held my stomach flat when I breathed. "OK," I mumbled, terrified inside that this strange man had come over to talk.

After a few minutes in the water, he returned to sit down next to me, while his friend went over to sit closer to the other girls. Feeling shy and nervous, I tried to think of something to say. "So where are you guys from?"

"Well, my name's Sam, and we're home on leave from the Air Force. We don't get much chance to talk to girls where we are."

I watched my friends talking and laughing with these men and I tried to imitate them. Sam asked me to go to the movies with him that night and, when I hesitated, his friend asked if one of the other girls would go with him, as a double date. Diane volunteered immediately and, after some more conversation, we gave them my grandparents' address. That night Sam and his friend picked us up.

I was seventeen years old and this was my first date. Sam and I were together in the back seat as we pulled into a drive-in theater. He told me Florida was his home, but he was stationed in Hawaii. He wanted to know all about me, and thought it was great that I would be going to nursing school. He suggested that we could write letters to each other. Then he moved closer.

I watched his hand move toward me, his arm around my shoulder. I began to push his arm away, and whispered, "No. Stop." He leaned closer to kiss my cheek. "No… please."

He stopped. We just watched the movie.

This had never happened before – sitting next to a man who wanted to touch and kiss me, but didn't do it if I said "No."

I am in love.

Although our brief stay in Florida did not allow for more times to get together, Sam and I exchanged addresses and agreed to write each other regularly after he returned to his Air Force assignment in Hawaii and I returned home. A picture of him in his uniform is still in my scrapbook.

JUN . 61

Gary, Dorene and Me

Mom has told me that, in the spring of 1958, with their divorce finalized, my father found it hard to live alone and see his children only on weekends. He loved the Colorado Rocky Mountains of his childhood, reasoned there was nothing left for him in the east, and decided to move back home, near his family and the places where he grew up.

When I had visited the History Room of the Colorado School for the Deaf and Blind (CSDB) in 1994, I read the October 1958 edition of the newsletter, *The Columbine*. The paper reported:

> George Culbertson, a 1932 graduate of the School and a 1937 Gallaudet College alumnus, is back in Colorado after his long stay in the east. He is working at the School as a physical education instructor, football and basketball coach, science teacher and Scoutmaster. He says, "It's good to get back home," and vows that he "no more will roam."

A two-page article in the May 1959 issue is an annual report by George Culbertson, Scoutmaster, titled "Boy Scouts, Troop 7." He tells us that 100 percent of eligible boys enrolled, twenty-six Scouts, and that the troop went hiking, camping, and bobsledding. They also won a blue ribbon at the Scout-O-Rama. And there they are, in a black and white photograph, wearing their uniforms, flanked by an American flag, every right hand raised in the three-finger Scout salute. The tall, handsome, dark-haired man in the back row is my father.

Now, in April of 1995, a few weeks after Freeman and I made our visit to Dorene in Ohio, Freeman drives me to the airport so I can travel to Colorado again. He can't go with me this time because he needs to stay home with our youngest son, Gabe. He waits with me at the gate until my flight is called, and sends me off with a comforting hug and words of love.

My High School Yearbook Photo

I have scheduled interviews with faculty and staff – both hearing and non-hearing – who worked with my father at the CSDB from 1958 until 1962. In the letters I sent them six weeks ago, I deliberately avoided mentioning any questions about his pedophilia and child molesting. I do not know who knows about this side of my father's life or whether they will be hurt or defensive if I am the first to tell them. So I explained my interview requests by saying truthfully that I didn't know my father well during the thirty years before his death.

I notice that this portion of my journey to piece together my father's life feels decidedly different. Exploring my father's childhood, college and family life involved talking with people who knew me and knew my mother. During those interviews I found that I was treated kindly and gently. Now I am apprehensive. The people I will be meeting on this trip are my father's friends and colleagues, people who mostly met my father only after my parents' divorce. They do not know me. How will they respond?

Wanting some sense of familiarity and comfort, I drive my rental car from the airport to the same motel where I stayed last summer. There is a coffeepot in the lobby and an indoor swimming pool, and I am given a spacious room with a desk. I have intentionally planned not to visit with my aunts and cousins this time. Being required to engage in small talk and family rituals feels too difficult during a trip focused on trying to learn about my father's assaults and violations of other children.

After organizing my desktop, I feel ready for the next morning, my first day on this trip's assignment. As I finish these preparations, the telephone rings. It's Freeman, calling from Virginia. He reports on life on the home front and wishes me luck.

For dinner, I go to the Chinese restaurant next door to the motel, order my favorite dish – shrimp and broccoli – sit alone, and read the local newspaper. This, I imagine, could have been the way George Culbertson spent his first evening alone in Colorado Springs in 1958.

I reflect that after my father's hospitalization, diagnosis, and treatment for molesting me, our legal system had no requirement mandating required public identification of child molesters or pedophiles. No labels could be permanently associated with persons identified with my father's condition. There were no mandatory rules for reporting his previous behaviors to the authorities when he moved. Nor, in those days, did institutions ask for background checks or psychological profiles of employees hired to instruct or serve in parental and teaching roles with children.

My mother, however, had been close to Daddy's sisters, Elizabeth and Eleanor, during their eighteen-year marriage, and informed them of the reason for the divorce. "I had not intended to tell his family why he was in a mental hospital," she explained to me. "But when he began to play on their sympathies, I decided his sisters at least should know the truth. They soon decided to tell their mother. All of them, naturally, hoped I would take your father back, because they were convinced that he was well now. Since he left home so young, I realize they never really knew him, so could not understand very much about his condition. The whole Culbertson side of the family was deeply hurt by the outcome of his illness."

To his credit, my mother's minister, Dr. Stuart, also had engaged in specific correspondence with Daddy's elder sister Elizabeth.

"I do not think it is wise for Mrs. Culbertson to receive her husband back," Dr. Stuart wrote. "Before you condemn her, try to put yourself in her place. Imagine the things that have happened to her and her children happening within your own family.

"My judgments about your brother are based on information given to me by competent psychiatrists and are the result of long consideration. I have no doubt as to the sincerity of the religious experience Mr. Culbertson has shared with you, nor do I doubt that it has made a sweeping change in his life. But a religious conversion does not eradicate an emotional disturbance, especially one as serious as that which your brother has had. In addition to whatever help he has received from religion, he needs the continued help of a competent psychiatrist. He is unwilling to admit his need for further help at this point, and therefore, Mrs. Culbertson is extremely reluctant to receive him into the family fold.

"I am impressed by the caution Mrs. Culbertson has used to make her decision to be separated from her husband. I do not think divorce is by any means the ideal solution, and I never in any way condemned George when I met with him," Dr. Stuart continued. "But I'm deeply concerned about the seriousness of the emotional disturbance through which he has been going for several years. I regret that he is not more willing to admit his wrong and, more basically, that he will not consent to continued psychiatric care. He cannot be helped if he does not want to be."

My father truly needed further psychiatric supervision. At the conclusion of his Spring Grove Hospital record, just as he was being discharged, there is a most

This had never happened before — sitting next to a man who wanted to touch and kiss me, but didn't do it if I said "No."

disturbing clinical anecdote. The hospital social worker, who had met often with my father, wrote, "Mr. Culbertson was originally referred to me six months ago, in July 1956. Before Mr. Culbertson left the hospital, I became administrator of his residential cottage, and within this time I did not feel Mr. Culbertson changed in any appreciable way what so ever. I felt he was still sick, particularly in the way in which he tried to manipulate people. In his religious grandiosity, I had the feeling that in many ways he was including himself with God.

Daddy

"He was still insisting, even shortly before he was paroled, that there had been nothing wrong with what he had done with his daughter, and that he could not see why anyone had made a fuss about it, much less put him in the hospital because of this. Last month, however, I attended the doctor's discharge conference, and it was felt at the time that Mr. Culbertson was not psychotic and had not been psychotic in the past. Consequently, we could not keep him. It was recognized that he was sick but, hopefully, if we would parole him, he would follow through with outpatient therapy with the private psychiatrist whom he had started to see shortly before he left. Because he was in therapy, and because he was not psychotic, I was ordered to parole him, which I did."

This entry makes clear the danger my father presented as he left the East Coast. I realize, though, that because my father's family and friends chose to keep all of their information about George private, and because no one at the time had access to his records, there could be no way in which students, Scouts, and other children he would now come in contact with could have been protected from him in 1958.

When I arrive at the school the next morning, I learn that the CSDB no longer has my father's personnel file, since it has been over thirty years since he left. State employees' record archives are kept in Denver. My calls there, later, will reveal they had no remaining details other than the dates of my father's employment and dismissal. Still, I hope to unveil from people's memories details of his life that no written record will contain.

My first meeting at the school is with Ed Wilson. In 1958, he was a new teacher, and only twenty-five years old. Now, in his small office in the gymnasium building, he tells me he is approaching retirement as the school's Director of Physical Education. He emphasizes that my father loved sports and wrestling, outdoor life and nature. He also recalls that they worked as wrestling coaches together, and fondly describes George Culbertson as his friend and mentor.

Mr. Wilson acknowledges he doesn't know why George left his job at the school in 1962, but confirms that afterwards he didn't come back to visit very often. "I heard that George decided to sell the business he started in town. He moved to the mountains and sort of isolated himself. One year before he died, he asked me to come up to his cabin to see him. But I never got the chance to get away," Ed Wilson says sadly.

He says there is a quotation by Tolstoy that makes him think of his friend: "Nature is a friend you will never lose until death… and when you die you disappear into nature." Today, he feels, George might be one of the deer, or a fish, or maybe a tree.

When we finish talking, Mr. Wilson shows me the gym, locker rooms and classrooms where my father once worked. I feel curious as I see the active and playful students and the attentive and friendly staff, and I try to imagine George Culbertson, at age forty, returning as a teacher to this school where he spent his adolescence.

Today, before I leave the Colorado School, I again visit the History Room and find newsletters and yearbooks from the years my father taught and coached here. *The Colorado Index* from October of 1959 tells of the faculty's summer activities.

George Culbertson reports his summer doings this way:

> "The highlight of my summer vacation was when my three fine children, Joyce, 14, Gary, 12, and Dorene, 8, came out from Maryland to spend a month with me. Only time and money prevented us from seeing all of Colorado. After the children returned east, I ran the wheels of my pickup off investigating mountain real estate for sale. I plan to acquire a ranch if possible in the near future."

Soon after, in January of 1960, the *Index* reports:

> "George Culbertson has contracted to buy a 160 acre mountain ranch located just thirty miles from Colorado Springs near Woodland Park. He has big plans for developing this beautiful ranch for the use of deaf people from far and near. Already the deaf Boy Scouts have used this ranch for a two-day, two-night campout. They think it is a very interesting place to go. There are over one hundred beaver dams on the stream through the ranch, and a short distance above it is Pike National Forest."

George was still insisting that there had been nothing wrong with what he had done with his daughter.

169

Gary Learns to Drive

For just sixty dollars an acre my father purchased these rolling hills, rugged rocks, fields abloom with yellow and purple flowers, and a stream winding through the center whose beaver dam formed a small natural lake. He moved his tiny one-room house trailer up next to an old wood shed so he could spend weekends and holidays away from the city. He named his new home "Silent Valley," and shortened it to "Silva."

We did not see Daddy during the school year, but we exchanged newsy letters regularly. He sent us photos of himself and his students, his scout troop, and his football team. He also sent a picture of his rented home, a small four-room cottage near the school, and wrote about his activities in local and state social and political groups for the deaf.

He also wrote about his plans to bring people to share and enjoy Silent Valley with him; his plans to fix his loneliness. He will have a fleet of snowmobiles so people can come in both summer and winter. He will have cabins for families to rent with horses, swimming, hiking trails, and campfires. He will subdivide the land into lots and sell home sites to other deaf people so the deaf can have their own resort, "Silent Valley." He will develop a recreational park for use by the hiking and outdoor groups whose activities he has started to attend and enjoy.

None of these big plans ever came to fruition. But Silent Valley would become the site of other plans my father chose never to share with other adults. Here, I am to learn later, he would engage in one of the most active phases of his pedophilia.

Some of Daddy's students have responded to my query letter, and I am able to find their pictures in the yearbook. Each confirmed that George had been their science teacher and noted that he was the Boy Scout leader. One remembers that the Girl Scouts and Boy Scouts went to picnic and hike at the Garden of the Gods in Colorado Springs and that Mr. Culbertson helped the girls and boys to climb the rocks. Another woman recalls, "I was a tomboy at school, so I asked him why I couldn't join the Boy Scouts too. He just laughed and said, 'You'd be a good Boy Scout, but that would be against regulations, because you are a girl.'"

Another student recalls that "Mr. Culbertson took three girls and three boys to his ranch. He showed us his home and beautiful land. He took us there hiking and sledding for two years." I find myself searching students' faces in the yearbook, trying to imagine which six students might have spent all that time with Daddy at Silent Valley. There are some questions I just cannot answer.

Aside from numerous reports and photographs of football and basketball games and teams, I find only one other article in the *Index* that mentions my father. In the issue from January of 1962, I read:

> "The most popular course in our school is probably Driver Training. Instructor George Culbertson is happy to see this enthusiasm because when boys and girls truly want to learn something they do so quickly, easily and well."

The report says there were six girls and five boys taking the course. I recall what happened to me, and to my sister, when we were alone in a car with my father. Did these students ever ride alone with their instructor, I wonder? If so, what else were they learning?

There seems to be no further information here in the History Room to add to my search. Tomorrow I will meet with five different people who worked here with George Culbertson through 1962. I have seen their pictures and names here in the yearbooks and newsletters.

That afternoon, back at my motel, I go to the heated indoor swimming pool to try to relax my body and my mind. The body is easier. My mind is trying to come to terms with the lack of information or evidence regarding any molesting behaviors during these years when my father taught in this residential school. Did it not happen? Did it happen, then get forgotten? Did it happen, and is it not forgotten but still a secret?

Silent Valley would become the site where he would engage in one of the most active phases of his pedophilia.

Damp and tired, I return to my room, lie down for a restless nap, and then call Freeman. It is two hours later in Virginia and he has already made dinner for our son Gabe and is helping him with homework assignments. I tell him of my lack of clues and he encourages me to be more direct in my questioning tomorrow. After all, the people I will be talking to were not the young students who might have been involved, and they are retired from their positions at the school. They will have less reason to be secretive.

We catch up on news about the children and his work. Spring is coming to the Blue Ridge, he announces – the redbuds are in bloom! Perhaps this weekend he will take a canoe trip on our nearby river. He tells me he misses me and loves me and says, "I'm proud of you. If people seem hesitant to speak, just ask them directly what you need to know. It's not easy to be the one who breaks the silence."

Grateful for his support, but weary from today and anticipating another long day tomorrow, I go for a walk to a restaurant several blocks away. It is not spring here in Colorado Springs. The early April air is gray and chilly. So is my mood.

Before leaving Virginia for this trip, I had received a letter from a colleague at CSDB, who wrote:

> "Mr. Roy Steele was superintendent of CSDB when I was hired as a cook in 1954, and was in charge there when George started to work in 1958. Mr. Steele had been an F.B.I. agent during World War II and he was strict in having the schoolteachers, employees and students follow rules to order.

> "George took the Boy Scouts on many outings and they stayed overnights. George had permission to get food from the kitchen, which I always got ready for him to carry on their outings. They also went skiing and snowmobile riding. Somehow George broke a school rule and Supt. Steele had him come to his office for an explanation. George told me he made a mistake in talking back to Supt. Steele instead of accepting correction, and therefore was fired. That's when he moved on to set up his welding business. He committed suicide by shooting himself in Woodland Park. I was very sorry to hear about that, as he was a good friend."

My first four meetings the next day are with men who, like Mr. Wilson, were teachers and coaches with my father. They all agree he was "a gifted person," "innovative," "always pleasant and cheerful," and "positive all the time." They say that he took the students on hikes up in the mountains, on overnight camping trips, on sledding trips.

"He was friendly," one man tells me. "Outgoing. If the kids got out of place he would take care of it, but he wasn't mean to the kids. He was very kind."

Another says, "He would give little talks to the Scouts. I remember one time when he was encouraging the deaf kids, when they were old enough to have jobs, to put away a little bit of money each week or whenever they got paid. Then I remember so distinctly him saying 'and when you need something then you can go to the bank and get the money and pay for it.' And the kids were listening so intently. You could see they were looking forward to the day when they would have a job and be able to put the money aside."

How bizarre, I think to myself, recalling that my father never had a spare penny his whole life.

One man tells me, "On weekends we would take them up to George's place, because some kids lived too far to go home, so we would take them up there just for a change of scene."

Then, looking somewhat confused, this elderly man, my father's friend, looks at me and says, "I didn't know he had a daughter. He never talked about his family."

With each of these men, I find an opportunity to ask if they know why my father was not re-hired after June of 1962. One remembers, "George and the Superintendent got into it over something." George was questioning the superintendent's authority, he says.

This seems to confirm what I had heard by letter. However, the other men will give me different explanations. The second man I interview recalls that at one point George decided he couldn't afford an apartment and was sleeping in the school gym, and believes that may have been the cause of his dismissal. The third says George bought too many supplies for the camping trips and did not return the leftover supplies, as he should have.

But the fourth adds, "Overall I would say he was quite friendly with most of the people, both students and staff. I don't know of any disagreements or any problems George had with others around the school."

I decide to take Freeman's advice and ask directly, "I have heard that my father had molested some children. Do you know if this ever happened while he was a teacher at the School for the Deaf?" Each of the four friends and colleagues states definitely that they never heard about any problems. They are not upset or defensive, just matter-of-fact. These men, I realize, have no secrets they can share, or none that they recall.

My last interview for today is with a woman who worked at the Colorado School as a house parent in the boys' dormitory. "It was when your father was a coach as well

My father never had a spare penny his whole life.

173

Daddy

as the scout leader and gym teacher – I think from 1958 to 1962," she muses. I confirm that she is remembering the dates correctly. She lives alone now in a one-bedroom apartment and has some difficulty getting about, but she is friendly and affectionate. As we talk she shows me pictures and offers me a piece of cake.

This woman confirms all the stories and descriptions I heard earlier today about Daddy's activities and personality. But when I ask if she knew why he left his teaching job, she tells me, "He thought he should also teach the boys about sex. I had to tell the Superintendent about his trying to teach this subject without the school's knowledge."

She knows about other incidents also. At one time, she tells me, George was reported to have molested three children of friends at a picnic. Then it was discovered he had molested the children of other faculty members from the school.

There were two families involved in this incident in 1961 and she gives me their names.

Although I am not surprised to find this confirmation of my suspicions that my father continued to molest children during these years, I marvel at how this woman can know so much when my father's other colleagues seemed to have no knowledge of George's sexual behavior. How easily such crucial information is kept secret, even while it is violently altering the lives of children.

I thank her for her openness, tell her that my father also molested me, and explain that I am trying to find out about other children he abused during his life. She expresses sympathy and gives me a warm hug as I leave, inviting me to return and join her for dinner later this week if I have the chance.

When I later write to these faculty members whose children my father molested, I will learn that they trusted my father as their friend, that Daddy visited their homes many times and became friendly with their children. One of these correspondents reported, "He was a brilliant man. Yet there seemed to be something amiss; he tended to be a loner and kept pretty much to himself on his ranch when he wasn't working. Still, until these events, we had liked George and enjoyed his company."

A second former CSDB colleague was more specific about my father:

"There were incidents that shook our world apart, concerning my daughter. He asked her to touch his private parts when riding in his Jeep. There was another little girl also; she seems to have been more involved than my daughter.

"The father of the other child confronted George immediately, sometime in the middle of the night. George left an apology on their door. Immediately the next day George placed himself under the care of a psychiatrist. The mother of the other girl and I went to the police. But the District Attorney explained that because George placed himself in psychiatric care that he was unable to get an arrest warrant served. Later George dismissed himself from the hospital. George never was trusted or accepted by the deaf here at the school again.

"But it was some kind of shower room incident in the gym that caused George's dismissal," this former teacher adds. "He was employed in the physical education department. If I recall, he was caught checking on girls, watching them taking their showers after class.

"I heard about your father's suicide. I have a strong feeling that his past finally caught up with him, and he was afraid of the consequences. I'm sure he died with little remorsefulness. He never even mentioned being sorry for the victims. George was always trying to defend himself."

How easily such crucial information is kept secret, even while it is violently altering the lives of children.

The
secrets
have a
familiar
sound.

The sound
of silence.

One of these deaf colleagues whose daughter was victimized remarks that fellow Gallaudet alumni, their own friends who were living in Maryland at the time Daddy returned to CSDB, knew his child molesting was the cause of his and my mother's divorce. She asks, in retrospective anger, "Why didn't anyone write, or inform us back then, about George and his illness? If we had only known, so much could have been prevented."

Reports of "something amiss," molesting children at picnics, having a girl touch his private parts, violating children of colleagues and friends, "teaching the boys about sex," checking on the girls taking their showers – these stories have an all too familiar sound. The secrets have a familiar sound, too. The sound of silence.

Of the six staff and faculty I have talked with, only one was even aware of their colleague's inappropriate behaviors with children. Although more and more people knew about my father's behaviors, as the years passed and the list of abuses grew, many who worked most closely with him remained in the dark about what he did. This active pedophile, with access to numerous children, was still not visible to those who knew him.

The layers of secrecy and silence were becoming thick and tangled.

Me Horseback Riding

Me

Chapter Eleven

Filling in Blank Pages

(1962-1965)

"Crazy,
I'm crazy for feelin' so lonely…
I'm crazy,
Crazy for feelin' so blue…
I'm crazy for tryin,'
And crazy for cryin',
And I'm crazy for lovin' you…."

– Song by Willie Nelson

Sitting now on our concrete porch in my weathered wooden rocking chair, looking out over the spectacular colors of the Blue Ridge Mountains in mid-October, I try to focus on what happened after I graduated from high school. For this next three-year period of my life, I can find no clues, no puzzle pieces, no stories that I can connect. Until this time, relatives and friends who had been part of my home life have been able to tell me their recollections and perceptions. Now, as I examine the years after I moved away from home, there are no people who were there with me to add their memories to my limited personal collection and help me fill in the pictures.

In September of 1962, Mom drove me to Sibley Memorial Hospital in Washington, D.C. and helped me move my few belongings into the student nurses' dormitory.

I realize that Mom, Gary, Dorene and I never lived all together again after that day when I left home. We saw each other a few times each year and had some holidays together. Soon after I came home to live after three years at nursing school, Dorene

Gary

left high school, joined the Air Force, and married. Gary had been drafted into the Army and was stationed in Oklahoma.

Later on, as we pursued our own adult lives, Gary and I would visit at each other's home several times a year, doing very little, saying very little. A few years before he died, I had begun talking with him about my memories of the incest and about my therapy, but I didn't know at the time to ask him about his own memories and experiences. And he didn't reveal them. I wish he were here now to talk with me and tell me more about his childhood and its effects on his adult life.

I lean back in the rocker and close my eyes, imagining that Gary hasn't died, that he is here, now fifty years old, visiting with me in Virginia.

"Hi, Gary!" I'd say. "Where have you been? Why didn't you call? It's sure good to see you. How about a hug? Want a beer, a shower, a nap?"

Finally I'd tell Gary about finding out that Daddy had molested my children – Gary's nephew and niece, Joe and Jenny. I'd tell him how I had realized that our father had molested many other children, too. I'd ask Gary what he thought about my idea to write a book and if he would help me by telling me what he remembers. Would he tell me what happened to him? "Do you have secrets, too, Gary?" I'd ask.

In my mind, I review what I know of Gary's life. Mom says Daddy was always hard on Gary, always critical, never satisfied. He told his son that he wasn't tough enough, didn't work hard enough, wasn't manly enough. Dorene and I received help and encouragement, but Gary was punished for his mistakes – spanking, belting, switching with willow branches. Mom is so sad when she thinks about those times.

I know that Gary and I shared a bedroom from the time he was born until after our parents' divorce. After Dorene was born, Gary and I had bunk beds and Dorene was on another twin bed in the same bedroom. Every single night, my mother has confirmed, Daddy used to come to "tuck us in." Sometimes I think I can remember his footsteps coming up the stairs, but neither Dorene nor I remember anything about stories, prayers, or other bedtime rituals.

Did Gary have memories of what happened? I wonder if Daddy molested him too, had oral sex with him, or had Dorene and Gary and me do sexual things with each other, as he did so often later with other children?

I wonder if Gary was in the basement at Langley Park when the neighbor kids and I were "playing doctor?" If so, did he remember Daddy being there? Did he remember whether our father told all the children to get undressed and then took photos of them, as he did later on with the kids in Colorado?

I wonder what Gary thought when Uncle Harold came to school to get us and said our father had gone to the hospital and we had to go away to New York. Daddy never came back to our family. Gary was nine years old when his father went away. I wonder if he thought it was his fault – because he didn't put the tools away right, or because he walked home too slowly after Cub Scouts and was late for dinner, or because, when Daddy wrestled with him, he cried instead of "fighting like a man."

I know that in high school, Gary's friends called him "Jesus." He laughed when I asked why and said it was because he was "always suffering." I wonder if Gary could name his sorrow, or had he blocked out his memories like I did?

I know that by the time Gary was in tenth grade, Mom was concerned about her adolescent son growing up without a father. He was failing in school despite his near-genius IQ. He refused to do chores. He seemed unmotivated. These days, maybe they would recognize that Gary was depressed. At that time, though, she didn't know what to do, and wondered if military school would help. She wanted so much to be a good mother and do the right thing for her son, so with financial help from her parents, Mom sent Gary to a military academy. It wasn't far from here, actually – just north of where I live now. Seventeen days – that's all he was able to stand of this father substitute, or maybe of the separation from his home and family.

Everyone in our family knows the story of how Gary left the military school dorm through a window in the middle of the night and walked alone for three days and nights through the Blue Ridge mountains and D.C. traffic to get home. When he walked in the door, hungry and exhausted, Mom took him in her arms and made him safe again. "Please don't make me go back," he cried.

She still wanted to be a good mother, to do the right thing, so Mom took Gary to a psychiatrist to get advice about whether her son needed to go back to military school. The doctor told Mom that Gary didn't have to go back, that he wasn't messed up, that she was doing a good job raising him. Gary told me years later, when I asked if he knew about Daddy molesting me, that the psychiatrist asked if Gary had any questions for him. Gary asked, "Do you know why my parents got divorced?"

"It had something to do with sex," the doctor said, evasively.

He told his son, Gary, that he wasn't tough enough, didn't work hard enough, wasn't manly enough.

Fifteen years later I would tell Gary that the "something" was Mom discovering Daddy and me in the bathroom.

After withdrawing from military school, during the three years I was away at nursing school, Gary barely managed to graduate from high school. In the fall of 1964 he tried a year of college.

My drifting brother could get an A in philosophy, but only manage an F in health! He was certainly intelligent enough to continue, and Gary knew that if he dropped out of college he would be drafted and might be sent to Vietnam. Yet in spite of his objections to the Vietnam War, Gary did leave school. Perhaps college just seemed pointless, since he had no vision or ambition for his future. I imagine him numb inside, caught between two impossible choices.

After leaving college, my brother was, in fact, soon drafted, but instead of Vietnam, he was assigned to Fort Sill, Oklahoma. Mom was so relieved. She didn't need her son to be a hero or, maybe, to die. Neither did I.

In the thirty years until his death, my brother and I would always feel safe and close and happy to see each other whenever we visited. I would cook his favorite chili dinner while he played with Joe and Jenny. He would listen to my search for memories, flashbacks and therapy, always believing me and accepting my healing journey.

I would hear about his travels out west, his jobs and adventures. Part of him seemed to be on a spiritual quest – occult books, mystical practices, devout groups. He tried so many things to relieve what seemed to me to be his inner suffering. Recently, through Internet research, I learned that one of the groups Gary joined for over a year, the Children of God, is said by ex-members to have promoted sex with children, saying this was "God's will." Maybe Gary was looking here for a belief to help him understand and justify what our father had done. But Gary left this group. I believe he wasn't able to reconcile his own search for love with the disturbing practices they advocated.

"Please don't make me go back," **he cried.**

Our shared childhood bedroom, our father's documented history of molesting both girls and boys, Gary's sadness and hopelessness, and the fact that Gary was part of this religious sect are among the reasons I am certain Daddy molested Gary, too.

After two years in the Army, after leaving the Children of God and hitch-hiking around the country, Gary, then in his late twenties, spent over a year living next door to his father, who was operating "Culby's," a welding and sharpening business in Colorado Springs.

Gary told me, "I went out there just hoping to get to finally know him. I guess I was trying hard to work out my relationship with Daddy." I think he meant he was trying to get his father to understand him, trying to earn his approval. I believe now Gary spent that year trying to come to terms with and heal from his own experiences of incest.

Finally Gary gave up. There was no getting his father's approval. Gary's hair was too long, "like a girl." His beard was disgusting; "a man shaves every day." He read too much "sissy stuff, poetry and religion." I don't think he understood that although Gary was not weak, he was definitely scared.

Before Gary died, it hadn't occurred to me that Daddy had molested other children besides me, including boys. It didn't occur to me that he might have molested his own son, so I hadn't asked my brother questions. Our timing was all wrong.

Gary

I wish I had known to ask. I wonder what it was like for Gary when he heard my incest story. Did he not remember what happened to him? Did he remember, but kept it a secret? Did he ever tell anyone?

Oh, Gary, how I wish you were here on the porch to talk with me today. If you were here, you could help Mom and Dorene and me go back to that time when we all lived together, in the debris after the "bomb." We could search together for memories and understandings.

Last evening's reminiscing helps me focus on changes that were occurring in our family and inside myself during the years after I graduated from high school, the years after Daddy was fired from his teaching position at the Colorado School for the Deaf.

I am ready this morning to continue my gathering of clues and spread out my meager resources - my senior yearbook and a single scrapbook with just a few items pasted in.

In the yearbook, I see the faces of my small class of sixty-five young women. For three years, 1962 – 1965, we lived and worked together twenty-four hours a day at Sibley Memorial Hospital in Washington, D.C. My friends and classmates would have known only the visible, available part of me. I was friendly, but serious; responsible, but not ambitious; shy in conversation, but outspoken in writing. None of them would know my secret history of incest or my secret way of surviving – not being present in my body or my feelings. After our graduation, these friends would come to my wedding and my baby showers. We would exchange birthday and Christmas

Daddy in front of his shop

cards and occasionally meet for dinner.

But ten years later, when my body and feeling memories had returned with a vengeance, when I was divorcing, drinking, and depressed, I had no ability to communicate my inner world and describe the emotional storms that were ravaging me. I broke off contact with those friends who had known me. I moved and moved and moved again, losing any traces of addresses and phone numbers. I no longer know anyone who can help me discover this part of my story.

As I open my nursing school yearbook thirty-five years later, I see my senior class picture. As in high school, I am surprised to see all the activities listed beside my name: yearbook committee, religious committee, Bible class, student recruitment, publications committee (editor), ways and means committee (chairman), Senior Class Vice President, State Student Nurses Association (treasurer), National Student Nurses Association delegate.

The academic and clinical part of nursing school came easily and naturally to me. Organizing and prioritizing patient care tasks matched my inclinations for order and control. Even the menial work of changing the sheets on a bed, cleaning the stainless steel patient utensils, and filling the water pitchers gave me some sense of accomplishment and satisfaction.

On the other hand, dormitory life was exhausting and bewildering. Sharing a bedroom with another person, taking showers in the group bathroom, listening to chatter and giggles about boys and sex – all these normal activities of daily life provoked fearful, guarded feelings in me.

Not being aware of my anxiety, I maintained control by carving out a serious and sedate routine – study, read, edit the school paper, baby-sit Friday and Saturday evenings, and write letters to my "boyfriend," Sam, from my post high school Florida vacation.

Our letters were so friendly and affectionate that by the spring of 1963, Sam and I were "going steady by mail." He used his leave from the Air Force to come east and visit me during my spring break, which I spent at Mom's house. She didn't want Sam to stay in our home, so he got a motel room nearby. For five days, Sam courted, teased and tried. I have only three real memories of this time. We rode together on a Ferris wheel at a local carnival and then held hands on our way to the car. We drove to Great Falls, parked to watch the river, and then Sam asked if he could kiss me. "OK," I said and turned my face toward him. He carefully pressed his lips to mine.

"It would help if you kissed back," he said gently.

"I don't know how," I said in embarrassment. And as always, I watched my awkwardness and his patient disappointment from above and behind my right shoulder.

Then, on Sam's last evening, we watched TV together in Mom's living room. After she went to bed, Sam slipped his arm around my shoulder. He tried another kiss and, woodenly, I tried to kiss back. Then, ever so gently, he put his hand on top of my sweater at the side of my breast.

"It would help if you kissed back."

I drew back in horror, shaking with fear. "We come from different worlds," I explained righteously. Sex is for marriage and babies. Unless you're a child – then it's for your father. "You have to leave now."

Sam went back to the Air Force, and I went back to nursing school. We wrote anguished letters trying to explain and fix what had happened. Finally we wrote "good-bye." I never saw him again.

"I don't know how."

I was eighteen years old and had thought I could simply be "in love" until I graduated, at which point I would then get married and have sex and babies. Now, I realized I had made a mistake. Most men, at least the one I had dated and kissed, did not realize how serious and sacred sex needed to be.

This was the behavior and thinking of a young child. I took a few poorly understood words - love, marriage, sex – and tried to use them to form a logical plan. I understood them only in cartoon fashion – large categories with nothing in them. I didn't know these words referred to complicated feelings.

In the summer of 1963, after completing my first year of nursing school, I traveled to Colorado with Gary and Dorene for our sixth and last trip together to visit our father. From this summer, I have a small memory fragment. Somewhere – I think we were sitting in his truck at a mountain overlook – Daddy and I were alone and talking. He told me that he was dating a woman named Irene, and that, like him, she enjoyed outdoor activities and flying airplanes.

I asked my father, "Why did you do that to me?"

"I never did anything to hurt you," my father responded. "I didn't come inside you like most men would, because I love you."

"The real problem," he went on to explain, "was that your mother was not affectionate enough. I needed a lot of affection, so I had to get that from you kids. I'm sorry you're still upset," he concluded, "but I didn't do anything wrong. It's just that our society doesn't approve."

I didn't know, then, to be stunned, to be outraged. At that moment, silence was all I could manage. I can still see this scene, and hear these words. They sounded like all the other words and moments in my life when Daddy assured me that he loved me and that Mom was to blame for everything that went wrong.

Today I know he was wrong.

Now I understand that Daddy's selfish actions, coupled with the kind of illogical reasoning that lay behind them, caused me an almost total confusion about love, sex, and marriage for decades afterward.

The sense of losing Sam, the first man who had showed me tenderness and respect, brought on feelings of sadness, which welled up inside me and turned into waves of intense grief. To avoid and make numb this pain, I began to eat constantly. I snacked on candy bars while I studied, raided pantries for chips and cookies when I baby-sat, and took emergency trips to the store for quarts of Swiss chocolate almond ice cream. In the next six months, I gained thirty pounds. I outgrew my initial student nurse uniform. Friends questioned whether I might be pregnant from Sam's visit last spring.

The part of me that was still the "good girl" kept getting A's and editing the nursing school newspaper. She watched the Beatles with friends and chose Ringo as her favorite. She started to go to foreign films and art galleries and symphonies with classmates, discovering a new world of intelligence and sensuality. She was drawn to the Civil Rights movement and the emerging struggle against oppression.

Although I had not heard of bulimia, by now my over-eating was almost constant and I was taking laxatives to have diarrhea and lose weight. I was swallowing No-Doze to stay awake at night to study. Sometimes I would get dizzy and my hands would

All the normal activities of daily life provoked fearful, guarded feelings in me.

shake. I had started reading my medical texts, sure that I had a fatal disease and trying to figure out what it might be. I still had no language for my disconnection from my body or my mounting anxiety.

I was intellectually interested in psychiatric theory and decided it would be "interesting" to talk to a doctor about my "compulsive eating."

Plus, I could miss class once a week.

Dr. King's office was on Connecticut Avenue, near the National Zoo. I had to travel across the city by bus to her elegant third floor office. The doctor looked like a grandmother – petite, gray-haired and kind.

"So, why are you here?"

"Well, I eat constantly. I think it's called a compulsion. For breakfast I have scrambled eggs and sausage and biscuits, and then for a morning snack I eat donuts, and then at lunch I get lots of extra rolls and butter and two desserts, and in the afternoon a few candy bars."

As I sat talking, my arms, which were resting on the chair, would begin to feel very heavy and grow larger and larger. Dr. King did not seem to notice that both my arms had swelled to four times their normal size. I could not lift them and could not move my body because my arms were so big and heavy.

Gary

I know now that the American Psychiatric Association defines this experience as "depersonalization," a form of dissociation, which may include perception of "an uncanny alteration in the size or shape of objects, sensory anesthesia, and a sensation of lacking control of one's actions."

Although I didn't know it then, this feeling was caused by the anxiety of sitting face to face with this psychiatrist and continuing to deny my feelings and my story.

Once I said, "I wonder if my eating is connected to what happened with my father?"

Dr. King didn't respond. She was asleep.

For several months I went faithfully every Wednesday at 4:00 p.m. to tell Dr. King what I had

My Classmate and Me

eaten since our last appointment. About halfway through each session, she would fall asleep in her chair. I would sit, my enormous arms keeping me still in my seat, until our session was over at 4:50 p.m. "Dr. King, it's time for me to go."

She would wake with a start, meet my eyes and say, "I'm sorry."

"That's okay," I'd respond. "I know you've had a long day and you're tired. Now you can go home. See you next week."

No needs of my own, no hurt, no anger. Just kind, patient consideration for her needs.

After each session, in the fading afternoon light, I would wander through the zoo, looking at the caged birds and animals, thinking I could understand how sad and lonely and frightened they felt. As I walked, I ate caramel popcorn and peanuts and candy bars until my arms got back down to normal size and I was able to get on a bus and return to my studies of psychiatry.

Psychoanalysis was the accepted treatment for most emotional problems in 1964. The prevalence of child sexual abuse had not yet been acknowledged by the medical community. There were no easily prescribed anti-depressants.

I could see that listening to my weekly lists of meals and snacks was boring for Dr. King, causing her to fall asleep and then feel apologetic. I was tired of making the bus trip and was becoming bored myself with the predictable ritual. I told her I wanted to stop coming.

After our psychiatry studies, in the spring of 1964, my class of student nurses went for three months to Children's Hospital to study pediatric nursing.

I already knew this was where I wanted to work, and had applied for a Registered Nurse position available there, to begin immediately after my graduation next June. I was near completion of the pediatric nurse part of my script, the one I had planned since I was a young child.

By 1965, I clearly knew the profession I'd be pursuing. But what about the marriage, the sex, the babies? I had not dated since Sam touched my breast. I had gained enough weight that guys didn't look or whistle anymore. It was as though one part of me was determined never to be vulnerable to any man again, while another part needed a safe new role to play. I had learned

186

about the wife-role in Home Economics, and on the surface was ready to try out for the part. How, exactly, does one get a husband? I knew I needed to date boys, like my friends did, to learn how to joke and flirt.

Clearly, I didn't have a plan that involved being single. My friend from third grade, Joan, was going to be an Air Force nurse. She wanted me to come with her. It was just one week until graduation, and I was sitting in my dorm room, reading the pamphlets and trying to decide. Live at home with my mother and work at Children's Hospital, or join the Air Force with Joan?

Claire burst into my dorm room. "There's a guy on the phone. I met him in a bar. He's a lot of fun. Come talk to him." She pulled me by my arm, led me to the shared phone in the hallway, and placed the receiver in my hand.

Reluctantly, I lifted it to my ear. "Hello."

"Claire says she's busy but thinks you'd like to go out with me," a friendly voice said.

I was shocked. How could Claire do this to me? "No, I don't think so. This Sunday is graduation and then I'll be busy working." I'll live with my mother or join the Air Force. I'll be busy forever. I won't go out and be alone with a man.

I had no idea what to say, but there stood Claire and two other friends watching me. "Just say yes," they were giggling. Under pressure from their urging, somehow I began to speak. The name of the voice on the other end of the line, I learned, was John.

He laughed, talked, asked questions, and wouldn't say good-bye until I agreed to a date the Friday after graduation.

He would pick me up at my mother's house. I was twenty. John's twenty-seven-year-old charm and sophistication were exciting and reassuring.

"I'm not pretty," I warned him. "I wear glasses and I'm fat."

"Hey, that's okay," he said. "See you Friday."

Gathering information about my own life during 1962 to 1965 was challenging because it was a period of limited family involvement and no enduring friendships. During these same years, my father also moved into a transitional phase of his life.

After being dismissed from his teaching and coaching position at the Colorado School for the Deaf and Blind in June of 1962, George had to find a new job. He no longer had his familiar campus life and his familiar work colleagues. In addition, his social life was affected by reports and rumors of his molesting of the children of friends and faculty.

I didn't do anything wrong.

It's just that our society doesn't approve.

From interviews with my aunts, I know that he was in regular contact with his family during these years. His sister, Elizabeth, and her husband, Andrew, had retired and moved from California back to Gardner, Colorado. George explained to them that he had been dismissed from the School for the Deaf due to a misunderstanding with the superintendent, and kept from them knowledge about the sexual abuse incidents with the children of his friends.

He then moved the trailer to his property at Silent Valley.

He began, once again, to do odd jobs in Colorado Springs – about thirty minutes away – especially lawn mower repair, saw sharpening, and welding. Word of his skill, efficiency, and friendliness spread and soon he developed a steady supply of customers.

Elizabeth and Eleanor relate something my father had always told us during summer visits. They knew their brother dreamed of developing Silent Valley into a recreational site for the deaf, for those who shared and understood his silent world. George began by building a small, beautiful, rustic cottage with a moss-covered rock foundation and natural cedar siding.

This cottage would be the initial community center of George's retreat, which he named "Silva Acres." But beyond this first dwelling, beyond his damming of the creek to create a picturesque pond at the valley's center, this plan for "Silva" never materialized. Later I would learn he molested even the children of these friends he had hoped would become charter members of his community.

His sisters know, too, that George's cousin, Brad, had brought his wife and four children to Silent Valley many times. George also visited their home frequently.

When I ask if I might interview Brad, they tell me he has been dead for several years. Elizabeth's photo albums show me, Gary, and Dorene visiting this cousin and his children and having fun. I regret this boyhood companion of our father's isn't here to share his memories.

When we are alone, Elizabeth confides in me that, many years ago, she learned from Brad's wife that George had molested Brad's daughter, Phyllis. She has never told this to her sister Eleanor, because she didn't want to "bring up George's illness." For my elderly aunts, I see that talking about their brother, even years after his death, is so upsetting, still.

With this piece of news, and Elizabeth's help, I find Phyllis's phone number in Denver and call to ask if I can talk with her about my father. A man answers the phone. Phyllis is not home. Phyllis doesn't return my calls or answer my letters when I try to contact her after I get home. I accept that she must have decided not to talk with me about her father's cousin, George. This silence is familiar, but without talking to

Daddy's social life was affected by reports and rumors of his molesting of the children of friends and faculty.

188

this distant relative, I cannot know if it is due to privacy or pain.

The other event from these years that Elizabeth and Eleanor tell me about, one I myself recall, is that my father was briefly married to a younger deaf woman. They know her name was Irene, but they don't know how to contact her.

Again, the remarkable network of the national deaf community makes itself available to my research. When I had talked with the Brooks, my parents' friends from the early years of their marriage, we had discussed what became of George after he moved to Colorado. These friends had not heard about his molesting of children during the years he was a teacher, but they did know about his re-marriage.

"He married Irene Johnson," Mrs. Brook remembers. "She lives in Portland now. I know her mother. I'll get her address and phone number for you."

A few weeks later, I receive a kind note from Mrs. Brook. She sends me current information about how to contact this woman who had ever-so-briefly been my stepmother. When he first met Irene, Daddy had written to me about how happy he was to find a woman who loved the outdoors and sports and, especially, his favorite activity, flying.

This is the same woman I remember him talking to me about on a Colorado roadside, when he divulged his impotency to me. I had seen pictures of her – short, slender, casually dressed. She looked girlish, like my own mother when she first got married. I even have a picture of my father and Irene visiting me in the summer of 1965 after I graduated from nursing school; but, because of my ongoing dissociative condition, I don't remember being with them.

I write a short note to Irene, apologizing for intruding in her personal life after so long and explaining that I want to learn more about my father's life in the years after he left our family. I do not know intimate details about their marriage and their divorce and, again, I wonder if there will be some tension or guardedness.

A few weeks later, I receive a call on my teletype machine. As I attach the telephone receiver to the electronic printing device, I assume this is a call from my mother, ready to make plans for our next get-together. I sit down next to the small table where the TDD sits and type: "Good morning. Joyce here."

As I watch the screen, blue digital letters move across it: "Good morning, Joyce." This is Irene Johnson in Portland. I got your letter and was so delighted to hear from you.

The casualness of this encounter astonishes me. Although it lacks the familiar voice and background sounds of a telephone call, watching a conversation take form in print creates its own sense of connection and intimacy.

That was the beginning of the nightmare.

189

Me

"Hearing from you brought back memories – some good and some bad. I will go back to the days when I was with your father and answer as much as I can," Irene types.

"Can you please tell me how you and my father met and any memories you have of him?" I ask.

Irene responds: "I was a student at Gallaudet from 1952 until 1957. This is when your parents lived in the D.C. area. I heard of George's adventures. (You know how our deaf grapevine system is!) He was a risk-taker in a sense and I admired him for defying the odds. I always admired George but didn't meet him at that time.

"After I graduated, I taught in South Carolina for two years and then I moved to Santa Fe, New Mexico where I took up flying. We read about each other's love of airplanes in some of our deaf newsletters; that was the common denominator that attracted George and me. We also found we had a lot of other interests in common – driving a jeep (I had my own), camping, outdoor activities, great fans of sports (particularly wrestling – your father excelled in wrestling).

"I started dating him in 1962, and we went together for around three years. He was the only man who could get me to tie the knot – even when my guts told me it would be a mistake. I did not quite know myself at that time, but he had a way of putting words in such a convincing way – he was convincing. He convinced me to marry him and leave New Mexico. We were married in February 1965. I moved to Colorado in June 1965 and began teaching at the Colorado School for the Deaf and Blind.

"I always told folks that if our marriage lasted beyond one year it would have gone on. Your father was a model hubby – picked up his clothes, wiped his shoes, changed his shoes for the house, cooked his breakfast, washed the dishes – I was the slob! HA!

"George was also a great companion. I enjoyed his company so much. We did things together and I came to appreciate his brain. He was a very brilliant guy with great writing skills. He taught me a lot, too. Now I tell some people that it was George who taught me about living together, being committed to a relationship, dealing with values, money, ideas, emotions, etc. I really admired him.

"I also want you to know that I never regretted knowing your father although there was a sad ending. Something was amiss that created a big problem for us eventually. Even though, like I said, he was a wonderful companion, I would say it was more of a marriage of convenience."

Irene stops writing, and my eyes return to one line: "Something was amiss." I have heard that before.

Urging her to go on, I type: "When I once talked with him about his dating you, Daddy told me he was impotent."

"Yes," she responds: "I have to admit that was something of a problem in our relationship."

The door to being more personal seems open: "Do you know about him molesting me?" I ask in blue digital letters.

"I didn't know when I married him. I knew he had a mental health problem. I heard that much, and many people were against my marrying him. But I never knew the nature of his problem. I'm not sure I would have married him if I had known. After he molested the daughter of our best friends and it became clear that other children were involved – then he admitted that he had molested you, too.

"At that time I realized he needed psychiatric help, so we found a doctor. He worked with George, and I met with the doctor from time to time. In those days there were no interpreters so we had to resort to writing. It was really difficult for him to talk with the doctor. It was hard for him."

"Can you remember what happened with your friend's daughter?" I ask.

"He molested her when I was not there. I think I was away for a short period of time. I can't remember. Then the daughter told her parents. They came to our place that night and asked to talk with him in private. That was the beginning of the nightmare.

"I could see he needed help, and we managed to stay together for awhile, but when I came home from my job teaching at the Colorado School for the Deaf, he could see something was wrong and he asked me what it was. I said the superintendent at the school had told me to keep George off the premises. This meant that we could not go together to watch football, basketball, and wrestling. That tore us up. At that point your father just up and said he would leave me, because he knew I was loyal and could see I would not leave him.

"Our friends did not press charges. I believe they did that for me. That was so painful for me. I've only seen them once in the last ten years."

When he talked about molesting our friends' children, he said he felt he was not hurting the children.

He considered it a form of affection.

191

Irene's story is connecting to the story I heard from an earlier visit to Colorado. My father had molested the children of friends. But now, I learn there were further consequences. Although no charges were filed, Daddy suddenly found himself banned from the campus community of his deaf peers, banned from social events and from viewing the athletic events that he so enjoyed.

I type: "What about his students? Do you know why my father was dismissed from his job at the school?"

"I never heard of sexual abuse with the students. He was not teaching at the time we married. He was terminated before I married him. He was working odd jobs and then landed a job with Hewlett Packard. It was a wonderful place, but he was terminated there, too, during the time I was dating him.

"I know that when George was working at the school he was always horse-playing with kids and he would end up in some accidents. Also, he had a jeep and one hundred sixty acres in the mountains. It was a great place for fun, but, remember, I said he was a risk taker.

"The school administration got fed up with his recklessness when two boys broke their legs during a time he took kids tobogganing. It was the third time he let some kids get hurt, and George broke his leg too. He defended himself on the basis that he made 'calculated risks.' His perspective was just in conflict with a school administration that frowned on his radical activities. That's my understanding of why he was dismissed."

"That's helpful," I say. Finally, what I think are the last pieces have dropped into place. Now I know the actual series of events that saw my father dismissed from his four-year teaching career, the four years when so many children were around him every day.

As one last question, I ask: "It sounds like there were never any charges about molesting the students at the Colorado School. Can you remember anything else about his sexual abuse of your friends' children?"

Irene types: "When he talked about molesting our friends' children, he said he felt he was not hurting the children. He said that he was only fondling their genitalia, nothing like penetration or something like that. He considered it a form of affection. That was when I realized he needed help. And I have always wondered about how much he must have hurt you or both you and Dorene.

"I guess there is no way we will ever know who else he hurt. After he and I separated, he moved into a boarding house where there was a young woman with Down's Syndrome. I worried he might molest her, too. I confronted him and asked him to explain what he was doing in such a place, where temptation was inevitable. He

For the first time, I have actually glimpsed the wounded and terrorized and silenced little boy who grew up to be my father.

192

denied any sexual activity with the young woman, and swore he needed another chance to prove himself.

"I still wonder if he abused that unfortunate girl.

"I hoped that he had learned his lesson. Oh well... I know that is just my own wishful thinking."

I suppose there are some things about Daddy I need to accept that I will never know.

"There is one more thing I need to tell you, Joyce," Irene suddenly writes. "George told me that when he was a boy, he spent summers on a farm in the country – maybe in Colorado. He went to someone's home. I think he said it was his uncle – by blood or marriage. He was sodomized by his uncle, but he never told anyone. You know how macho he was.

"When he was telling me about it, he held his buttocks and said 'ouch.' He tried to make his own abuse an understatement. I think he tried to bury that memory, and I'm not sure if that was the only incident."

I am stunned by this revelation. For the first time, I have actually glimpsed the wounded and terrorized and silenced little boy who grew up to be my father.

For the moment, I maintain my composure, as I ease this long and very helpful conversation to a close. Irene seems now not a remote and unknown stranger, but a generous and courageous friend. We will talk again.

After signing off and disconnecting the teletype machine, I move slowly toward my comforting retreat, the rocking chair on the front porch. Rocking gently, my arms wrapped around my stomach to hold myself, I weep softly.

My father began spending summers on his Uncle Ralph's farm in Leadville, Colorado, when he was a four-year-old little boy. He went every summer until he finished high school. I believe he was describing anal rape to Irene when he held his buttocks and said "ouch." How many times each summer? How many times over those long years from age four to age sixteen?

On my porch, rocking and crying, I imagine myself holding that frail and mischievous little boy, George, who has been abandoned by his father, who lives with his mother and two sisters in impoverished circumstances. I know this little boy longs so much for male companionship. Suffering from tuberculosis, he has been sent away to spend his summers with his aunt and uncle so he can benefit from the fresh air on their farm.

Me, my own children, many other children, and now, I discover, even my father. Too much sadness. Too much.

Too much sadness. Too much.

My anger

for what

my father

did to me

and my

children

swirls

inside

my heart,

mixing

now with

compassion.

After a while Freeman comes to join me and finds me crying. He holds me and then sits quietly holding my hand as I tell him of Daddy's secret. More pieces of this tragic story begin to fall into place as we talk.

Elizabeth and Eleanor had on several occasions described Uncle Ralph as mean and angry, a man who would go off into the hills to spend days drinking with the miners, a man who left his wife to do most of the chores around the farm. I have no difficulty imagining this man assaulting his visiting nephew.

With no available evidence, I can only guess at the duration of the abuse. I assume that these assaults began when George was young. In George's own assaults on children, he would show a sexual preference for children ages four through sixteen, the ages I now believe he himself was sexually assaulted.

This abusive treatment by his uncle, his father-figure, combined with abandonment by his own biological father and the violence of his stepfather toward his mother, helps explain George's harsh and sometimes cruel treatment of his own son, Gary.

Since the only fathers Daddy knew were men who treated their families abusively, it is easier to understand the mental and emotional processes by which George could convince himself that abuse really was a way to say 'I love you.' He knew that men should love their families, but the only forms of physical attention he saw from husbands and fathers was abuse.

Perhaps, then, it was not such a large leap for him to connect love and sexual abuse.

Now, too, when my father told me, "I didn't want to hurt you, because I love you, so I didn't come inside you like most men would," his self-exoneration fits into the picture. He was saying, "I didn't want to hurt you like Uncle Ralph hurt me. I didn't come inside you like Uncle Ralph did to me."

There are other pieces that look like they belong here. Brad, my father's cousin whose daughter, Phyllis failed to return my phone calls, spent childhood summers with George, at their uncle's farm. Could it be that Ralph abused these boys together, the way my father would later molest children in pairs or in groups?

When I was visiting my aunts, Elizabeth told me, "Uncle Ralph died young. He committed suicide by going down to the creek and cutting his wrists, when he was only fifty-three. He had ulcers and we think he killed himself because he was in pain from them."

These aunts also believe my father shot himself because of his arthritis. I don't believe their explanations for the suicides of either man. How many other parallels might exist between my father and his uncle? I wonder if someone threatened to report Ralph's assaults on children and, like his nephew, George, would do later,

Ralph decided to commit suicide rather than face the consequences of the truth.

Discovering this ongoing family tragedy drains me. I will never know the facts of what happened to my father. I will never know exactly what Uncle Ralph did to cause George, almost forty years later in his life, in a macho and almost clowning way, to put his hands on his bottom and say, "Ouch." But I have painful suspicions.

My anger for what my father did to me and my children swirls inside my heart, mixing now with compassion. What is the name, the color, the sound of this heartbreaking sorrow?

Daddy's dreams for his new life with Irene came to an abrupt end. Shortly after his re-marriage, he sold his one hundred and sixty acres of land, Silent Valley, to buy a small four-passenger plane that he could fly with his new wife.

However, after the molesting of their friends' children was discovered, the marriage was annulled. He no longer owned his retreat at Silent Valley, the land he had planned to develop for his friends and leave to his children. Soon after the end of his marriage, he crashed his airplane, and although he was unhurt, the plane was demolished. His only remaining possessions were his truck, his snowmobile and his little trailer.

He was alone again, and he began to become more bitter and isolated. As far as I have been able to discover, he never told his secret to anyone else.

Daddy

Chapter Twelve

Just Playing Roles

(1965-1973)

*"She makes his coffee,
she makes his bed.
She does the laundry,
she keeps him fed.
When she was twenty-one,
she wore her mother's lace.
She said forever
with a smile upon her face."*

-Song by Mary Chapin Carpenter

My Wedding Day

I begin my writing work this spring morning in 1998 after another reverie on the front porch. Sipping orange juice, I let my mind wander back to those seldom-recalled early days of my first marriage, the Sixties. Although I was still reading women's magazines, with their constant beauty tips, fashion updates, and meat loaf recipes, I was also noticing the Beatles and the developing hippie and "flower-child" culture. Civil Rights marches, the Vietnam War, and the Women's Movement were just outside my daily world.

In June of 1965, I had graduated from nursing school and had my first real job waiting for me as a nurse at Children's Hospital. I was about to go on a blind date with a man with whom I had talked for only a few minutes when I was still living in my dormitory. I was wholly unconscious of the inner dimensions of my life.

Auditions for the roles of husband and wife began on our first date. John pulled up in his white Volkswagen "Bug" and, watching from the dining room window of my mother's house, I could see his wavy black hair, deep dark eyes, muscular arms, and confident walk. After coming into the house briefly to meet Mom, John escorted me

196

to his car, held the door while I got in and smoothed my cotton skirt, and then drove us to a nearby neighborhood park. He spread out a blanket so we could sit and talk and watch the sun go down.

Twenty-seven and previously married, John seemed worldly and sophisticated to my naïve twenty-year-old self. He had lived in Chicago, held jobs, rented apartments, been to blues clubs, ridden on a subway. He smoked cigarettes and drank Scotch. And he was charming. I sat, legs folded up under my skirt and hands in my lap, watching from behind my right shoulder, as John told me about his life and asked me about mine – parents, brothers and sisters, pets, schools, jobs.

I learned that not only was John dark-haired, muscular and friendly – like my father – but he had also been abandoned by his father as a little boy, grown up in poverty, dropped out of high school, married young, and was recently divorced. He had some of the same undercurrents of sadness and loneliness, masked with humor and bravado, which were so much a part of my father and my childhood. Without realizing it at the time, now I can see that I was meeting a man I already was familiar with, and whom I sensed needed me.

Perhaps he sensed my tension, or perhaps city guys just said these things, but as the sunset colors moved across the sky John interrupted the friendly flow of our conversation. "Since it's our first date," he said, "and so we won't have to be wondering all evening, I'll ask you now. Do you want to go to my apartment and make love later?" His casualness and directness were both shocking and a relief.

"No," I stated flatly. "I don't believe in sex before marriage." Want to? Why would I want to? After marriage I'll have to.

"Okay. Just thought we'd get that over with."

For the next two weeks we courted constantly – eating at restaurants, going to amusement parks, watching movies, taking walks around the lake, talking on the phone, giving and receiving flowers. John opened doors for me to walk through, offered his arm for me to hold, pulled out my chair for me to sit. I was able to accept his hand to hold and his arm placed around my shoulder. He offered kisses and accepted my avoidance. He took me to see his apartment and gently led me into dancing in the living room. I felt safe, protected, and even pretty.

After just two weeks, John asked me to marry him and I accepted. I was working night shift – 11:00 p.m. to 7:30 a.m. – at Children's Hospital, living in my old bedroom at my mother's house, and still trying to decide about joining the Air Force. Marriage was the obvious and natural next step, and John wanted me. We planned our wedding for December, just six months after our first date.

Soon after telling our surprised and apprehensive parents about our sudden decision

"No," I stated flatly. "I don't believe in sex before marriage." Want to? Why would I want to? After marriage I'll have to.

to marry, I realized there might be a problem that I hadn't considered. The next time John came to Mom's to pick me up, I asked him to come into the back yard and sit down next to me on the old concrete bench under the shade of the oak tree.

I faced my kind fiancé, who was nicely dressed and looking forward to the date we had planned, a concert at a popular blues nightclub. But I wasn't in a going-on-a-date mood, although I was wearing my favorite dress. I remember feeling embarrassed and not being able to look him in the eye. I knew there was something wrong with me, knew that women were not supposed to have sex before they were married. I felt the need to make a confession, and my face must have reflected this worry.

"What is it?" asked John with a concerned look in his own eyes. "What's wrong, Joyce?"

I knew that what Daddy had done to me had something to do with sex. I knew I had broken the rules and felt frightened that now the man I was going to marry might reject me.

> *When I was a little girl, my father used to touch me and kiss me, and make me do it to him.*

"There's something I need to tell you," I said, fidgeting anxiously, and with a sense of inner desperation. "When I was a little girl, my father used to touch me and kiss me, and make me do it to him. I wanted you to know, in case you wouldn't want to marry me." Thinking I was somehow broken or damaged, I made my confession and was ready to accept the verdict.

"Hey, that's OK." John smiled gently. "It happens to lots of girls."

Over the next few months, gradually and respectfully, John coached me on kissing and hugging and touching and holding. His advances made me feel attractive and the closeness and comfort felt good. Eventually, at his request, I was even able to lie next to him in his bed. He accepted my "no sex until marriage" rule, and being naked and being touched felt familiar to me. I had no physical responses, no arousal or desire – just an obedient response to expectations.

We set our wedding date for December 19, 1965, my twenty-first birthday. I looked up the rules and lists of "things to do" in bridal magazines and watched myself plan the wedding. It was a small, informal ceremony, with Gary escorting me down the aisle and Dorene as my bridesmaid. Mom and her Potluck Group friends, my classmates from nursing school, and John's family were the only guests. I still have my album of wedding photos, but I only remember one moment from the event. I remember standing next to John, facing the minister, and looking behind him through the window, which faced a patch of leafless woods and a creek. There was a large, fluffy collie playing near the water, and I imagined myself outdoors with the dog.

After the ceremony, John took me back to our newly rented apartment. I was still in my white bridal gown. He took off my coat and led me by the hand into our bedroom.

I have no memory of making love with John on our wedding day or at any other time during our eight years of marriage.

John recalls I was a good lover but that I never had an orgasm. He says that each time we had sex, I would cry for a long time afterward. Because John knew my sexuality with my father was what caused my parents' divorce, he believed that when we had sex together it made me feel guilty about breaking up their marriage – and that's what caused me to weep.

I know, today, that being touched in a sexual way by my new husband re-stimulated deep feelings of anguish concerning the way my father had touched me. This is what brought on my tears.

I do remember that I read marriage manuals to try to find some information about marriage and sex. I read about orgasms and, on a visit to my gynecologist, after four years of marriage and one pregnancy, I confided in my doctor that I had never had an orgasm. My book said that I might be "frigid." I wanted his advice.

Without asking anything about my childhood or sexual history or about my relationship with my husband, the doctor replied casually, "Just drink a glass or two of wine before your husband wants sex."

Our marriage, house and family script unfolded smoothly and predictably. After one year, with a loan from my grandparents, we made a down payment on a house and settled into suburbia. I had lessons on lawn care (there was a neighborhood war on crabgrass), invitations to ladies events (Tupperware parties and recipe exchanges), and continued my familiar cleaning, laundry, and cooking routines from childhood.

At Children's Hospital, I was now a nurse on Central 3, the infectious disease unit. Each morning, I would report to duty at 7:00 a.m. in my white uniform, white shoes and white cap. Caring for seriously ill infants and children, each one lying alone in a separate room, I would put on and take off the isolation gown and mask at each doorway, wash my hands and move on. One day, as I entered the next room on my assignment list, I looked at the frail toddler's body, turned and walked out, hung up the gown and moved rapidly down the hallway to the nurses' station.

"Doctor," I said calmly, tapping the handsome young resident physician on the shoulder, "the child in room eleven is not breathing."

The doctor darted toward room eleven, called for emergency assistance, and revived the child by pumping oxygen into his lungs and giving him firm thrusts to the chest to return the heart to its independent beating.

I have no memory of making love with John on our wedding day or at any other time during our eight years of marriage.

Me and Joe

Afterward, he walked toward me, tired and bewildered. "Joyce," he said, "don't you ever get upset about anything?"

This was a new question, and I realized the answer was "no." I wasn't even surprised as I came to this revelation, and just shrugged my shoulders and quietly shook my head.

I am never afraid, or sad, or angry. Also, I am never excited or pleased or happy. I don't have feelings. I just do what I'm supposed to do.

Life in the nation's capital in the late 1960's was increasingly fervent and intense. Civil rights protests and opposition to the Vietnam War were gaining momentum. Seeds of change and activism were being planted in my consciousness without my realizing it.

My brother and many of his friends were being drafted into the military for a war that – deep down – they could not understand and did not believe in. They came home and began growing beards and long hair, listening to folk and protest music, "turning on and dropping out." Vietnam veterans marched against the war, and on television I saw pictures of little Asian children and their families, burned and bombed.

I bought a Women's Strike for Peace medallion, which said, "War is not healthy for children and other living things."

One day, feeling overwhelmed and helpless, I sat on the front steps of our house and made the decision to do something positive, something hopeful. I decided to have a baby. Raising a child to be gentle and peaceful would be my contribution toward changing the world.

John wanted to begin our family and readily agreed that it was time. We painted our extra bedroom a soft yellow and bought the crib, changing table, diapers, blankets, and other supplies we would need. For her new grandchild's room, Mom made curtains from a bright blue fabric printed with large, vibrant yellow butterflies.

With expanding belly and thrusts of little hands and feet inside, I began, for the first time, to really notice the feelings in my body. They were mysterious, sweet, eternal feelings. Pregnancy brought me into connection with myself and with others in a new way. I began to imagine myself as a mother, to imagine the miracle of a new baby.

Born in May of 1969, named for his father's grandfather, Joe began to change my life. The very process of his birth was a moment of wonder and transcendence like nothing I had ever known.

How could this be? This tiny, helpless, precious life was created and given to me to love and protect.

In the moment of Joe's birth I was transformed into a mother. I experienced his vulnerability and the awesome power and responsibility given to parents as caregivers and protectors of their children. Perhaps this was my first role as my own person, as an adult, rather than as a child, or as a wife following a child's script.

Baby Joe got an enthusiastic letter from his grandfather:

> "Bask in your glory, Joe! Your family is the most important one in the world, today. When you get to know me, soon, I hope you'll call me 'Grampy,' not 'Grumpy,' or 'Grandpa.' And here's a few words to your parents: Now that you both have this whole new set of responsibilities, I pray that your family will be an exception, and stay intact. It's we failures at marriage who can often give the best advice. Experience is a thorough teacher."

I changed my nursing job to the evening shift, 3:00 p.m. to 11:30 p.m., on the pediatric unit of another local hospital. That way I could be home in the daytime with Joe, and his father could be with him in the evenings. John and I began to develop separate lives and separate schedules, each orbiting around Joe and around our own jobs, occasionally intersecting on weekends.

My fascination with Joe stimulated inquiries into child development, psychology and spirituality. Reading voraciously during his naps, I discovered intellectual and emotional companions in existentialism, Zen, humanistic psychology and feminism. Increasingly the world of literature, music, art and politics drew me in. Not since learning about DNA in high school had I felt so curious and excited.

Joe, for his part, gave me the unmitigated joy of observing and responding to his growth and learning. Each day was a new adventure, a new accomplishment for him – finding his foot, stretching to reach a desired toy, pointing to his body parts, climbing steps, learning to say "No."

Being a mother also required a new extension of myself socially. Gary had introduced me to Ellen, a friend of his from his semesters in college. "You two have a lot in common," he said. "You're both pregnant."

Now I called Ellen, whose own little daughter was just Joe's age. She began baby-sitting for Joe from 2:00 p.m. to 5:00 p.m. each day, neatly covering the overlap of John's and my work schedules. Each day, I took Joe to Ellen's house on my way to the hospital, visited over a cup of coffee while Joe settled in, and went on my way to work.

In the moment of Joe's birth I was transformed into a mother.

*I had
completed my
high school
script:
"Get married.*

*Have sex
with your
husband.*

*Iron your
husband's
shirts.*

*Have
babies."*

Ellen began referring to me as a friend, saying she felt close to me and valued me in her life. I watched and listened, trying to learn what it meant to be an adult and a friend, to be "close." It was different than sharing toys and homework.

In the summer of 1970, at my father's request, John and I visited Silent Valley, bringing Joe to meet his grandfather.

Daddy led us on his motorcycle out to the local airfield, and posed with his sixteen-month old grandson in front of the plane he rented for recreational flying.

In following years, Daddy invited himself to come back East, to see old friends as well as his grandchildren. He made three such trips so our children could "get to know their Grampy." I have photographs from all of these visits, but I don't remember them.

In the fall of 1971, when Joe was two-and-a-half and I was almost twenty-seven, Ellen urged me to come with her to a meeting of mothers who were trying to organize a play group for toddlers. As we sat around the table in the church basement, we were instructed, "Say your name and tell us about yourself."

When it was my turn, I began to shake. "My name is Joyce. I'm a nurse. My son is two years old." That was all I knew, but it was a start.

Being a mother was drawing me outward, requiring adult contact with other parents and, although it felt awkward, I was able to do the expected tasks – bring a snack, supervise children at the sandbox, wipe up the spills at the sink.

After a few months in his weekly playgroup, Joe began three mornings a week in a co-op nursery school, where my adult socialization continued. I was expected to participate in the classroom several days each month, attend parent meetings and serve on a committee. I recall feeling intense anxiety each time I was expected to speak or initiate some action.

Mothers and fathers worked together in the classroom serving juice, setting out paints and blocks of clay, gathering children into a circle for story time. It was here that I met my second adult friend. Like Ellen, Pat was friendly, easy to talk with, and she and her son David enjoyed spending time with Joe and me. Pat shared my interest in child psychology, and we began exchanging books and theories and morning visits.

Early in 1972, six years after our marriage began and now fully settled into our roles as husband and wife, father and mother, John and I moved into a traditional Tudor-style brick house in an old, established residential neighborhood. We rented out an upstairs apartment for extra income. In this simple and tranquil house, we felt ready to have our second child, and hoped for a baby sister for Joe.

202

My pregnancy with Jenny was a delight. I had been pregnant before, delivered a baby before, taken care of a newborn before. I was comfortable in this role and knew I could do it well.

When Jenny arrived, beautiful and alert, on February 1, 1973, my world felt complete. Joe was a willing and loving older brother. Jenny held his finger in her tiny hand and smiled at his attention.

I had completed my high school script: "Get married. Have sex with your husband. Iron your husband's shirts. Have babies."

Pregnancy, childbirth, breast-feeding, rocking and cuddling with my children – these tender and intimate experiences were creating new and unfamiliar physical and emotional sensations. Gradually and gently the distant, dissociated observer was being coaxed back into her body. I began to feel and to say, for the first time, "I'm so happy."

Having reconstructed the early years of my first marriage, my investigative focus once again shifts to the rest of my family as I try to assemble the time line of all our lives. It was during this time that my sister Dorene dropped out of high school, joined the Air Force, married and moved to Ohio.

Her two sons were born in 1976 and 1980. Dorene and I had only a few brief holidays together at Mom's house during these years when our children were little.

Although she and her sons' father divorced by the end of 1980, I would not learn until I interviewed her for this book that domestic violence was a regular part of this marriage, and the cause of their divorce. "He hit me only one time before we were married," Dorene told me matter-of-factly, "but afterward it happened whenever he was angry with me, which was often. Since I was more skillful than he was at fighting with words, he justified hitting me as the only way he could have equal power."

Dorene says she never accepted that the violence was her fault, or that she deserved the abuse, but was afraid to leave him because she feared his anger.

"But when I came out of the emergency room with my arm in a splint and stitches in my head, I knew I finally had had enough," she said firmly. Her husband had beaten her while their six-month-old son sat on her lap, and the four-year-old watched.

It is disheartening for me to learn that as I entered a peaceful and love-filled stage of my life, my own sister was experiencing, at the hands of her own husband, physical abuse similar to what Daddy in his boyhood had to watch his mother, Hannah, endure.

During this same time period, when Dorene and I were beginning our marriages and

Her husband had beaten her while their six-month-old son sat on her lap, and the four-year-old watched.

Gary was drafted, our father was moving into a new phase of his life as well. His marriage to Irene had ended in divorce after less than one year together. Knowledge of his molesting the children of faculty at the Colorado School for the Deaf and Blind and the children of members of the Colorado Springs Deaf Club had spread. People in these two groups argued about his guilt or innocence, and the conflict meant he was no longer welcome in the deaf social community.

He was involved regularly with his sister Elizabeth's family in Gardner. His other sister, Eleanor, also invited him to join her family in nearby Walsenburg for dinners and holidays. Elizabeth's daughter, Liz, and Eleanor's daughter, Karen, my cousins, and both my age, were often part of these gatherings. By this time, each of them was now married and had young children who were close to Joe's and Jenny's ages.

During my visit in 1996, Elizabeth tells me that she thinks George felt "left out" with the family, because they did not use sign language and he did not read lips. She reflects that, "George was so active and fun though, and when he played with the children he could relate."

My aunts have pictures of their brother George and his nieces' young children taken during these years. They also have photos of George with their cousin, Brad, and his four children. I recall from my last visit that at least one of Brad's children, Phyllis, is known to have been molested by my father. I suspect that the others were as well, but, remembering that Phyllis had not returned my calls and letters, I decide not to pursue interviewing her brothers and sisters. I want to respect their privacy.

Elizabeth's and Eleanor's husbands are able to tell me some of their memories of being with George during these years. As always, there are stories of risk and adventure. Elizabeth's husband, Andrew, recalls going on a motorcycle ride with George. He was riding behind him, holding on and watching while George went over 100 mph. Andrew shakes his head and laughs, "George liked to be scared and thought others would like it too. That wasn't for me."

Stuart, Eleanor's husband, remembers George as a man who was innovative, but who lived in isolation, and who was a "dare devil." He went on an airplane ride with his brother-in-law once, but vowed "never again."

Although he was working in Colorado Springs during these years, George lived in his trailer at Silent Valley, so he was able to continue his active outdoor life, taking people with him on weekends for hiking, camping and snowmobiling expeditions. Elizabeth, Eleanor, their children and grandchildren spent time with him often there, and they have pictures of him riding on a motorcycle, driving a jeep, and chopping wood to heat his shop.

Learning about my father's ongoing activities with his family reminds me of George S. Kaufman's words, "The trouble with incest is that it gets you involved with

George "loved being outdoors with people and was really affectionate with children."

relatives." This is not a quote I can share during these interviews.

Eleanor's daughter, Karen, now grown and living in a beautiful community north of Denver, remembers that her Uncle George "loved being outdoors with people and was really affectionate with children.

"Mom once asked me if George ever touched me inappropriately," Karen informs me. "I told her nothing ever happened with Uncle George." What her mother didn't tell Karen was why she was asking, that she was concerned for Karen because she knew about George molesting his own daughter.

Karen's oldest son, Bruce, says, "Uncle George was always around – mostly at Christmas and other holidays, at family reunions, or to help with repair and building projects on our house." He remembers trips to Silent Valley for snowmobiling, and says he tried to learn some sign language so he could talk with his mother's uncle. He says he has good memories of George.

Joe and Daddy

Bruce and his younger brother, Paul, were the ones who came to Silent Valley with their father to help pack up George's things after his suicide and Gary's death. I ask how I might get in touch with Paul, but his parents tell me they don't want me to call him. "Paul is going through a hard time in his life right now," they tell me, so I don't pursue contact with him any further.

In 1973, George moved down from Silent Valley to live in Colorado Springs once more. He rented a small basement apartment in an industrial neighborhood. The apartment was next door to a building containing several small workshops where he opened his own business, "Culby's," specializing in sharpening saws and welding.

Last time I was here in Colorado Springs, talking with people at the School for the Deaf, my father's colleague and friend, Ed Wilson, had suggested that I try to contact Calvin Harris. "Calvin is also deaf," Mr. Wilson told me. "He was probably your father's best friend after George left his teaching position at the school."

Following Ed Wilson's directions, I drive to the shop where my father's old friend still works. He has his own woodworking business in this same small industrial park where his friend, George, had set up a welding shop. When I go inside, I am greeted by a young, hearing man.

"Hi, I'm Bill Harris, Calvin's son," he says after I introduce myself. "I remember your father. He and my dad were really good friends."

I explain the purpose of my visit, and Bill takes me into the back office, where his father is seated behind his desk. Mr. Harris is pleased to meet his best friend's daughter and invites me to sit down. Bill's wife, Gail, a hearing woman, also works in the family business and is proficient in sign language. I ask her to be the interpreter for our conversation and she readily agrees.

I begin by asking, "Can you tell me how you first met my father?"

Mr. Harris tells me he first talked to my father at picnics sponsored by the Colorado Association of the Deaf. After seeing each other there in 1958 and 1959, they became friends.

"Since we both lived in Colorado Springs, we began to get together to talk. He told me a lot of his ideas. We had a lot of the same beliefs and that is why we got along fine. I think George was very smart."

Mr. Harris remembers that they talked about my father's years as a student at Gallaudet, as a worker in a Virginia shipyard, and as one of the leaders of the deaf in Virginia and in Maryland. "George could talk so well," he tells me. "Since I don't write real good English, I depended on him all the time because he was so good at writing. He helped me a lot.

"George told me he wanted to open his welding and sharpening shop and had heard that I had a wood-shop in my basement at home. He couldn't afford to rent the whole building and wanted us to go halves on the two separate rooms. I was afraid I really couldn't afford it, but I moved in and we were both successful. Today I really thank George because if it weren't for him, I wouldn't be here.

"We really enjoyed George. He was a lot of fun. We used to have a great time up at his cabin. I will never forget that. One time we got up there, I think on a Saturday, and he had hacked out a new hiking trail for us. He was always trying to help people have fun."

Mr. Harris turns to his son, Bill. "When you were a small boy, you thought the world of George. Am I right?"

They recall that one time George took the whole family, the parents plus Bill and his younger sister, Sarah, for rides in the airplane. They also tell me about the pet monkey that George kept caged in front of his shop, thinking that people, curious and amused, might stop to see it, bringing in some new customers, or at least some folks to talk to. Everyone laughs at this memory, agreeing that the monkey "smelled awful." George was never able to really tame his novelty pet, which even bit Bill's

Pedophiles find children easier to have fun with.

206

sister once. Finally he had to take it back to the pet shop. Mr. Harris smiled. "This was typical of the unusual types of things George would always think up."

When I inquire, Calvin hesitantly acknowledges that he and his wife had heard of George's molesting Deaf Club members' children. Because of this, his wife refused to let their children be alone with George.

When it is time for me to leave, he adds, "You know, I guess I have another regret – that I never went snowmobiling with George. He and my kids always tried to get me to go but, well, this was a one-man shop at that time. I was always working. I'd tell George, 'I'll come next time.' But next time never came, and then George killed himself."

I think to myself how much my father needed the companionship of adult friends like Calvin, but I know that pedophiles often have a hard time making such relationships happen. They find children easier to have fun with.

Bill tells me that in addition to our fathers' two shops, this row of businesses also housed a snowmobile shop, where George met a lot of people. Although Sarah is out of town this week, Bill gives me several names of other people from the area who might remember my father from his time operating his shop.

Offering thanks for these reminiscences, I leave the Harris's and walk back to look through the windows of my father's old shop. Behind the shop, I see the tiny cottage where Gary had lived during the year he worked as Daddy's assistant without ever gaining his father's approval. This is my first time seeing the place where my brother had lived, and I feel I should be more curious, perhaps walk to the window and look inside. Instead, recalling my brother's despair over this era of his life, I turn and walk away.

I mull over what I have just learned. Yet again, George has been depicted as an innovator, a friend, and an apparent extrovert who was easy to like. How much at odds this is, I think, with the secret damage he was doing to children during exactly the same time frame.

Following up one of Bill's leads, I telephone Debra, the daughter of a neighbor near the shop, who was about eight years old when she knew George. She does not want to meet me but agrees to talk on the phone.

"I met your father while I was playing outdoors – I must have been riding my bike or walking down the block. He was always friendly and invited me into his apartment to show me funny and interesting things. I remember his monkey, too.

"When I was in the apartment he would want me to get undressed, and he would get undressed, too. He said it was good for people to be naked. Then he would take

She is still afraid of talking – afraid she will hurt someone, afraid she will not be believed, afraid she will be blamed.

Me, Dorene and Mom

pictures of me and get me to hold his penis. Sometimes he would touch me or have oral sex with me."

Debra tried, when she was young, to tell her mother what their neighbor, George, was doing, but her mother blamed Debra, saying she shouldn't have gone into his apartment, so she has never told anyone her whole story. She is still afraid of talking – afraid she will hurt someone, afraid she will not be believed, afraid she will be blamed.

Debra has two daughters now, four and five years old. She can see that they are innocent and that it is not right to blame a child when sexual abuse happens. Still, it is hard for her to see that she was not to blame for what George did.

She notes that one effect of her abuse is that she is "vigilant" about her children. She has never had a baby-sitter for them and is worried now that they are almost old enough to go to school, where she can't be with them constantly.

Debra says she knows she should deal with her feelings about the abuse. She has handled it intellectually, but she is afraid to lose control. "I have spent my whole life trying to be in control," she says. "I don't know what would happen if I stop."

Gently, I say back to Debra what she has said to me. "Children are not to blame for harmful things adults do to them. Even if the child doesn't refuse or doesn't tell, the adult is responsible. Young children cannot separate play and affection and love and sex, and cannot know that the sexual activity is harmful. You know this from watching your own two daughters."

I know, though, that this rational, verbal explanation does not relieve the guilt and shame that Debra acquired when she was a little girl. "If something like this happened to one of your daughters, would you take her to talk with a counselor?" I ask.

"Of course," says this devoted mother.

"Well," I gently suggest, "maybe your own little eight-year-old girl, the one who was molested by my father, needs someone safe to talk to."

As I hang up, I reflect that an unexpected effect of my research has been to reach people like Debra who have not fully healed from my father's abuse of them. I am grateful for Debra's willingness to talk with me, despite her pain, and I hope that my few words over the telephone are able to help her with her recovery.

My next phone call was from Carolyn, another person Bill had suggested I talk with. As a child, Carolyn lived near my father. Her call was even more painful to hear. "When Bill called me and told me George's daughter was visiting in my hometown, I went into shock just hearing his name. I was shaking and crying. He gave me your number, and that's why I'm calling. I never knew that George had kids."

Bill had encouraged Carolyn to meet with me, telling her, "George's daughter is a neat lady. You'll like her."

Carolyn reached me at my motel room in Colorado Springs after Bill had phoned her at her job. Carolyn worked for an attorney in Santa Fe, New Mexico. "I'd really like to meet you, Joyce," she tells me. "Maybe if I could just talk to someone else who knew George, it would make me start to do something about this problem," she said over the phone.

I tell her that in two days I am driving to Albuquerque to visit my son Joe, who is in the first year of his Master's degree program in Public Health at the University of New Mexico. It will be easy for me to overnight in Santa Fe, and I want very much to meet her.

When I arrive in Santa Fe, after a drive through the unforgettable scenery of the jagged San Juan mountain range, I phone Carolyn at work and give her the address of my motel. She knocks on the door of my room soon after, and enters in a friendly, almost professional, manner, wearing the comfortably fashionable skirt and blouse that is typical of her paralegal profession.

She is a slender, graceful woman of medium height, with dark, wavy hair down to her shoulders. "I have loads of briefs to update and prioritize once I get home," she explains, adjusting her glasses after introducing herself, and indicates the bulky briefcase she is carrying. Carolyn initially appears competent, composed, and friendly. She asks if she could use my bathroom to change into more comfortable clothing, and emerges wearing black slacks and a comfortable sweat shirt.

"I've been sick to my stomach ever since Bill called me," Carolyn says. I notice that now she appears sad, even a little frightened. "I felt like I'd been punched in the gut. What you shared on the phone about what he did to you, Joyce, that tore my heart out. And, like I told you, I never knew that George had any children of his own."

Carolyn tells me that her own father was an alcoholic. He beat her and her mother, "drunk or sober," and he molested her when he was drunk. "Outside our home, though, no one knew," she explains. "Everyone thought my dad was a great guy."

Carolyn's husband knows that she was molested by her father, but she hasn't told her family, or even her husband, about George. She recalls she met my father because her parents were snowmobile dealers, and George used to visit their shop to buy spare

Children are not to blame for harmful things adults do to them.

parts. Their common outdoor interests led, within a few months of meeting, to a close friendship lasting many years.

"Our family all used to go together to Silent Valley over many years when I was a child – camping, hiking, lots of things," Carolyn recounts. "We were always around your dad. The first time it happened was when I was riding with George on a snowmobile. He put my hands on his penis, to 'keep my hands warm,' he said."

Carolyn says that her parents allowed her to go with George "any time." He would come and pick her up, and they would go back to his shop, and then to his basement apartment.

"That's where it happened," she tells me. "We would have oral sex – both ways. And we would look at his Playboy magazines together while I would masturbate him.

"Once when I was fourteen, and my sister was eight, he asked us to dress in mini-skirts and then he took us to a carnival. He wanted us to walk around the carnival with no underwear and to pick up guys. He said he wanted to watch."

Carolyn also knows of two other children whom George molested. The first boy, who was Carolyn's age, told her that George stood next to his bed at night and groped his penis. But the kid sat up and angrily asked, "What do you think you're doing?" George made an excuse, saying, "I'm seeing if you're warm enough."

Carolyn also tells me about her friend, Barbara. "George had sex with us together," Carolyn says, adding that Barbara is now married to her fourth husband.

If anyone ever molested my child I would kill him.

"Barbara made me furious," Carolyn tells me. "When her daughter told Barbara that her step-dad had been molesting her for three years, Barbara refused to believe her daughter. Yet I can remember when we were kids together. When Barbara told her parents about George abusing us, they believed her immediately. They protected Barbara. In fact, after Barbara told her parents, George disappeared. I never saw him again.

"But now, even after all that happened to us, Barbara won't help, or believe her own daughter. I am so mad about it!" Mentally, I make a note to contact Barbara during my next visit to Colorado Springs.

"I'm married to a wonderful man," continues Carolyn, "but sometimes I'm not sure that he really loves me, because he never beats me or demands sex."

She also has four children now, ages five to sixteen, and she is very protective of them. "I'm always telling them to tell me if anyone tries to touch them. If anyone ever molested my child I would kill him. I would cut his penis off and shove it down his throat."

When we began our conversation Carolyn had appeared agitated, but, despite the anger of this remark, she is gradually relaxing her body and making more eye contact. "I'm glad I came to talk with you, Joyce," she says. "That feeling is gone from my stomach now.

"I've never told anyone what happened between me and George. I couldn't ever talk about the oral sex and the other things. I know it's sick. I feel like, somehow, I'm sick, because I liked going with George. You see, he never forced me. He was fun and affectionate, and he taught me how to do things. I felt that I had a choice."

I remark that she had a choice between staying home with her father or going with George, but not about having sex with an adult man. "Would you have liked to go with George and have fun without sex?" I ask her.

Daddy

"Sure!" Carolyn says immediately, but she seems surprised and confused by the question, as though she had not realized this other possibility.

Carolyn says that before she was married she used to "have sex with anyone. I used to pick up men to have sex – anyone who paid attention to me. I know it's sick." Now she still wants to flirt and seduce men, but says, "I wouldn't do it, because it would hurt my husband."

"I drink a lot," she remarks, "often until I pass out. Also, I lose my temper with my kids and my husband. Often I feel suicidal, or like packing my bags and going away. I wish I knew how to stop feeling this way.

"Once I confronted my Dad and asked him why he had abused me. But he just refused to answer the question. I didn't go back to see him for three years after that."

Like me, Carolyn also has a story about the difficulty of forgiveness.

Her father died a few years ago and she saw a counselor after his death. The counselor said she should forgive her father, because if she didn't her father wouldn't go to heaven.

"But to me, it's like he was a murderer on death row who had killed children," she tells me. "I need somebody to talk to, somebody who knows what he did. I can't forgive him. That will be up to God."

She has only told three friends about her father and my father molesting her, but she hasn't told them any details. One suggested that she should see a counselor to help her get over it.

"But that's not what I'm after," Carolyn tells me. "I don't need someone to pat me on the knee and give me advice. I just need to be able to say I was molested – to talk about it – and to have the other person listen."

"You know," Carolyn says, as she prepares to leave, "a pedophile forges chains for the victimized person, and when the chains are forged over too long a time, the person holds on to the chains and imprisons herself."

Carolyn's story is achingly familiar, and so similar to my own. I reach for her hand to offer comfort, and say, "You aren't sick or crazy. Sick and crazy things happened to you. Your responses are perfectly normal."

"Can I call or see you next time I come to New Mexico?" I ask as we say good-bye.

"Sure, Joyce. I'd like that," replies this gentle woman, who might be my friend or my sister. "It's been good to talk with you and to tell the secret. I've been alone with it for too long a time."

The memory of this powerful meeting has haunted me ever since. I haven't seen Carolyn again, but in our two-hour visit I felt she and I knew each other, completely, in deep, dark places few can understand.

Assembling interviews from these years, 1965 through 1973, I see that my father had re-constructed the visible part of his life. He had new friends, a new apartment, a new business. He also had new victims. I am able to document four young girls he was actively and repeatedly molesting: his cousin Brad's daughter Phyllis, his neighbor's child Debra, Carolyn, and Barbara. And Carolyn told me about one other boy who was molested at least once by my father. Probably there were other children as well.

Meanwhile, I am married and having sex with my husband without being present physically or emotionally. Gary drifts from the military to a religious sect which teaches that sex with children is "God's will." Dorene is in the Air Force, being beaten by her husband and essentially disconnected from her family.

In 1972, George's father, Samuel, whom he has not seen since he was three years old, sixty-three years before, died alone in California without ever again seeing his son.

This family legacy of abandonment, violence, betrayal, and secrecy has been passed through too many generations already. I want it to stop with my children.

This family legacy of abandonment, violence, betrayal, and secrecy has been passed through too many generations already. I want it to stop with my children.

Joe and Jenny

Chapter Thirteen

The Earthquake

(1973-1975)

*"There's a land that I see
Where the children are free,
And I say it's not far
To that land from where we are."*

Song by Bruce Hart and Stephen Lawrence

In 1998, twenty-five years after Jenny's birth, I visit the house in Takoma Park, Maryland, where John and I lived with our two children. It is still a charming brick Tudor cottage, its trim painted deep red, azalea bushes nestled around the front porch, and a large oak tree in the yard, with brown leaves drifting slowly down to the ground.

I walk around the outside of the house, trying to "find" my memories. The shaded back yard, with a small creek and patches of bare dirt, was Joe's play area. His yellow Tonka steam shovel and bulldozer dug up the dirt. The little dump truck hauled it away. Sticks and gravel were carried in for construction projects. Water and mud were always involved.

Wooden steps head up to the back porch, where there are two doors into the house. The door on the right opens into the small kitchen where I cooked and washed dishes. From here, I could keep one eye on Joe in the back yard and my other eye on Jenny in the dining room, where I would watch her grow from infant seat to wind-up swing to play pen.

The door on the left is the entrance to the second floor apartment, an artistic sort of garret with sharp ceilings and small, unexpected alcoves. John and I chose the house because the income from the apartment would help pay our mortgage. We didn't anticipate that the tenant would be involved in ending our marriage.

Walking around the side of the house, I see the first floor windows belonging to the two bedrooms – one for John and me, one for the children. When I became pregnant in 1972, John and I talked with Joe about babies and pregnancy and sex, about wanting him when he was born and now wanting another baby for our family. The new baby would share his bedroom, and Joe helped us prepare by making space for a crib, a changing table, a diaper pail, and special toys. We were all getting ready for the change in our family life.

But there was no preparation for the changes that were happening in my psychological world. Just as earthquakes can happen without advance warning, just as they are measured and explained afterwards, while the casualties are counted and the debris is gathered, so the fault line in my soul unexpectedly split apart. And, as with many tragedies, the beginning was subtle, innocent, and even beautiful.

From the two first floor windows, my gaze moves upward to the window of Richard's bedroom. He had moved in soon after we did. Richard was a Vietnam veteran, now enrolled in college. From his apartment, I could often hear haunting classical music, especially violin sonatas, that touched my own deep sadness.

Our porch and driveway conversations set off sparks of intelligence, philosophy, and humor in my mind and heart, sparks which had never previously been ignited. His face, body, and voice moved through curiosity, amusement, sarcasm, bitterness, delight and despair – a range of emotion and vitality completely new and unfamiliar in my own inner world. He took pleasure in nature, art, good food, and books. And when I was near him, my body began to experience something new and unknown. As we stood on the back steps, talking and laughing, Richard touched my belly to feel the baby kick.

"I think pregnant women are so beautiful. It won't be much longer now," he said.

I smiled and nodded my head. "Pretty soon, I hope."

I was twenty-eight years old, married eight years, pregnant with my second baby, and infatuated like a fourteen-year-old. I can describe my experience now with my clinical theories and language as "projection" – seeing in Richard the parts of myself that had gone away so many years ago. I was drawn to his intensity, his sensuality, his love of literature and art and music – each of these qualities part of my own unconscious, "shadow" self.

As my pregnancy progressed and my conversations with Richard continued, I began

Just as earthquakes can happen without advance warning so the fault line in my soul unexpectedly split apart.

215

to re-enter my body and emotions for the first time since I was three years old. Noticing the feelings in my body was a change that had begun subtly with my first pregnancy but was heightened now by the combination of my second pregnancy and my newly awakened inner self. I was feeling sexual, feeling happy, feeling ready to burst – with pregnancy and with joy. As I stand here now, on this unseasonably warm November day, twenty-five years later, my memories of the eruption are wistful, tender, filled with awe. As with earthquakes and their tidal waves, there was ultimately an inevitable surrender to the larger power and mysterious forces beyond my control.

When the psyche has been well defended and fortified for decades, through denial, repression, eating disorders, amnesia, and dissociation, even a slight crack in the structure of numbness and control can lead to a disastrous collapse.

I walk around to the front of the house. The number "13" is still there above the door in large brass figures. John and I had joked about whether it might be bad luck to live in number thirteen, but we bought the house anyway, assuring our safety with optimism and determination. In the end, the number itself didn't really bring the bad luck; the fault lines were already there, and my own inner foundations began to shift. A rupture was inevitable.

The two large windows beside the front door look into the living room. In the far corner of that room, by the bookshelf, the four of us posed for the happy "new family" photo soon after Jenny was born in February of 1973. Richard took the picture for us, smiling warmly from the other side of the camera, happy to be included in this domestic intimacy.

And there, right under the windows, was the couch where John sat for days, immobile, staring out the window, deep in depression just six months later. In August of 1973, our perfect marriage, family and home were shattered, and the resulting rubble was strewn everywhere. The crack in my psyche had split wide open and twenty-five years of emotions, bodily sensations, dreams and flashbacks began to escape. There was no intention, no control, and no stopping the devastation.

Sexuality and joy escaped first. In May, when Jenny was three months old, I returned to work as a nurse on the evening shift, while John continued to work days at his construction job. Arriving home around midnight, I would often encounter Richard sitting in the back yard or on the porch, enjoying the moon and the stars and the gentle breezes through the tall trees, and listening to the violin sonatas which drifted softly from his upstairs window. With John and the children asleep inside the house, I would often join Richard to talk and unwind after my evening at the hospital. I looked forward to these thoughtful, playful, and, sometimes, simply quiet times together.

Our perfect marriage, family and home were shattered, and the resulting rubble was strewn everywhere.

Like the flash of fireflies that began to join us as the weather became warmer, unfamiliar feelings began to flicker through my body. I experienced quiet flashes, almost unnoticeable at first, of warmth, tingling, and openness. I had had these feelings before when I was reading books or watching movies. And sometimes, as the dawning of the Women's Movement encouraged me to explore my body, they came as I first experimented with touching myself. But I had never had them in response to being close to a man and, at first, I didn't even realize these were responses to Richard.

Slowly, tentatively, I moved into a new and unknown part of myself. As Richard and I began to sit closer, to hold hands, to hug good night, my young, innocent, and unconscious self was discovering adult arousal and desire. I was also experiencing overwhelming confusion. These were feelings and behaviors that were supposed to be part of marriage, but I didn't have these feelings for my husband.

Over the previous year, during my pregnancy, John and I had joined some of our friends in reading and discussing the book *Open Marriage*, which had been recently published and which suggested that married couples could successfully have other close and intimate partners. This was an exciting possibility in these early, post-birth-control-pill, pre-AIDS years of "the sexual revolution."

As my body continued to respond to Richard's closeness and I felt longing and joy and excitement for the first time, I talked with John, matter-of-factly, about experimenting with "opening" our marriage – about my thoughts about being sexual with Richard. John, himself, had enjoyed making advances to other women through the years of our marriage and was enthusiastic about this permission to proceed with and act on these flirtations.

I look back now and see that even in the throes of romance and desire, a part of me still needed to be a "good girl," to "do it right," to ask my husband's permission. The next time Richard and I were together in the back yard, as we held hands and he stroked my arm and face, I asked him if we could go upstairs to his apartment.

Richard had had these feelings before, and he knew what they were and how to respond to them. As he began to kiss and touch me, my body surrendered to him with a passion and abandon I had never known. No thinking, planning and deciding were involved. I was not observing from above. I was in my own body, and this time my body was in charge. For the next few weeks, night after night, we shared intense lovemaking intertwined with music, poetry and wine.

At first supportive in the trendy current fashion of our "open marriage," my husband soon gave way to grief and anger as he witnessed his marriage and family collapsing. Witnessing his pain, I was nevertheless unable to stop or turn back the process of becoming conscious and feeling alive. Nor could I see that my initial feelings of

As he began to kiss and touch me, my body surrendered to him with a passion and abandon I had never known.

Kids Playing

elation were soon to be followed by "aftershocks," wave after wave of deeper and older feelings – terror, heartbreak, rage, confusion, and emptiness.

Realizing our marriage was in trouble, John and I made an appointment with a counselor, who first interviewed both of us together. Then he talked alone with John. When I went in for my individual session, the counselor asked me directly, "Do you want to stay in this marriage?"

"I don't know," I replied numbly. "If he wants me to, I guess I will."

"Let me ask you in a different way. What is it that *you* want?"

"I don't know."

"Is there anything you want for yourself?"

"I'm not sure. Maybe someday I'd like to learn to swim, or even to play the piano."

The counselor concluded by saying, "It's so clear that you have been taking care of everyone in your family, but you don't know very much about taking care of yourself. Would you like me to take care of John for you?"

Tears escaped from my eyes.

I was so tired. I had married John because my inner self was programmed to be a caretaker. Today I understand it was this caretaker part of me that had been attracted to John, a man who was so sad and lonely, so like my own father. Other women, later, would discover fine and different qualities in John. But caretaker was the only role I knew when I met him.

I nodded, gratefully. "Yes, please take good care of him."

We saw our counselor again, came to agreements, informed relatives and friends. John moved out of our house in October, just eight months after Jenny was born. He took the VW bus and I kept the early American furniture. We agreed to sell the house and use the money to pay off our sizeable bills. There were no assets to fight about, no disagreements about children or schedules. We had been married for eight years with almost no conflicts.

"But why?" my mother asked. "Why? He's a good father. He doesn't drink. He doesn't beat you.

He brings home his paycheck. Why do you want to divorce John?"

"Because," I said slowly, meeting her gaze and feeling the earth begin to shake, "when I have sex with John, I feel like I'm having sex with Daddy."

She became silent.

Our marriage ended with aftershocks of anguish and confusion. There was no possibility of repairing the damage, and so we let it go. We had shared an illusion of happily-ever-after, but the energies of my childhood abuse, combined with John's childhood abandonment, were the primary emotional realities that bound us together – the carpenter and the nurse and their perfect children, being a perfect family.

Undercurrents of dissatisfaction had drawn us to experiment with "opening" our marriage. This was the '70s! Freedom was the promise – civil rights, Vietnam, the women's movement. All the old rules and structures were crumbling. And so were the marriages.

Ours was one of the first to go.

My being good and quiet and self-controlled was over. From age three to twenty-eight, for twenty-five years, I had been absent from my body and my emotions, dissociated, unconscious. Now I found myself the single mother of a preschooler and a toddler.

Once, Joe, Jenny and I were on our way to the laundromat at the corner, me pushing a laundry cart with one hand and a stroller with the other. As we walked, Joe looked up at me and said, "Last night I had a dream that our house disappeared. And then I couldn't find you and Dad anywhere." My little boy turned his eyes toward mine, re-experiencing the sadness and fear of his nighttime reality.

I stopped walking, and, crouching down beside him, I took his small hands in both of my own. Calmly and lovingly I gave him the "right" response: "Dad and I are getting a divorce from each other. That means we won't live together or be married. But we will never divorce you, Joe. You will always have a home and two parents to take care of you. What's happening between Dad and me is not your fault. Grown-up things are sometimes very complicated."

How simple, even magical, parenting seemed in 1973. I thought that I understood child psychology and was proud that I could accept my four-year-old son's feelings. Now I notice the similarities between Joe's dream and the one I myself had just after my father was taken out of my family. In my dream, an atomic bomb destroyed my family; in Joe's, his family simply disappeared.

Not until years later would I realize that the distance between first speaking about

The distance between first speaking about pain and eventually healing that pain can be a terribly long journey.

pain and eventually healing that pain can be a terribly long journey.

After John left, I was unable to continue working as a nurse due to lack of suitable child care. I put an ad in the paper:

> **Day Care – Pediatric nurse will watch your children, ages three months to five years, in her home. Emphasis on play, age-appropriate learning, development of autonomy and self-esteem. References provided.**

I was seeking parents who were eager to know their little ones would be lovingly nurtured and appropriately guided throughout the workday. I was astonished at the number of responses I quickly received, from both graduate students and working couples.

Four children came each morning during breakfast and left just before supper. Over the coming years, their parents and I would become an extended family for each other. We were all exploring childhood and parenting issues. Child development was our religion. The title song, "Free to Be You and Me," from the album of empowering children's music produced by Marlo Thomas, became our anthem.

I can still vividly recall this time.

Four-year-old Paul arrives first, so his mom can get through rush hour traffic to her job in the child nutrition program at the Department of Agriculture. He joins Joe at the breakfast table for some Cheerios and bravado four-year-old style. They can hardly wait to finish eating so they can go pee, practicing their new trick of making an "X" with their streams. Then they're out to the back yard to push the big yellow dump truck and bulldozer through the dirt, no doubt ending up wet and muddy by lunchtime.

I see the children's freedoms and choices, but I do not see mine.

Kenrik and Jeremi come next. Their mom has an early class to teach at the University of Maryland where she is completing a Ph.D. in Human Development. Kenrik joins the big guys in the back yard construction project while Jeremi and Jenny, the toddlers, begin the morning's curriculum on sharing and taking turns – beginning as always on the Creative Playthings wooden slide in the living room.

"Jeremi, you have to wait 'til Jenny goes down."

"Jenny don't push Jeremi – he might fall."

"Jeremi, do you want to crawl through the hole while she comes down the steps?"

Just arrived – the third toddler, Justin. His Dad brings him today, and then will go back to work with his wife on their new business – a children's book publishing house.

These two former Head Start teachers see a need for books for young children free of gender and racial stereotypes. Justin has trouble saying goodbye and sobs until he sees Dad drive off in the car. Then he's into the mayhem at the slide.

"OK, Jenny, now Justin needs a turn."

"But Justin, you have to wait 'til Jeremi gets off."

"No, Jeremi, you can't push Justin with your foot."

"Jenny, Jeremi's coming down, so you can't come up the slide right now."

"No biting!"

"Time for Sesame Street!"

Jenny is in the high chair, Jeremi in the feeding table, Justin in the walker – Bert and Ernie are cleaning their room on TV. "C" is for crayon and candy…and another cup of coffee.

"Joe, Paul, Kenrik," I call out the window, "time for a snack! Sit at the table, guys. Look, it's Cookie Monster!"

Kids Jumping with Joy

"Cookie! Cookie! Cookie!" they demand.

We all sing "I love trash…" with Oscar the Grouch, and I settle the toddlers into "safe" places – playpen, swing, walker – and the four-year-olds into drawing, blocks, and puzzles. They talk to each other, laugh, trade toys.

I change diapers, wipe faces, clean up spills and try to remember what the book said about "choices." Give kids choices.

"Jenny, do you want the hammer toy or the bell toy?"

"Jeremi, do you want to walk or be carried?"

"Kenrik, do you want to read on the floor or in the chair?"

It's about "autonomy," the book says.

Can a mother have autonomy? I wonder.

Lunch, more diapers, bottles, naps – every bed and room is in use. Joe and Kenrik can't sleep. "Your choices are drawing or reading – quiet things."

I hold tight to my afternoon coffee – "it just sits there getting cold – didn't really want it anyway – just something warm to hold," one of my records sings. The children begin to wake up. Three o'clock – still two hours to go.

"Play 'Free to Be You and Me,' they clamor. The four-year-olds dance, the toddlers stand up and fall down. I sing along. It's both exhilarating and confusing for me to sing, "Free to Be You and Me."

Me and Jenny

I never heard this song when I was growing up.

The four-year-olds play Uno. The toddlers pick up, put down, taste, push and roll everything they can reach. There is nothing breakable or valuable left in the house. It's been "child-proofed." Up on high shelves, only my books and records remain as evidence of an adult life.

Late at night, after Joe and Jenny are sleeping, I listen to folk music, sip Burgundy, and dance quietly alone in the darkened living room.

I see the children's freedoms and choices, but I do not see mine.

Everything in the building spoke of money, glamour, happiness, and success. On my right as I entered, was a travel agency displaying a poster in which a slender, tan woman in a bright orange bikini lay seductively on the sand as a muscular, adoring young man in blue briefs handed her freshly picked orchids. To the left, was the bridal shop. Lace, pearls, satin – from dresses to garters, everything the virginal young maiden needed to walk down the aisle, marry her tuxedoed prince and live happily ever after.

Directly in front, in the center of this shopping promenade, was a water fountain jetting three stories high. I watched, mesmerized and strangely calmed, as the bursts of water shot up from the lower level. The water rose past us here on the first floor, reaching up to the next floor where men in suits and women in high heels were carrying on business in their law, real estate, and retail offices.

There was something strangely ludicrous about this setting. I was only just beginning to experience the awareness that this world of television and magazine advertisements was not my destination – today or ever.

Using most of my remaining cash, I had been delivered here by taxi, since I didn't have a car and public transportation did not make this connection. My faded jeans and long sleeved brown jersey shirt, bargains from my favorite thrift store, made it clear that I was not here to shop in the boutiques or to work in the professional offices. The directions I had received on the phone said "lower level." I continued to stare at the fountain as the jets of water spouted three stories and fell gracefully as dewdrops and prisms back into the pool below. I wanted to turn and leave, or, preferably, just disappear, be gone from here and from everything.

"Lower level," I said to myself. "It must be down there by the fountain pool." I saw the steps and descended slowly, reluctantly, wondering what it would be like.

The lettering on the door read, "Department of Social Services." I paused. Would these people be dressed in elegant clothes, serve their visitors hors d'oeuvres, perhaps pay a string quartet to play soothing music for us? Something in keeping with the upstairs ambience?

Walking into the office was like entering another reality. I was in a different world now, with different rules, different attitudes, and different customs. I had no money and no power, so no one was trying to please me. It would be my job to say and do the things that would please them.

There was a sign that read, "Take a Number," so I did. Then I sat, waited, and watched. Women came in with children, with elderly relations, with a friend or simply alone. Women asking for help – some tearful, some angry, and some, like me, just numb. We were black and white and yellow, young and old, frail and stout. We all would do whatever we must. We had children to feed.

"Fill out these forms."

"Children, names of fathers, ages, school environment, relatives, work history."

"Wait."

"Show birth certificate, yours and your children's."

"Wait."

"If you go the bathroom, and your number is called, you will lose your turn."

"Wait."

Not only did I feel like I was going crazy, but now the world seemed crazy, too.

I am a refugee from the middle class. I used to have a job, a car, and a savings account. I paid my bills, bought groceries, and sometimes went out for pizza. Clerks and receptionists were friendly and respectful. So maybe this was what it was like to survive an earthquake – dependent on others for assistance and permission. Perhaps this was how some people become homeless. Or perhaps some of these people had always lived this way.

"Come into this cubicle. Sit there. Your forms say you are a nurse, you were working full time. Why are you here? Why do you want to go on welfare?"

"I don't want to go on welfare. Really, I don't. I want to work. I have two children. They are not in school yet. I used to work evening shift and their father was home. He fed them and put them to bed. Then I was home with them in the daytime while he worked. We managed. We worked hard.

"But now, their father and I are getting a divorce. There is no childcare available when I work nursing shifts and weekends and holidays. I have to stay home and take care of them. I've also started taking care of several other children during the day to try to earn some money.

"No, I didn't know I need a license to baby-sit. How do I get that? I'm sorry. I didn't mean to break the law. Please, could you help me? If I don't pay the mortgage we'll lose the house. We're trying to sell it to pay off our bills. No, I didn't know the house was an asset."

Her survival required that she leave her body to avoid knowing what was happening.

All I know is I'm in the middle of an earthquake and my children need food and a place to live.

"Why are you divorcing your husband?"

Well, like I said, there was this big earthquake and I lost everything familiar, everything I knew about myself. Now I'm in shambles, huddled in a dark corner of the basement, terrified, mute. My husband is my father. I am a four-year-old child. I don't know the words.

"He left," I said. "He won't be back."

She added up the numbers and fit us into the formula. "Here are your food stamps. You'll get a check in the mail. Come back next month with receipts of your childcare business, your expenses and bank account now that your husband is gone. Be sure to get a day care license or else I'll have to report you."

I passed the reception desk as I left. A woman was crying. "Please, can't I get an emergency check? They're going to turn off our water today if I don't pay the bill. I can't take care of my children without water."

I walked out past the three-story water fountain that tossed water up and down all day for the pleasure of visitors on the promenade. Plenty of water. Plenty of money.

I stepped back into that other reality – the "normal" world. But my soul had entered a new struggle. Not only did I feel like I was going crazy, but now the world seemed crazy, too.

Perhaps I had always had two separate lives. The daytime child played with paper dolls, rode a bicycle, learned to jump rope and walk on stilts, was a good student in school, helped Mom take care of my brother and sister. The nighttime child waited silently in the dark for Daddy to come, allowed him to do things to her "because I love you," agreed to keep the secret "because they won't understand."

Moving Out

Even though Daddy had been taken away when I was ten, this inner separation of day and night selves continued through high school. By the time I went away to nursing school in 1962 and then married John in 1965, the two separate selves were more fused and unconscious. The "daytime" child was now a full-time person. Pleasantly, cooperatively and responsibly, she became a nurse and a wife. The two roles she had known since childhood would be her destination. Caring for children as a pediatric nurse, trying recipes from her wedding-gift cookbook, attending the neighbors' Tupperware parties, responding to her husband's sexual needs, deciding to become pregnant.

The banished "nighttime" child continued to keep the secret, not just from others but even from herself. Her survival as a little girl required that she leave her body to avoid knowing what was happening, that she have no emotions, no fear, no anger, no needs.

How to describe repressed memory, dissociation, or post-traumatic stress disorder to someone who hasn't experienced it? Words are so inadequate.

It was as if there is a dungeon where bad things are locked up, kept safely under control.

As if a very large dam is built to hold back a powerful river.

As if there is a toxic waste dump for discarding poisonous substances.

The psyche tries so hard to defend us from pain. It uses denial, rationalization, minimizing,

I struggled

to patch

the cracks

in the wall of

psychological

defense

systems that

had protected

me for so

many years.

obsession – everyday defenses for everyday problems. Like our physical immune system, the psyche responds naturally and predictably to stressors. And, like the immune system, the psyche can be overwhelmed and debilitated. Severe trauma can cause a shutdown. When the available responses are inadequate, the pain is locked up, dammed up, and dumped. This defense works. It protects us through tragedy, disaster, and horror. It is a generous blessing.

Generous until the dungeon is no longer large enough to hold any more bad things; until the force of the river begins to crack the dam; until the toxins from the waste dump begin to seep into our drinking water. My defenses could no longer protect me.

Although today I realize that I was experiencing post-traumatic stress disorder, what we have come to call PTSD was not an official medical diagnosis until 1979, when the Vietnam Veterans educated us all about the aftermath of war. They did not experience depression, substance abuse, flashbacks, nightmares, and triggered outbursts of rage or terror before they went to Vietnam. These symptoms were a direct result of their experience in a war zone.

We used to say that soldiers, men, had "battle fatigue," while women with the same symptoms had "hysteria."

Now, as the Vietnam Veterans named their trauma and recognized their severe, overwhelming, life-threatening experiences as the cause of their symptoms, the Women's Movement helped us realize that survivors of childhood sexual abuse had similar symptoms in adulthood in response to the abuse they had experienced years ago. Whatever the root cause, we now acknowledge that PTSD persists for years after the trauma.

By the mid 1980's, research into the long-term of effects of trauma and violence began to receive more attention. Studies of amnesia, dissociation, memory distortion, flashbacks, depression, addiction, and attachment disorders began to yield valuable information and understanding.

As I became aware, inside myself, of PTSD symptoms such as these, I struggled to maintain an interior separation. My daytime Self was a single parent, a welfare recipient, and a family day care provider. I woke at six, dressed and fed Joe and Jenny, welcomed the children whose parents were on their way to other jobs.

Throughout another year, still unknowingly driven by a deep fear, I struggled to patch the cracks in the wall of psychological defense systems that had protected me for so many years.

With Joe and Jenny and all my day care children gathered around me, we'd watch Mr. Rogers' Neighborhood, listen to him sing, "It's a beautiful day in the neighborhood," and feel secure as he reminded each of us, "You are special."

After playtime outdoors, I'd supervise lunch, clean up messes, and, just before nap time, show the children's favorite video, *Free to Be You and Me*. And when the big football-player, Rosey Grier, sang, "It's all right to cry, crying lets the sad out of you," I'd lead the kids to sing along. I was lavishing care on so many children, and perhaps upon a part of myself, so long unloved, not by others, but by me.

An important moment from this period comes back to me.

In the evening, after their playmates go home, Jenny sits in her modern, white Scandinavian high chair, finger-painting the tray with green and orange tones of her pureed foods. Joe, in his OshKosh B'Gosh overalls and Beatles-style haircut, builds a complicated Lego town, providing dialogue for the Playskool inhabitants.

On our dining room wall, a cheerful and carefree drawing by Picasso depicting two hands giving and receiving flowers is prominently displayed. Jackson Browne's "Fountain of Sorrow," playing softly in the background, is my companion for the evening.

I contemplate freedom, choice, responsibility, and transformation. The next ten years of my life will be both the best of times and the worst of times, but I do not know this yet.

I savor my cup of coffee, tentatively touch and explore my new book – it's like nothing I've seen or experienced before – mysterious, forbidden. It is my first book of food stamps. And, soon, a government welfare check is due to arrive in the mail.

So this is the Great Society!

Later, I prepare dinner, do dishes and laundry, put away toys, bathe Joe and Jenny, read them bedtime stories, and wait watchfully and tenderly until they are asleep.

And, then, the nighttime Self, no longer dissociated and unconscious, but still separated from the day Self, combs her hair, puts on a clean blouse, walks through the kitchen and opens the two doors – one to our kitchen, one to Richard's upstairs apartment. With doors open to listen for children, to connect the two separate worlds, I spend the rest of the night listening to music, drinking wine, making love, sleeping close. But by morning I am always back downstairs, ready to re-enter the daytime world.

Gradually, inevitably, the collapse of the wall between the two separate lives and two separate parts of my self occurred.

Soon Richard began joining the children and me for dinner, coming downstairs to spend the evenings with me, sleeping in my room so we could wake together. As we began living together, as my sexual and emotional self was no longer denied or

Fear, sadness, anger, jealousy – anything could trigger outbursts for which I had no explanation, not even a name.

Daddy in Front of His Shop

restricted to a separate time and place, the wall within my psyche gave way. Although sexuality and joy had been the first feelings to leak through the cracks, now other physical and emotional feelings began to break through as well. Fear, sadness, anger, jealousy – anything could trigger outbursts for which I had no explanation, not even a name   Confusion, apprehension, helplessness – I was immobilized, watching my sense of self begin to crumble.

What was happening to the nice, responsible, good person, the one who always was cheerful, calm and in control? Who or what was this other woman? The me who cried and yelled and sometimes threw things seemed so mean and ugly, so scary.

Up until now, I had essentially remained dissociated. But since my second pregnancy, since my first opportunity – with Richard – for sensual, sexual feelings, I suddenly found myself overwhelmed with waves of emotion, physical sensation, flashbacks, and dreams, not yet understanding that these represented the accumulated residue of my childhood sexual abuse.

Recently, in a lecture on post-traumatic stress disorder, I heard a psychiatrist say, "Men have to be sent to war to experience what women and children can experience right in their own homes."

Richard had just returned from Vietnam; I had been repeatedly sexually abused. We were both survivors of horror, we both had PTSD, and we had no language, no communications skills, no strategies to use to recover from our respective traumas. Though each of us hoped to create a solid relationship and longed for the other's tender caring, soon our dream turned into a nightmare.

I can see how little I comprehended, then, about the difference between sexual attraction and real love. Richard and I were both lonely and frightened and, in addition, he became angry easily. He drank a lot, and I began to drink also, both to keep Richard company and to armor myself from being afraid when he yelled or got enraged.

I knew, too, that Richard wanted to be a husband and a father, to have a family. He adored baby Jenny and tried to assume a fathering role with Joe, reading, showing him how to do things. But Richard also began to punish and criticize my young son simply for normal child behaviors. This was too much like my father's treatment of Gary.

I was desperate, and then I was given a way out. A buyer wanted the house. Dreams of Richard and me staying there as a couple disappeared. Instead, John and I sold the house and paid off our bills. Richard stayed on in the upstairs apartment, a tenant for the new owner. I found a small house for Joe and Jenny and me, and we packed up everything that was left of our life: Tupperware, Tonka trucks, and tears.

During these years of my psychological and emotional earthquake, as I was leaving my marriage and going on welfare, a single mother with a five-year-old and a toddler to raise, my father was re-establishing his life.

He was continuing to operate his repair shop in Colorado Springs, spending weekends at Silent Valley, and had joined a hiking and outdoor club that had regular social events, including overnight camping trips.

Sarah Harris, the daughter of my father's friend who shared his shop space, reported things about Daddy during these years that were much less lighthearted. Her mother had heard about George molesting children of other friends, and her parents argued about whether it was safe for Sarah to go on rides with George.

"I felt my Mom was sometimes overprotective," Sarah told me.

I found myself wanting to tell her that more parents need to be cautious, exactly like her mom had been, and I listened with concern for what would come next.

"Your dad used to flirt with me and tell me I was pretty, but he never approached me sexually. I do know, though, that my cousin Barbara was molested by George. Since those days, she's become a very angry person," Sarah said thoughtfully. "I don't think she will be willing to talk with you.

"I feel sad George had this problem," she continued. "I think he was just lonely. Of

Tupperware, Tonka trucks, and tears.

course, I expect I might feel different if he had molested me."

I asked Sarah to contact Barbara again to see if I could interview her, but just as Sarah had predicted, her cousin would not talk with me.

I remember that Carolyn, whom I interviewed during my trip through Santa Fe, also had mentioned Barbara to me, telling me Barbara had married an abusive man who had molested her daughter. I am saddened, but not surprised, that this victim of my father will not, or simply cannot, speak of it.

I suspect that her refusal may be because she has not found a way to deal with or heal her own abuse. Once again, as with Carolyn, I wish there were a way for me to repair the damage my father has done. I hope that completing my research and book is at least a step along that path for women like Barbara, as well as other survivors.

During this period, George shared daily conversations with his "best friend," Calvin, and he had an active social life, with access to the children of numerous friends. I suspect Phyllis, Debra, Barbara, and Carolyn continued to be molested. Maybe there are others.

And during this same period, I exchange newsy letters, from Maryland to Colorado and back, with Daddy: "Joe got an excellent report card in first grade. Jenny is learning some of her alphabet letters. I had to get new tires for my car."

"Well, I've been trying to fix up an old motorcycle. I just can't get this pet monkey tamed. What a lot of fun I've been having with my friends and family and all their children."

Neither of us truly writes about what is going on in the secret and hidden parts of our lives.

Chapter Fourteen

Dancing in the Dark

(1976-1979)

Me

"Rosie goes to La La Land
When he turns out the light.
Reaches with his cold hard hands
And she takes off in flight.
Driven by the darkness
And the pounding in her brain,
Rosie goes to La La Land,
And never feels a thing."

– Song by Terri Allard

The madwoman slept in the dungeon in the basement. During the day, she came slowly up the steps, made her first pot of coffee, sent Joe off to school, and welcomed the day care children. Jenny was three years old now. She would be old enough to go to school in three more years.

One of the parents from these years has helped me recall the world I lived in at this time.

Kids Playing

"You masterminded a day care service for kids and, since all of us parents could sense that our children were in good hands, your clients became your friends. Undisputedly, you were the best facilitator with kids in groups I had ever met. It's almost as though, out of the dunghill of your abuse history grew this flower of 'beauty in action' with children.

"Your house, in Hyattsville, MD, was situated in a well-worn and comfortable suburb of Washington, D.C. Mostly there were brick and cinder block houses built in the forties, each with three to five bedrooms, a basement, back yard and front porch.

"Inside your house I remember an efficiently furnished, noticeably uncluttered interior. Two whole rooms, the living room and the dining room, were dedicated solely as the play-space of children ages one to seven. There was plenty of stuff to play with, and more than enough shelves. Each day, I was delighted watching how the house bustled with the activity of children growing and having fun."

This was a good job for a madwoman. The children didn't seem to notice her disability. They asked for juice, crayons, puzzles, and books. She could provide those. The children never asked what she was thinking or feeling, which was good because the madwoman had no words. In fact, she had no understanding at all of what was happening to her mind, her heart, and her soul.

Some friends had stopped calling or visiting her after the earthquake. They blamed her for causing it by having her affair with Richard. Others the madwoman avoided, because they were tiresomely cheerful. They seemed to fill all the space in the room, until she felt she might suffocate. They pretended not to see that she was a refugee living in rubble, surviving as best she could, day to day.

Only Pat, mother of Joe's best friend, David, continued to visit. Pat, too, was recently divorced, so the two women would get together for suppers or weekend trips to parks with their children. Once, the madwoman told her about Daddy, about what he did to his daughter. Mostly they talked about their own children, about giving children chores, about discipline without hitting, about helping children talk about their feelings. They talked about the challenges of being a single parent, about exhaustion, about managing money, about wondering if they would ever date or re-marry.

Around her friend, Pat, the madwoman didn't have to pretend to be constantly cheerful, helpful and nice.

The madwoman's mother kept visiting too. Mom would never abandon her or stop loving her. She would come for coffee, they would talk about news and weather, and then the children would ask Grammy for a story, and she was always willing to read them one. Mom knew her daughter was hurting but didn't know the questions to ask or any way to help.

Joe and Jenny's father, John, determined not to lose his children, was kind to the madwoman. He didn't understand her. She had wounded him deeply. But he cared for her, and helping her would help the children. He visited regularly, stayed with the children when she went grocery shopping, made small repairs around the house, and took the children to his new home every other weekend.

Pat, Mom, and John made a small circle of caring and acceptance and help. The madwoman didn't pretend to be happy, but neither did she tell them about the nights, the dark, the terror, and the craziness.

The thoughts and feelings were always inside her – in her scrambled brain, in the constant stabbing pain in her shoulders, in the heavy blood clots of her menstrual blood. Mostly she dressed in loose, shapeless clothes that hid her body. Mostly she wore brown and gray and horizontal stripes, creating a sort of prison around her body. Her body was always heavy, always tired. She watched the children playing in her home – so little, so innocent, so spontaneous, so happy. She didn't understand how they could live in such a carefree way.

The children never asked what she was thinking or feeling, which was good because the madwoman had no words.

At night, after Joe and Jenny were sleeping, she drank a glass of wine while she folded clothes, another glass of wine while she wrote checks to pay the bills, and another glass of wine as she sat at the table and stared vacantly at the Picasso print hanging on her wall. She hoped the flowers, the hands touching, the bright colors and delicate lines would offer an explanation for what was happening to her life.

Finally, numbed enough to go to her bedroom, the madwoman would descend the basement steps to her dungeon where she kept the bad things locked up.

It was a small house. Joe and Jenny each had a bedroom on the first floor. There was a kitchen and a dining room. The living room had a couch but was mostly a day care room with shelves and cabinets full of toys, and a green and red climbing/crawling structure in the center. The bathroom had potty chairs, step stools, rubber and plastic bath toys.

The only space left for her own room was a small part of the unfinished basement. Down the steps, to the left of the washer and dryer, a roughed-in drywall room with a door. There was space for her bed, her dresser, and a nightstand to hold her diary.

The wine numbed her enough to go into her bedroom alone, but it also softened the control she managed to hold onto during the day.

Thoughts, feelings, memories and questions poured into her diary, night after night. Some of what she wrote turned into poems, while other writings became graffiti written on her wall. Often she cried as the words escaped.

Mostly, she told the diary, she was alone, in the dark, lost, hiding from monsters. She saw Joe and Jenny being seven and three, yet didn't know if she herself had ever been a child. She had no memories of childhood. If she had no childhood, maybe she didn't really exist.

She longed for love, to be taken care of, to be safe. Inside her mind it was sad and frightening and very, very dark. Other diary entries were written in frantic attempts to capture her experiences:

The madwoman didn't pretend to be happy, but neither did she tell them about the nights, the dark, the terror, and the craziness.

She would write until she fell asleep. In the morning, the alarm clock demanded that she open her eyes, get out of bed and take three steps to the dresser to make it be quiet. She knew to keep moving. Don't stop. Don't think. Don't look back at the diary lying on the bed stand in the wake of last night's outpouring.

Time to go up the steps to the day.

My writing was a forum for me first to air my pain, and then to remind myself of why I was needed – in this case, to take care of my children, who not only needed me but who also symbolized something I yearned for – love and happiness.

In those days, treatment for depression was not a familiar topic. This was before Prozac, before this psychological condition, which is suffered by one of every six people, was commonly understood or discussed. Instead, people used terms like "nervous breakdown" or "the blues." Electro-shock therapy, MAO inhibitors, and tricyclic antidepressants were considered effective, but were used sparingly due to their serious side effects. Even "substance abuse" and "alcoholism" were not in the public vocabulary. Drinking was something people did, but they didn't necessarily talk about it with others.

Wine was the medication for my depression – it helped numb the sadness and the fear. Now, however, we know that alcohol itself is a depressant. Drinking can cause depression, and make existing depression even worse.

I can see that by 1976 I was spiraling into a deep clinical depression. Each day was darker and more exhausting than the one before.

The diary, the dungeon, were being filled with the bad things I had spent more than twenty years holding back. How much longer could I keep them locked away in the dark?

Years of practice at calm, controlled behavior helped me keep a sane face for the daytime world. I had received my day care license from the Social Service Department, and each day for three years I cared for four children, in addition to my own, in our home.

Me

One day, lingering to visit with me as she came to pick up her son, one of the mothers said, "You know, you have such a natural understanding of children. You are so calm and controlled, so capable. I think you should go back to school and get a degree in child psychology. Did you know there are government loans that could help you pay the tuition?"

I began researching college loans and grants and was able to fully cover the cost of tuition. In the fall of 1976, I was accepted into a combined BA/MA program in Developmental Psychology at Antioch University in nearby Columbia, Maryland. The program was designed for working adults, with classes held three evenings each week. Mom and John agreed to take turns coming to the house to feed Joe and Jenny, now ages seven and three, and tuck them into bed. I felt both exhilarated and terrified. High school and nursing school had been easy academically – mostly I was an A student. I worried that college would be much harder. Maybe I wasn't smart enough.

I was worried that I did not know how to interact with other people as this new adult woman, a woman with thoughts and feelings, but with no memories and no clear role to play. I was deeply depressed, drinking nightly, writing diary entries and poems about misery and craziness. But somehow my routine had begun to seem normal.

To go into the world again meant to meet strangers, smile, talk – to be asked who I was and what I planned to do. I didn't know the answers, but I knew I had to go. College, with all the new interactions and learning it involved, seemed like a life raft that I couldn't refuse.

It couldn't be worse than what's happening now, I thought.

I was wrong. Ambivalently, shoulders back, smile adjusted, books gripped tightly, I entered college and lost control.

Thirty-two years old, dissociated and unconscious until age twenty-eight, hidden away in my house and my depression since then, I encountered a classroom full of lively, intelligent, articulate adults; adults of all ages, sizes and colors; adults who were friendly, who introduced themselves

Joe Camping

and asked about me. Why was I here? What were my plans? What did I think about this or that professor? Did I like that textbook? Wasn't that a wonderful poem? Wasn't the snow beautiful? Would I like to have a cup of coffee? Did I want to take a walk between classes. Would I tell them about myself?

I was in a daze. I didn't know the answers. I didn't know myself. I just tried to do whatever I was supposed to do next, and then at night I drank and wrote and cried.

That man who's smiling at me – his eyes – they're so sad; he must be very lonely. He looks so much like Daddy; he needs me. I should take care of him.

Waves of nausea were in my stomach.

That other man – he's looking at me – what does he see? Uncross my legs, keep my knees tight together, bend over my papers, keep my eyes down – try to become invisible. If I can't disappear, I'll be forced to have sex.

And that woman – she's wearing a dress with yellow flowers, soft and low at the neck, flirting with the professor. Laughing.

My fists clenched, my forehead hurt.

I was in a new and different world, one of adult men and women laughing as friends and talking of intellectual investigation into other people and feelings; talking about classes on art, literature and poetry; of discussions of normal, healthy child development – trust, attachment, autonomy, gender roles. My senses and defenses gave way completely under shock wave after shock wave. Again, as when I first entered depression, I was unaware that new Post-Traumatic Stress Disorder symptoms were beginning to emerge.

Tearfulness, panic attacks, nightmares, regressing to a three-year-old child's feelings. What initially seemed to be a life raft, now seemed to be taking me under again, the waves rising higher and higher.

Then, at church one Sunday, another life raft appeared. A member of the congregation, a licensed therapist, announced the formation of a spiritually oriented psychotherapy group – a place for those who wanted to experience "safety" in relationships and with themselves.

I hadn't been in any group before, except for the various clubs I had numbly belonged to in school, and none of those were groups where people got together to be themselves. I was frightened and exhilarated again. Like college, this group seemed a necessary part of my survival. I signed up to attend.

We all took turns introducing ourselves. "My name is Joyce."

"Why are you here?" asked Chris, our leader.

"I don't know," was my simple and honest reply.

As we came to the end of this first session, Chris suggested that we stand in a circle for a "group hug." I tried to figure out what to do – watch the others, three steps forward, arms out – hands on the backs of people next to you.

There were two hands on my back. I felt frightened. Then numb. "Everyone take deep breaths," said Chris. I breathed and the numbness and fear washed away as I began crying. Chris saw my tears. "It's okay," he said. "Crying is okay. Everyone take another deep breath."

Tears gave way to sobs. Still the hands were on my back, the group in a circle. No one critical or frightened or shocked. No one asking me to be happy and nice. A few more minutes – breathe, breathe, calm, calm.

"Joyce, can you tell us what was happening?" asked Chris after I had calmed down.

"I've never felt safe being touched before," I said, my eyes meeting each person in the circle. "Thank you all."

Each day was darker and more exhausting than the one before.

237

If only one sweet session of "safe" touch and tears could fix a broken childhood. For three tortuous years, from 1976 to 1979, college and group therapy helped me cleanse the old toxins, the "bad things," the rage and terror and shame and self-doubt. But the cleansing meant feeling, remembering, talking with others.

Trying to obtain further details and memories about his group, I telephoned Chris, with whom I have kept in touch over the decades since his therapeutic wisdom first helped penetrate my emotional fogs and detachment. I ask him if he knew that at the time I was in his therapy group I was drinking several glasses of wine every night, just to be able to go to sleep.

"I had no idea you were abusing alcohol. Back then, you initially seemed so devoid of feeling," he remembers.

"It was only when our group engaged in some vigorous activity, some exercise for externalizing feelings, that you were able to break out of this frozen state. I do recall you were finally able to express, to the group, the anger you felt toward your mother. You blamed her for not knowing what your father was doing to you. But you were too frightened to ever express any feelings you had toward your father.

"In fact, when our group first met, you couldn't even say the word 'No,'" my former therapist recalled. "We practiced exercises in assertiveness, asking for what we wanted, saying 'no' to what we didn't want. This was merely a role-play within a circle of safe people, who asked you things like, "Can I borrow a thousand dollars? Will you give me your car? Will you paint my house for me? You just would become silent and lower your eyes." You couldn't utter the word 'no.' So we had to begin by helping you feel safe just shaking your head in the gesture 'no.'

"The most striking thing," Chris concluded, "was that you'd talk about something obviously painful, but you'd have a very pronounced smile on your face. No matter how intense an event you were describing, your voice was always gentle and soothing. It was as though these defenses were designed to protect your inner child, adaptations you were still holding on to from your own girlhood."

If I can't disappear, I'll be forced to have sex.

In the fall of 1976, soon after I began the new therapy group and my evening college classes, a man my age, taking the same required class in "Theories of Personality," asked if I would like to go to dinner with him the following weekend. I knew I needed to practice being an adult woman and that dating was something I knew very little about, so I decided to go.

After Joe and Jenny had left on Friday afternoon to spend the weekend at their father's house, I took a long shower, dried my hair, and stood in front of a mirror, trying on dress after dress, like a frantic teenager getting ready for a big date.

When Chuck arrived, I was dressed, but beginning to be very anxious. Trying my

Joe, Daddy and Jenny

new skill from my therapy group, I decided to tell him how I was feeling. "I'm nervous," I said. "I dated one man a few times when I was nineteen and then, when I was twenty-one, I dated the man I married. That was nine years ago. I really don't know what I'm supposed to do."

Chuck was kind and understanding. Recently divorced himself, but not so inexperienced as I was, he suggested a relaxed, informal evening – dinner at a Chinese restaurant, a walk in Rock Creek Park, and then a drive through downtown Washington to see the Jefferson and Lincoln memorials in their soft, nighttime lighting.

Feeling more relaxed and able to talk about school, children, and the news, I was still unprepared for what to do when Chuck parked the car under the autumn trees near the Tidal Basin. He turned slowly to face me and said softly, "Would you hold me?"

"Not there!" he said a startled moment later. I had placed my hand right on his penis. That was all I knew about men wanting to be held.

With a bemused smile, Chuck took my arms and placed them around his shoulders. "I haven't been held in a long time," he said.

"Me, either," I murmured, as I practiced this new behavior.

Chuck and I saw each other every few months for the next three years. We practiced post-divorce trust and comfort and tenderness and lovemaking, but never became involved with each other's lives outside of these liaisons. This was a new way of keeping my sexuality and emotions under control.

Looking back at these years, I see them as messy, tragic, and disastrous. Depression persisted, distorting daily life to an almost psychotic dimension. My thinking and decisions about daily life – my "reality testing" as we say clinically – were extremely poor.

I was driven by inner forces battling for my soul.

I was driven by inner forces battling for my soul. Some forces would have me reject old destructive patterns, while others would insist on new, even risky, possibilities. Reason, modulation, balance – even common sense – seemed out of my reach.

Chuck was my first date after my catastrophic loss of control and subsequent break-up with Richard. He was kind and gentle, although we had little else in common. I was still very confused and was trying to regain control by maintaining my emotional detachment from sexual activity, using a system of familiar logical categories – stranger, acquaintance, social companion, friend, sexual partner. Chuck, I reasoned analytically, fit the categories of companion and partner. So far, only women fit the category of friend. I did not yet know that qualities of vulnerability, trust or intimacy could be involved in sexuality.

Over the next few years, I took lover after lover, believing that desire and arousal, my own or the man's, required immediate response. I met men in my college classes, met single fathers of some of Joe and Jenny's friends, met strangers at social events. We would seldom be involved for more than a few weeks or months, sometimes just for one night. Sex didn't include friendship or emotional intimacy. I see now that I was compulsively taking sexual partners in the same way that my father compulsively had pursued sex with children.

Dennis was the exception. Dennis was my friend before we were lovers. He had been a high school and college friend of Gary's and Ellen's, so I had known him for over ten years. An infrequent but regular visitor, with or without Gary, at my home or at Ellen's, Dennis had known my husband, John, and had known Joe and Jenny since their births. He had been a bystander during my affair with Richard and during John's subsequent depression. He was Gary's friend in North Carolina, and Gary had moved so that he could live near him. After Gary's death, Dennis helped us take Gary's ashes out to sea.

Living alone with the children, now in a different house, I was surprised when Dennis arrived one spring day in 1977, unannounced as usual. He entered the house in the morning along with the day care children, smiled, nodded, and quietly made his way toward the smell of coffee. For most of the day, he sat and observed me and the children, occasionally helping out with clean-up, or joining in a puzzle or block-building activity.

It was with Dennis that I would finally experience an opportunity to share the joy of sexuality within the context of on-going friendship. I didn't know it was possible to have such a relationship with a man who – unlike John, Richard, and Chuck – knew me and liked me for who I really was. And my motivation for being with him, for the first time, stemmed from a need to be whole, rather than to split off into a caretaker or detached sexual activity. He would be the first man to know and care about ongoing parts of my life: my childhood family, my children, my intellectual and philosophical interests, and my commitment to developmentally appropriate education for young children. Dennis remembers:

> One evening, I joined you and your children for a simple supper and, after their bedtime, our evening featured glasses of wine, music and good conversation.
>
> Finally, in my direct manner, I asked, "Joyce, may I spend the night with you?"
>
> "Certainly, Dennis," you replied. "I'll get some blankets and the couch is available, or, if you prefer, there is a mattress you can put on the porch."
>
> "Actually, what I am asking is if I could sleep with you. Don't answer immediately. Give my request a few minutes for consideration."
>
> "Dennis, you're such a good friend. I don't want to spoil things by sleeping with you."
>
> "Does that mean you can only sleep with enemies or strangers?" I said, with a perplexed but good-humored laugh. "I can't quite understand what the risk is to our friendship here. To me, it feels like if we became lovers, I'd be able to know you even better."

I can remember now being touched by the honesty of his words, his laughter about a tender topic so serious to me. Dennis did stay, and we did sleep together.

He reminds me that, during those years we were together, sometimes after making love I would go into an emotional shutdown. At the time, he didn't know what was wrong, and I wasn't able to tell him because I hadn't yet learned to identify flashbacks. When I ask Dennis to describe those times, he says, "It was as though you were lost inside a big black thundercloud, and I was in a small plane circling around and around outside the storm. I felt helpless because I knew I couldn't go inside the cloud to be with you, or I would be destroyed."

Reason, modulation, balance – even common sense – seemed out of my reach.

241

We never discussed marriage. Neither of us had that goal. We both had other lovers as well – Dennis, because of his belief in "free love," and me, because I was still experimenting and learning. At least now my learning included safety and friendship and pleasure.

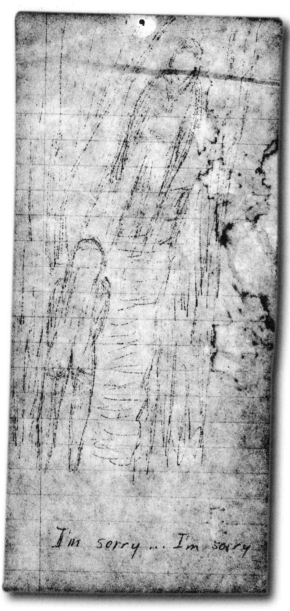

Drawing in My Diary

By early 1978, although feeling somewhat less crazy. I now drank at least a quart of wine each night in order to numb my panic and grief. I worked night shift at the hospital on the weekends when Joe and Jenny were with their father.

Now that Jenny was in kindergarten, I was working mornings as Director of the children's elementary school to pay for their tuition there, and I still worked every afternoon providing after-school childcare.

I couldn't sleep.

Finally, after three years of regular journal writing, I simply stopped. I had sunk into such a deep depression that I no longer had the energy to write. My last diary entry, dated February 11, 1978, states simply:

I did not know that tired and fatigued and
used up could be so comprehensive.

In the summer of 1978, my father visited me and the children in Maryland and convinced me to let Joe have "the best adventure of his life," a camping trip with his Grampy, cross-country on the back of a motorcycle. Today I ask myself what could have possessed me, no matter how numbed I may have been, to allow a nine-year-old child to go off on such a long, dangerous trip?

Equally heart-breaking and impossible to explain or repair, I began in the following summer to let Joe and Jenny go to Colorado to spend summers with my father, their Grampy. In my denial and amnesia, I would be unaware that my father had begun sexually abusing them, and that he would continue to do so for the next six summers.

Though I was exhausted and was deeply immersed in bodily and emotional memory, I had not made the verbal, logical left-brain connection that my pain was due to incest.

Nor did society know or talk about incest or pedophilia in those days.

I knew he did it to me. I thought I was the only one. I thought it only happened to girls.

I found a very faint drawing hidden in the pages of my diary, beneath which I have written the words, "I'm sorry... I'm sorry."

Are these my own or my father's words? Should I trust them?

When my father asked me to send his grandchildren to Colorado to visit him, just as I had done as a child, I agreed, but said, "You must never touch Jenny like you did me."

"I won't," Daddy promised. "That's completely in the past."

And I believed him.

In 1994, when I learned that my father's behavior was never "in the past," that it continued through his whole life, that it involved my children, I was engulfed by disbelief and remorse. My rage toward my father, now nine years dead, knew no bounds.

I wished he were alive, so I could be the one to kill him.

How could I know about Daddy, I ask myself, know about all he did to me, and yet not-know it at the same time? How could I have been, in 1978, so removed from present reality, from my own spirit? How could I be so enmeshed in the trance of denial and distortion my father created during my childhood?

I will never have absolute answers to these questions. I will never have complete resolution of the guilt and grief. But I can achieve some understanding of how this happened. I know in large measure that in 1978 I was still following my childhood script to please and take care of Daddy. My adult self was still not in control of my life.

After his death, I discovered among my father's few papers a handmade card which I worded, and helped my children create for their grandfather. Today, I cannot believe the tone of these words in their blind and childlike affection.

I continued to participate in Chris's "growth" group, which he called "The Holding Company," for two years. Due to my welfare and student status, Chris had given me a scholarship to the group, which otherwise would have been too expensive for me to join.

While my children were away for the summer, I attended a three-day weekend intensive group session. In one of our experiential activities, we were to role-play the "good mother" and "good father" to another group member. When it was my turn to

I found a very faint drawing hidden in the pages of my diary, beneath which I have written the words, "I'm sorry... I'm sorry."

G is for the Greatest guy around us

R is for Respect from the whole brood

A is for Adventures that surround us

M is for the Mouths requesting food

P is for the Pleasures that you gave us

Y is for the Youth you'll always be

Put them all together; they spell GRAMPY,
A special person, all of us agree.

be the "child," my "good parents" tried to approach me with affection and words of praise. "We love you. You are such a special little girl." Drawing my knees up to my chest, I wrapped my arms tight around my legs and turned my head away. Role-playing my father, Rob reached out and touched my arm. "I need you, Joyce," he said.

When I came back to awareness of where I was, I was lying flat and rigid on the floor. Chris and the trusted members of my group were gathered around me, calling my name and reminding me that I was safe, an adult, in 1978, with friends. Rob's touch and words had triggered an extreme dissociative reaction, a flashback, a flight into the frozen rage that had been my experience all through childhood. I had been "gone" for ten minutes.

Never before had I understood so clearly how all-pervasive the dissociation and numbness of my entire childhood had been. For the first time now, it was witnessed and discussed by others. I was no longer alone.

The group members' acceptance and Chris's steady and intuitive guidance continued to help me name feelings and feel safe to express them, to stay present in my body and experience the sensations in my stomach, shoulders, throat and head without having to leave by dissociating or regressing to childhood. And, importantly, the group had allowed me to receive current and realistic information, what psychotherapists call "mirroring," of my self. Shame, self-doubt, disgust, guilt were being replaced with words like brave, kind, smart, and funny.

In early 1979, after Chris moved away and the group ended, I couldn't continue in therapy because I had no money and no insurance. I continued my after-school child care, weekend nursing, and full-time college work. My professors and classmates, like the therapy group, contributed to a new confidence and belief in myself. "Creative, intelligent, articulate, professional" – such new ways of self-understanding. I began to wonder what this newly discovered woman would do next.

Financially, with my child care and welfare income, I had not been able to keep up with the mortgage, children, school, car, and groceries. I had paid most expenses with credit cards and, by the time I graduated with my Master's degree in Developmental Psychology, in June of 1979, I was deeply in debt.

Now, though, I had finished three years of evening classes. Joe and Jenny were older and were in school all day. I had a credential that would enable me to get a Monday through Friday, day shift job. Finally, life was easing into a more reasonable and manageable rhythm.

I began to look for a job where I could help make the world better for children.

"There's a land that I see where the children are free, and I say it's not far to that land from where we are." These words from our day care sing-alongs of "Free to Be You and Me" finally were resonating inside my own heart, my own life.

I was no longer alone.

However, I still had a hidden secret, whose shadow visited me quietly in the dark. My depression and alcoholism remained hidden, unnamed and unnoticed by others.

During this same time, with tragic irony, I helped ten-year-old Joe and six-year-old Jenny pack their shorts and shirts to fly to Colorado for their summer with Grampy.

I was not able to understand by their faces or their behavior what I was sending them to. Like a German soldier loading Jews into a train, none of us could comprehend the horror that awaited them. Grampy had already trained them: "Don't tell your mother. She won't let you come to visit me. Then I'll be so lonely I'll have to kill myself."

My father persuaded me that it would be good for Joe and Jenny to have a summer vacation and for me to have a break from my parenting responsibilities. I trusted Daddy, and there lies my unconscious complicity. No explanation suffices or makes it go away.

During these years, 1976 through 1979, my father's life stayed stable and, from all appearances, happy and successful.

He continued to live in his basement apartment and work daily in his lawn mower and welding shop. He continued to enjoy weekend outdoor activities with his friends and family and their children.

In 1977, Gary moved to live in a small cottage near our father's apartment and shop. He worked part-time with Daddy, who taught him how to weld, and Gary tried to create a better relationship with the father he had lost as a boy.

Gary's old friend from junior high school, Frederick, who spent time visiting Gary in Colorado, shared with me some of his memories. We reminisce about how Daddy hated Gary's long hair and beard.

My father has done terrible things.

"Your father was what I'd call 'abrupt,'" explained Frederick. "He made sudden, strong gestures and movements. They didn't get to the point of being frightening, but it was rather abnormal, so I tended to put some distance between him and me. He used more force than was necessary, and I wasn't that comfortable with him. Your dad was very strong. I remember that. Muscular."

Frederick remembers Daddy's lawn mower shop and knows that he shared his workplace with another man, but says he doesn't remember ever seeing any kids around the shop. I find this unsurprising, since I've come to realize my father more often molested children in family and friendship situations.

Hoping once again to find verification for my belief that our father also molested Gary, I ask Frederick whether my brother ever discussed his relationship with Daddy. "Gary never mentioned any specific problems with his father, either when we were in

Jenny, Daddy and Joe

high school or later. In fact, he never mentioned him at all. I never even saw any pictures. I never thought about his missing father at that time, because my own father was already dead. We usually, when we were together, talked about music or drugs or other people, but not family. Gary's friend, Ellen, provides the missing clue. She recalls that Gary always seemed to have ambivalent feelings about our father. "Once," Ellen says, "Gary told me, 'my father has done terrible things.'"

I meditate on this world of men I am exploring. Daddy, Gary, and Frederick, each of them "fatherless," manage somehow to never talk about their fathers with one another. For a full year, Daddy has his son living next door and working with him daily in the shop. Yet from what I have learned, I doubt they ever talked about Gary's childhood. I doubt that Gary was ever able to confront his father about the "terrible things" Daddy has done.

In the summer of 1978, after Joe and his Grampy's two-week camping ride through the south and across Texas, Jenny and I flew out to Colorado to meet them and we all went to Elizabeth's home in Gardner for the big Culbertson family reunion. Even Gary is in the photos of that event.

Again, I have no memory of being there.

Jenny

Elizabeth and Eleanor – during one of my visits to them – showed me pictures of Joe and Jenny spending Christmas of 1978 with their Grampy at his basement apartment in Colorado Springs.

This seems incomprehensible to me. I cannot believe that I actually sent my children to him for their Christmas holiday. I don't remember this at all.

The next photos are from the following summer – 1979. Joe and Jenny flew out by themselves to visit Grampy. There are many pictures of their activities, which look so similar to the photos of Gary and Dorene and me on our summer visits a generation before. I still have Jenny's postcards from this, her first summer away from me. She draws tears, and writes, "I miss you." Today I understand those tears and I feel them in my heart.

Liz and her children were there again for the summer. I ask Nancy, the twenty-five-year-old daughter of my cousin Liz to meet me for lunch. "I guess you want to ask me about George molesting me," Nancy says even before we order. She says that her mother asked her a few years ago, "Did George molest you?" Someone had told Liz that he had molested others and Liz was worried about her daughter.

Nancy says, "I told Mom, 'No.' I didn't do it to cover up or hide shame, but it was over with I didn't want to torture her." Also, Nancy says she doesn't enjoy being pitied and was afraid that would be the reaction.

"I can vaguely picture that there were ten to fifteen separate incidents over several summers, but I only really remember the details of two of them. One time occurred at Silent Valley with a group of kids, though I can't recall if he involved some of those others in the abuse.

"The other time happened in the garage at my grandparent's place at Gardner. That time it was real quick," she continues wryly, "sort of like an alcoholic saying 'just a sip.'"

Nancy thinks it's likely that her older brother, Charles, was also involved. "But," she adds, "I hope my little sister, Stephanie, was too young."

When I ask Nancy why she's kept the abuse a secret for so many years, she says, "Our family doesn't talk about things. If someone gets angry, we don't talk. We never discuss it after it's over."

When I ask if she thinks her experiences with her mother's uncle, George, have affected her, she says, "No. It's over. I don't think about it anymore."

As a clinician, I recognize how this mechanism of "not thinking about it" is indeed one valid option for abuse survivors. I reflect about other friends or clients who also have expressed that their childhood abuse is affecting their current life either minimally, or not at all. Generally, these adults report they are not experiencing depression or PTSD symptoms, and have successfully separated the childhood events from their present life and daily functioning.

I accept that some survivors believe that the events of childhood simply do not affect them much any longer. However I find myself curious as to how their capacities for personal intimacy and friendship, as well as the emotional openness implied by sexual relationship, have been affected.

I don't know what Nancy's response to these concerns would be, but I hope they are things she and other survivors consider when deciding whether or not to seek help about past abuse.

The other person who is in my father's photo album, whom he had written about in his letters to me, and whom Joe and Jenny also have mentioned and remembered, is Ruth Ferris.

From my motel room in Colorado Springs, I look through the phone book and begin dialing people named "Ferris." Finally, a woman's voice responds, "Yes, of course I know her. She's my daughter."

I ask her for Ruth's phone number.

I follow my directions to the address Ruth gives me on the phone, and a tall, slender, professionally dressed young woman meets me at the door. She has just come home from work, and invites me inside her comfortable, small, casually furnished living room. She says she is glad to speak with me, though I sense she seems a bit anxious and awkward.

She immediately asks about Joe and Jenny, who had been her playmates for many summer vacations. I update her about their recent lives, and explain that I am visiting Colorado because they have just told me about what happened to them during those summers, and that she too was involved. I notice she seems relieved that I have broken the ice about this difficult topic. Inviting me to sit down, she is eager to see the album I've brought with me.

"It feels so strange, looking at photos of George," she begins.

I've come to realize my father more often molested children in family and friendship situations.

249

Generously, and at length, she shares her girlhood memories of Daddy:

"George had been close to my family ever since just before I was born.

"It was a big surprise to hear that George had passed away, since I had no idea. I think I had always wanted to one day see him again and ask him why he did these things to me, when I was a little girl, over so many years. I just feel like, because of it, I can't remember lots of my childhood, and whether those memories be good or bad, I really want to have them back. So I've always wanted to go up to the cabin where he and I spent lots of time alone, and see what else I could remember.

"I truly can't remember when the abuse began; it was progressive. It's not like I can remember one certain day. Things just started to happen. And from the start, it felt uncomfortable. But it feels like George had always been there in my life, and my parents and I always trusted him. My parents let me go out camping or driving alone with George many times.

"My stepsister, Sherry, asked me why I hadn't said something to my mom about what he was doing to me. I told her, 'Well, when your parents trust somebody, it's not very easy to tell on them.'"

Then Ruth said to me, "I feel like all of us in the family sort of subconsciously knew the abuse was going on. We knew… and somehow, this was just something that was acceptable."

"We used to go on a four-day camping trip every year – just George with me, Joe and Jenny – up to Glenwood Spring. I know I began to feel more and more negative about it, but my mother would tease me, tell me not to be a mama's girl, that I wouldn't be homesick. She'd say, 'Once you get up there and are there for a couple of days you are going to be fine.'

"The first years, before I was six, I used to go willingly, and then it started to be where, because of the molesting, I had a problem with it, and didn't want to go. I can remember one summer Jenny talked with me; she didn't want to go unless I went. I was crying and crying, saying, 'No, I don't want to go; no, I don't want to go!'

"Jenny used to get furious at George.

"She would yell at him and say, 'I hate you.' Sometimes, Jenny and I would just walk off together and refuse to do what he said. When we would come back he would sometimes give in, and let us have treats even if we had refused to undress.

"I think now that his insistence on undressing was done so he could see the naked children, since when we were alone with him, George never wanted us to have any clothes on. He always wanted people naked.

When we were alone with him, George never wanted us to have any clothes on.

He always wanted people naked.

Daddy

"He used to say, 'God saw to it that we were born without our clothes on, and so that must be how God wants us.' He was always giving us that story.

"I can remember one incident up in the cabin at Silent Valley. Some kids that lived around there were over, and George said, 'Okay, let's everybody go skinny-dipping out in the pond.' And all of us were nervous, and said, 'No, no.' And then we finally did it, got naked. George said, 'Shhh, quick, hurry, hurry, hurry. Your parents are going to be coming soon. You guys are going to have to hurry up if you want to do this.'

"Another thing I remember is that when we were camping, in the tent, we used to always play cards. There was some kind of game that we always played, during which George used to drink something; it was Coke mixed with rum. Even to this day the smell of rum makes me sick. Naturally, we kids used to always want some Coke too, but unless we took our clothes off he refused to give it to us. Instead he'd make you drink milk, and I detested milk.

"It was always, 'If you want this, than you are going to have to do that.' When we were driving up to camp, Jenny would ride up front with him, but Joe and me would always ask to ride behind, in the camper. George would tell us we could, but only if we hugged and kissed, and would be naked and pretend to have sex. This was totally bizarre to us, but he always wanted to watch this,

Riding the Snowmobile

in the mirror, I guess. When we got in the back, Joe and I would ignore his rule, and begin coloring or playing with stuff we brought. George would get mad, pull over to the side of the road, and make us come sit up front.

"I don't think that Jenny ever particularly liked George. I wasn't afraid of him, but Jenny never really knew him, like I had, as a young kid, and all of a sudden she spends summers with him and the sex stuff started, so it was a different kind of relationship for her.

"I used to worry, 'What if somebody sees us?' George took photos of us all naked, and when I found a bunch of them once, I ripped them up. I thought, 'What if he ever got taken to court, and we have to go to court and tell about it?' Joe always promised me that he would never tell anybody.

"When I was alone with him, George would get into mutual genital contact, both touching and orally. He used to do a lot of stuff to himself, like have me masturbate him and stuff like that. That used to really bother me. I just thought it was totally disgusting. Later on in life I had a very hard time dealing with sex. I hated to be naked. In my first several sexual experiences, my attitude was like, 'We can have sex but you better figure out how to do it with my clothes on.' I think I hated men's bodies for a long time.

"When I was young, dad and mom were divorced and dad had married my stepmom, Juanita. So now I had a stepsister, Sherry, who was probably thirteen or fourteen. Once she and I went up to Silent Valley. We were sleeping in George's trailer, with him in the other bed. The minute we got in bed, we had to pretend we were asleep. Otherwise, I knew from past experiences that he would come to the bed and begin touching our privates.

"George used to come up to our home at Christmas, for holidays and things like that. He would baby-sit us during those visits, so that my folks could go out alone together. What he would do is walk around without clothes on. He'd be laughing, following us around the house. Then he'd start wrestling with us, and from that it went to putting his hands up our shirts, and touching us down below. For him, it was like a game, and he was enjoying it. For us it was sort of scary. Sherry and I would go hide in the closet to keep him from finding us.

"One time, we had gone driving, with dad and Juanita up front, and George sitting between Sherry and me in the back. And he had each of his hands down in our underpants, feeling our privates. We were so scared we were speechless. I guess we were just young enough to be naïve, but already old enough to know what he was doing wasn't right.

"Finally, when I was eleven, my parents found out what George was doing to me. He had begun asking me if my stepsister, Sherry, could 'keep a secret?'

"I didn't want him to get her involved in what we did together, and said, 'No, no, please don't tell her about us.'

"I can't remember exactly what he said to her then, something like, 'We do things you just can't tell your parents.'

"I don't know if George went on to touch her again, or anything, but when he kissed me one time that evening, George stuck his tongue in my mouth. So I told Sherry that had really bothered me. I may have been crying about it or whatever.

"Anyway, next morning, Sherry said we had played his game a long time, but she couldn't handle this anymore. It was the last straw, and she was going to tell our parents. I don't think we would have ever been found out if she hadn't said something.

"I was so afraid, because I knew George would get in trouble, and I didn't want that to happen. I remember just telling her, 'No, no, no… don't tell on him!'

"But she told, and then it was kind of like all hell broke loose.

"Dad was enraged. George had already gone back up to the trailer where he lived.

I hated men's bodies for a long time.

Dad drove all the way up there to Silent Valley. Thank goodness, though, George wasn't home. Sherry also went there, at a separate time, intending to confront George. But again, he wasn't at home.

"That's when my father filed the charges. The police confiscated some pictures of children that George had. Because they were photographs of minors, the officers basically took me into a room alone, just to identify that I was one of the children in the nude pictures.

"At this point, my mom also reported George to Social Services. So when Joe and Jenny came out for summer vacation, George took them on a road trip to visit their relatives, or to go off camping. That way he could avoid visits to his cabin by the social workers or his probation officer. I think one reason he visited our family in Golden was he already had been charged once before, and prohibited from having contact with kids at his trailer.

"My stepmom, Juanita, did try to talk with me right after George was arrested. She came to my bedroom and asked about what he had done, but I was so embarrassed I couldn't talk. I told her she could guess things, or name things he might've done to me. Then I would say, 'Yeah, okay, he did that,' or 'Yeah, he touched me here,' or stuff like that. But I couldn't ever just come out and say he did specific acts or things with me.

"Juanita also asked me how I felt about George, and I said, 'I have never had bad feelings. Even after everything came out, I was never afraid of him.'

I couldn't ever just come out and say he did specific acts or things with me.

"One of the things I've always wished was that George could have been able to get some help. He was not like one of those perverts that hang around bookstores and are real sleazy, the kind you always think of as doing things like George did. I still have no hatred for him. I just always remember him as being kind and loving.

"There's one last thing. I can't remember a time when George hadn't been like a real part of my family. But after Sherry and I told what George had done, essentially I just never saw him again. He was never mentioned. A year or two later, my sister Julie and I were going to the mall, and we spied him walking in to J.C. Penney's. We just totally freaked, but I don't think he saw us.

"Like I said at first, I never even heard until later that he had died."

After my long talk with Ruth, I find myself struck by comparisons of her abuse history and my own at the hands of my father. Like me, she knew my father from birth. Like me, she still sickens at scents that re-stimulate memory of him. And Ruth developed close friendships over five summers with my own children. She has provided a witnessing voice to their abuse which reopens wounds in my heart.

While the duration of our abuse is similar, my own exposure was almost daily, while hers was more intermittent. Is it this difference that has allowed Ruth to hold in memory graphic images of the abuse itself, while I have few of these? Like me, Ruth experienced a sudden, intense disturbance within her family, coupled with the disappearance of George from her life, when the abuse was discovered.

Later, I am able to confirm the core of Ruth's memories with her father, Leo Ferris, whom I reached by phone. He tells me his family enjoyed snowmobiling, and he remembered meeting George in 1972 or 1973 at the snowmobile salesroom, near George's repair shop. They started talking, struck up a friendship, and then George started going on outings together with Leo and his family.

"We became really good friends," he informs me. "I invited him often to join us for meals, holidays, even trips by car. So I was totally shocked when Ruth told me what George was doing to her for so long. He always appeared so very normal, but now I see this was his way of getting on my good side, getting people to trust him.

"After filing charges, I just felt so betrayed. How could somebody do that to you, to your children? I wasn't successful when I tried to find and confront him, and I never spoke to or saw him again."

I struggle within my mind to find words I can offer to Ruth Ferris and her father. In very different ways, each was betrayed completely by my father. My own world will never be free of the damning consequences of Daddy's selfishness, his lies to me, and his violations of my children. The Ferrises, I reflect, will be haunted, in similar ways, by my father for the remainder of their lives.

My own world will never be free of the damning consequences of Daddy's selfishness, his lies to me, and his violations of my children.

Intensive Care

"Maybe they're right.

Maybe I am crazy.

I didn't tell him to stop.

I just wanted him to love me, that's all."

From the film, *Nuts*

Drawing "Intensive Care" by Joyce's "inner child" 1979

Joe and Jenny

Chapter Fifteen

Hitting Bottom

(1979-1981)

"It's all right to know
feelings come and feelings go,
and it's all right to cry
it might make you feel better."

– Song by Carol Hall

Model Cities Child Care was a program for 100 inner-city children ages six weeks to six years old; a program specifically intended to provide free or low cost day care for welfare mothers.

This was part of the "Great Society," President Lyndon Johnson's domestic plan to eradicate poverty, and the idea was that if the mothers had childcare provided, then they could get jobs and earn money. The Center advertised for a nurse and a program director. With my pediatric nursing and child development degrees, I could fill both roles. I had been a welfare mother. I understood and cared about this problem. This was clearly my opportunity to change the world.

I'd never had a "regular" job – nine-to-six, Monday through Friday – or had an office with a desk. Hospital nursing was not like this; many jobs were not like this.

A normal day: drink coffee, drop the children off at school, drive to work and park, say "Good Morning," head straight to the bathroom, deal with my diarrhea, walk back to the lobby, say "Hi, how are you today?," slip into my office, close the door, put my head down on my desk, try to remember what day, what meetings, what forms. I didn't know then that this was called a hangover.

By 10 a.m., I'd checked the calendar and made my list of tasks for the day, had another cup of coffee, and begun my rounds of the classrooms.

Precious, curious, active children – babies, toddlers, and pre-schoolers. Dedicated, creative, hard working teachers. I loved them, loved this program, and loved the oasis of affection and play and working together.

Rudy, the Center's Director, let nothing interfere with his mission to do what was right and best for the children. At least, nothing he could control. Budget cuts, politics, and city legislation were constant challenges. We fought the battles and laughed to keep from giving up.

If only our country really meant it about ending welfare and poverty, meant it about taking care of children. These young mothers, living in small inner city apartments and houses, got up early, dressed, fed their babies and little children, and drove or took a bus to the Center by 7 or 8 a.m. Then they went to their minimum wage jobs. At 5:30 or 6:00 p.m., they would come back to the Center, take their tired little ones home, maybe on yet another bus trip. At home, there was dinner, bath, bedtime, dishes, laundry, then some sleep and another day.

I was all too familiar with this story, but at least when I had small children, my job had been in my house, where my children could stay with me. I had been able to return to professional work just as Jenny had become old enough to join Joe in elementary school and after-care. I had managed to make it through those six years, but barely.

I had learned how to stay poor enough to keep getting welfare because I knew I couldn't make it without that check. These women knew to stay poor enough to keep getting childcare because if they began to earn too much they would not be eligible for the program. They were up against a Catch-22.

But still the depression and alcohol abuse were hidden in the dark.

The Model Cities Center, where I worked for two years, still has a special place in my heart. I wish I could have stayed. I wish I could have changed the world.

Even with my administrative salary I could not pay my mortgage, a car, large credit card debts, and now my student loans. Without my welfare check and food stamps, there still wasn't enough left on payday. I resumed working weekend night shifts at Children's Hospital every other weekend, when Joe and Jenny were with their father. I put my house up for sale, hoping this move might get me out of debt.

My PTSD symptoms of overwhelming emotional memories, frightening dreams, and intense fear of men and situations that reminded me of my abuse had subsided, but the depression and heavy drinking continued.

My children were older and more independent by now. I had made some friends who had their own painful stories and weren't afraid of mine.

Finally I had friends who could let me be tired or sad, or need help. I knew people who I could simply talk with on the phone about our days, or get together with after a week's work for frozen fish sticks and French fries with the children. This valuable opportunity was new to me, and felt like such a blessing.

But still the depression and alcohol abuse were hidden in the dark. Not because I was trying to hide them, but rather because, almost like the incest, they were so well hidden that no one asked. And I didn't know to tell.

Me and Charlie

Every day I'd stop and buy just enough wine for that night – never more than a half-gallon – and always at different liquor stores, different convenience stores, or sometimes when I bought groceries. The automatic-pilot part of me never forgot this detail. My daily pattern saw me "relaxing" every evening with Charlie, our poodle puppy, my mind bound for oblivion. My drinking was unconscious yet conscious. I didn't think about it as part of a larger pattern or problem. Today I know this is called "denial."

One school year passed – weekdays at the childcare center, weekend nights at the hospital, mothering in the evenings, sleeping and housework on the weekends.

The depression was getting worse. The drinking was increasing. I was stopping before getting to work – a convenience store, a donut shop – anywhere I could get quickly to a bathroom, finish the morning diarrhea, maybe vomit, buy something, anything, and get back in the car. I'd walk into the Center – "Good morning. Hi, beautiful day isn't it?" – and enter my office, my hiding place. Door closed, head on the desk, I'd suffer with nausea and heartburn. It became harder and harder to make myself focus and go through the day.

Rudy, my Director and friend, says now that he had no idea I was drinking heavily. I never appeared hung-over, and he never smelled wine on my breath.

My friends, my mother, even Gary on one of his visits – they all say they didn't see it, didn't know about the drinking or the depression. So skilled at hiding my childhood, I now used those same talents to hide this adult darkness too.

Gary, Me, Jenny, Joe and Mom

In the summer of 1980, Joe and Jenny left for another summer "vacation" with Grampy. They had spent seven years now with a single mother who was doing and saying "all the right things," except she wasn't really there – she was depressed, she was drunk, she was hungover and she sent them to Grampy each summer.

That summer, while my children were away, during the disco-music craze and the beginning of Ronald Reagan's presidency, I filed for bankruptcy, sold our house, paid off what bills I could, and once again packed up our life into boxes.

Without consulting Joe and Jenny, I found and rented a tiny, unfinished basement apartment, telling myself it would be a good place for them – they could walk to school and best of all, it was in an ethnically diverse neighborhood. Better than some garden apartment in the suburbs, I rationalized smugly.

In reality, however, this was a terrible place for children. I am appalled, as I look back, at how lost I was and what I put them through.

The apartment and neighborhood were a mirror of my psyche, an outer manifestation of my inner hopelessness and despair.

Our apartment was one long narrow basement space beneath a rich family's elaborate row house. Unfinished concrete walls, uncovered plumbing pipes and electric wire, a cement floor painted brown, tiny high windows with black metal bars, even a barred gate at the entrance. It was our own private prison, which I filled with our familiar posters, books, and furnishings… and called "Home."

When Joe and Jenny came home for the new school year, this inner city locale was their new home and neighborhood. Joe was eleven, in sixth grade, and Jenny, now seven, was in second grade.

They were children functioning as virtual adults, taking care of themselves and each other before and after school. Now they didn't fall asleep so early or so easily. I waited until they were in bed to start drinking, but I no longer waited until they were asleep. That would have been too late.

One night, as I stumbled past his bedroom door, Joe called out jokingly, "Mom, are you bumping into the walls again?" I laughed, "No, just lost my balance. Go on to sleep."

I didn't think I could keep on going – I was too tired, too empty. I longed to die, but ruled out suicide because I didn't want Joe and Jenny to find my body. When I got this depressed, I "reasoned" that I would have to kill them first, and then myself. I just couldn't do that.

I began to imagine that I could stop working. Then I'd lose the apartment, we would be put out on the street, social services would come and take the children to a "good home," and I would be free to sit up on the corner with the other homeless people.

Alcoholics Anonymous calls it "hitting bottom." They say it's hard to begin recovery until you hit bottom, until the denial and delusion, the lies to the self and to others, unravel your world completely.

This was my bottom.

Joe knows about my drinking. Maybe Jenny knows. The secret is out. I thought I was taking care of them and protecting them. But they know.

I'd lost our house and most of what we owned. We had moved three times in six years. We lived in an underground jail cell. My life goal was to become homeless and have my children placed in foster care.

Oh, please God, I need help.

The pleas and remorse of an alcoholic are so plaintive and so brief. But God had heard me. I had admitted powerlessness, even if only for a moment. I had asked a Higher Power for help.

That weekend on my way to the liquor store, I wandered through the corner drug store. There on the pharmacy counter I saw the flier: "Community Health Clinic – healing body, mind, and spirit." My therapy group and my college classes had come just when I needed them. I suddenly felt that this clinic was my next, maybe my last, life raft.

In the second floor office of the health center, I met with a social worker and told her my story. I don't remember her name, her face, or what books or pictures were in the room. I only remember she was gentle.

I told her about being exhausted, wanting to die, drinking just to keep going. I told her about the incest but that I thought I had finished dealing with that.

"You'll need to stop drinking," she said. "I want you to join Alcoholics Anonymous."

"No," I said. "I can't do that. I've just found out I have a self. I don't even know who I am. I'm not going to start by naming myself an alcoholic."

The apartment and neighborhood were a mirror of my psyche, an outer manifestation of my inner hopelessness and despair.

261

For several weeks she listened patiently to me as I said I wanted to give up, and as I repeatedly refused AA. She worried I might have physical damage from the drinking and asked me to see the clinic physician.

The doctor too was kind, gentle, but firm. There was no liver or nerve damage yet, she said. But if I kept drinking there would be soon. "You might die," she told me.

"No," I said. "I won't go to AA."

I won't be an alcoholic.

"You are certainly abusing alcohol. It will kill you," the doctor replied. "There's only one other thing I can offer. There is a medication called Antabuse. It's dangerous and I don't want to give it to you. It won't stop your craving or fix your depression. What it will do is give you a reason not to drink.

"If you drink alcohol while you're taking Antabuse you will have a seizure, and that too could kill you."

The thought of seizures and death was somehow easier for me than an AA meeting. Depression was still affecting both my energy and my judgment.

That winter I stopped drinking. After the two weeks necessary to cleanse the alcohol out of my system, I began taking Antabuse.

Sober for the first time in seven years, I felt an immediate euphoria and also confusion.

What should I do in the evenings?

I suddenly had time to read more books and write letters to friends.

What should I do during the first hours of work in the morning?

I tried leaving the office door open. Things to do found me.

Easy, I thought. Now, I'm really fixed! The incest and the drinking!

The initial excitement sustained me for a few weeks, maybe through the holidays. But that soon wore off as I began to feel the full extent of my still un-named depression.

Without drinking and hangovers to preoccupy me – where to buy the wine, how to hide the bottles, how to find a bathroom – the symptoms of depression became more and more apparent, looming like a threatening cloud, always enclosing me in the dark and fog.

Now I succumbed completely. Tearful, irritable, hopeless, lethargic. Every action

I didn't think I could keep on going – I was too tired, too empty.

I longed to die, but ruled out suicide because I didn't want Joe and Jenny to find my body.

and interaction seemed exhausting. I kept going to the childcare center weekdays, working at the hospital weekend nights, taking care of household tasks whenever I had a spare moment. But those moments were barely enough to keep our lives functioning. Joe and Jenny were more and more on their own. Now, in the summer of 1981, my twelve and eight-year old children left again for their summer visit with Grampy.

As they left, I collapsed. Without the structure and responsibility of parenting I could not focus or motivate myself.

I began arriving late to work and then calling in sick. I lay in my bed, cried, slept, and stared at the ceiling. Nothing mattered, nothing made sense. I didn't eat. I didn't dress.

Depression is not a choice, not a matter of will power or faith. It is a severe medical illness affecting brain chemistry and, therefore, affecting thought and mood.

Desperate, I wrote a letter to relatives and friends, telling them of my fatigue and despair:

> August is now scheduled for rest and I am not available for family or personal crises, except in cases of hardship meeting the Federal disaster guidelines.
>
> I am taking the month off, sleeping lots, refusing to accept calls.
>
> I am very tired; it has been a long seven years, a lonely seven years, a well-hidden, ever-willing, can-always-do-a-little-more-when-you're-tired seven years. I will sleep, will dream, will stare at the painting on the wall, until autumn. Then the children return, school will start, we will find a new apartment and a new job.
>
> I will pick up my familiar role, and try to learn to dance more lightly!

My friends rallied around me, determined to shake me out of my state of fog and numbness. They forced me to shower, took me to the grocery store, called in the mornings to be sure I was up and on my way to work. They visited and helped with chores. Still I was empty.

I saw the social worker occasionally. It was too much effort to get to the clinic for the appointments. I remember at least one emergency phone call during a panic attack. I kept taking the Antabuse. I was sober. I was a dry alcoholic. As far as I can remember, medication and hospitalization were not suggested. Times were different, and these solutions were not regularly used then.

After a few months, as gradually as a fog lifts on a cold damp morning, the depression began to clear. I cannot say why.

Oh,

please God,

I need help

A war had been waged within my own mind and body. I didn't declare the war, and I couldn't end it. These seven years were, for me, like living in the emotional equivalent of a refugee camp, trying each day just to survive physically and emotionally. I took my children with me as refugees.

Now, finally, the war was ending. But there was still much healing and repair to be done.

I also finally could see that I had expected to be poor and exhausted as a parent, just as my mother had been. I had been making decisions to create that reality.

The social worker helped me realize I could not keep working two jobs, and that I couldn't support my children on my salary as a day care supervisor. She also insisted that I start looking for a new place to live – that we move out of our physical prison now that I was out of my emotional one.

I had always enjoyed my nursing job at Children's Hospital, but as a single mom I couldn't return if I had to work evenings, nights and weekends. A fortuitous opportunity appeared in 1982, when the hospital opened a new inpatient child-psychiatry unit, with room for ten seriously afflicted children between the ages of five and twelve.

I had been working weekend night shifts on the toddler medical unit for several years now. My supervisor knew I had gone to school and received my Masters in Child Psychology. She asked me to work full-time on the new psychiatric unit, and agreed that I could work day shifts during the school year, and do my evening and night shifts in the summer, when the children were away.

I was sad to leave the Model Cities Center, but with my new job and salary as a full time nurse, I could afford to move to a first floor apartment in a better area for the children.

I painted the walls and played new and happier music.

That summer of 1982, when Joe, thirteen, and Jenny, nine, were away at Grampy's, I began settling us into this new home. Mom and Gary helped, and for the first time since childhood, because I was not depressed, I was able to feel a closer connection with them.

I painted the walls and played new and happier music. I experimented with meeting friends for dinner and with taking walks in the park. I even had some real dates and went to concerts and plays. We had a tiny apartment, a rattly old car, and beat-up furniture – but we also had windows, and the sun was shining in.

1982 through 1985 felt deceptively calm and easy. This must be what people call "normal," I thought – work, school, household tasks, getting together with friends, occasional romance.

I had stopped seeing my social worker, but knew I was not finished dealing with the effects of my abuse history, especially my inability to develop close friendships and intimacy. I found a therapist who worked in a new way with memories and feelings, helping me express them through visual images rather than words.

I continued in imagery therapy with Marilyn weekly for the next three years. She helped me explore my inner perceptions of myself and my world. She helped me transform feelings and images of helplessness and vulnerability. Slowly, I became able to trust, to receive nurture, to develop a sense of autonomy and empowerment.

Joe and Me

It would not be until well after my father's death, however, that I would be able to express my deep and long-suppressed rage. This release came at a five-day intensive retreat entitled Life, Death and Transformation, led by Dr. Elisabeth Kubler-Ross. In a process called "externalization of feelings," I used techniques facilitated by her trained counselors for the release of blocked emotions such as fear, anger, and grief. In a moving moment in the dormitory one night, several group members gave me a bedtime story, a backrub, a song, a loving tuck-in, and a kiss on the forehead. At age forty-three, for the first time, my "little one" could feel safe to express all her needs and feelings.

With my therapist assistance, however, I began to move in new emotional directions. With my women friends, I learned that it was okay to not always be the strong one, that I was allowed to ask for help. For the first time, I sought out get-togethers for the intention of having fun rather than merely accomplishing tasks.

With men, I came to understand that our interactions could include safety, friendship, and commitment, not just sexuality.

Instead of songs about sorrow and despair, I found myself drawn to more joyful, energetic music. In the middle of my life, I felt myself opening and maturing, finally, into an adult.

Although these new relationships and therapy helped me to grow, interludes of confusion, sadness and fear continued. I still could find myself abusing alcohol. Sometimes during lovemaking, I still encountered emotional shutdown, with the sense of flashbacks to my childhood terror.

Mark, with whom I had an intimate relationship for over a year, and who remains a true and trusted friend, recalls the times I would close myself off. "I experienced you as being lost inside a very thick and tangled forest. Even though I wanted to help you, I was afraid that if I went into that dark place to rescue you, I might get lost too."

Recovering from child sexual abuse was an on-going and lengthy process. It was not easy, and it wasn't over. But my life was so much better than before.

I loved my new job on the Child Psychiatry Unit. It was challenging and stimulating. I absorbed information about child development, behavioral interventions, diagnostic criteria, medication efficacy, social service programs, and special education.

The patients I worked with had a range of problems. I remember one girl who had jumped out of a window, breaking both legs, while trying to commit suicide. More than one child had intentionally started serious fires. Several had severely injured other people. Many were depressed. Some were psychotic.

Children were not admitted to the psychiatric unit for having been sexually abused, although their medical records often included this factor as a contributor to their emotional or behavioral problems.

In the middle of my life, I felt myself opening and maturing, finally, into an adult.

For the first time, I became professionally aware of child sexual abuse. I learned about dissociation, depression, and PTSD in clinical terms. I learned about child protection investigations, foster care placement, and long-term family therapy.

Child sexual abuse was a new term since I had first studied pediatrics twenty-five years earlier. The descriptor was first used clinically in 1979 as medical professionals began to break through their own confusion and denial about cases they had seen of young children with gonorrhea and syphilis and lacerations around their genitals. Doctors finally began to realize or acknowledge that these illnesses and injuries had been inflicted on the children by adults.

I was so relieved to be past my own bad times. I felt professionally fulfilled and challenged, and each day brought such rewarding, healing work. To me, these profoundly injured little ones I was encountering as a psychiatric nurse had become children to whom I could give some of what I had learned from both my personal experiences and my growing professional knowledge.

After my own descent into utter depression, I had finally begun to rebuild my life with a much deeper understanding both of my past and of the decisions I was now making. Instead of being affected negatively by my history of abuse and depression, I was beginning to transform my own experiences into a positive force to reach out to and help others.

266

Daddy

Chapter Sixteen

Stabbed in the Heart

(1981-1985)

"The horror! The horror!"

By Joseph Conrad

While I was making changes in both my inner and my outer worlds, little had changed in my father's life. He had settled into his work rhythm in Colorado Springs, was active with his social and outdoor activities, and, unknown to others, was continuing to abuse numerous children. His shadow was spreading.

For seven years now, since beginning to write this book in 1994, I have been moving toward the moment when I must put the horror into words. My father's life story, an unfolding tragedy, moves inexorably toward its final years, which will culminate in his suicide. This morning, with excruciating honesty, I admit to myself that I do not want to write this part of our family's story.

My husband Freeman is away on a business trip and I wander alone through the rooms of our house, searching for sentences, explanations, and strength. I have vowed to assemble the final pieces of my father's life story before Freeman returns home. I want to be able to say that I am finished with this journey, this mystery, this anguish.

The family pictures on our walls and shelves bring no comfort. Seeing all the photographs – Joe and Jenny's faces as little children and as grown adults, Freeman and I smiling and embracing, his sons Dan and Gabe, now part of our "blended family" of six – only increases my deep sadness, my sense of how much pain and sorrow can be hidden from others.

Outside, winter is ending. The sky is gray and the wind blows the bare branches of the trees and the boughs of the evergreens. The grass is brown and dry. Yesterday, walking outside our mountain home, I saw that there are small yellow buds on the forsythia bushes, and three delicate purple crocuses have pushed through the soil in the garden.

But these signs of hope and resilience are not visible from where I stand now.

There is no escape, nowhere to go but into the end of the story. Seven years ago, I learned about the sexual abuse of my children at the hands of my father, and went through the shock and heartbreak of that truth. I have made trips to Colorado five times, talked with over one hundred people, typed and organized my notes, and diligently transcribed all of the details – moving ever inward on a spiral that I hoped would lead to understanding.

Now, at the heart of this journey to know my father, I must accept that I have not found any clear answers or explanations. All that will be waiting at the destination I now must move toward is dread, disaster and anguish. All that is left for me is the ability to will myself to go there.

From 1975 through 1981, my father had re-built his life in Colorado Springs with work, friends, and extended family. He had also been spending large amounts of time alone with Paul, his nephew, and with Ruth, the young daughter of his good friends. Beginning in the summer of 1978, he received annual summer visits and even a Christmas visit from Joe and Jenny, his grandchildren.

In the summer of 1981, as my life stabilized, my father began the descent into his final darkness. When he reached age sixty-five, and was able to begin receiving Social Security payments, Daddy closed his shop in Colorado Springs and moved to live full-time in his trailer at Silent Valley.

He would make his visits to sisters and to his nieces and nephews, and they would continued to visit him and enjoy outdoor activities together. On previous visits, they have told me that during these years their brother was developing arthritis and had begun to drink a little vodka each day.

"I'll never go to a rest home," he had told his sister, Elizabeth. "If the time comes when I can't take care of myself, I'll know what to do." Elizabeth says he never complained.

Friends and their children from Colorado Springs continued to visit for snowmobile rides and hikes along the trails George maintained. He also continued his active involvement with the Central Colorado Outdoor Club, frequently hosting their get-togethers, day hikes, and campouts at his isolated mountain retreat.

During this time period, from the outside, my father's life seemed as it had for decades. He continued to be perceived as a friendly, active, hard-working man who

In the summer of 1981, as my life stabilized, my father began the descent into his final darkness.

enjoyed people and outdoor activities. Now, as I went looking for information about these last years, I no longer expected to find new victims, and no longer felt I needed any more documentation to illustrate my father's lifelong patterns.

But it felt like something was still missing in my father's story. When did it all finally stop? Why did he kill himself? What were his last days like? I would have to go back to Colorado to find out. In 1995, I found myself on yet another trip to Daddy's mountains.

For this part of my search, I traveled to the picturesque Rocky Mountain town that is closest to Silent Valley. From a small motel room, I made daily excursions to look for more pieces of the puzzle. As always, the superficial outside segments, "the edges," were easiest to obtain and piece together.

After I identify myself, the teller on duty at the small community bank retrieves George Culbertson's records. She notes, next to the word "deceased," the line where I signed the forms to close the account after his death in November of 1985.

She tells me that one other place that my father had been active was the community library, where he had taught sign language classes. One of his adult sign language students at the library, writes to me her memory of my father:

"George reminded me of my own father. He seemed to be a very rugged country man, who carried inside him both tremendous strength and a tender heart, as well as sadness and a great depth of loneliness. He had very expressive eyes.

"He seemed like a person who could pick up a wounded bird and care for it, and at the same time one who could be ferocious as a bear when justly angered. At one point, I felt a great need to pray for him. A month later I read, on the ambulance sheet at the hospital where I work, that he had died – and I was so upset. I treasure the education he gave me; with his moving fingers of love and strength, he taught me a lot in a short time. Even now, I keep the alphabet sign language card he gave me, and use it on occasions when I meet someone who can't hear or speak."

His student's comments remind me that there's this place of mystery and wonder that surrounds my father still. I really recognize this part of him, a man people felt they could love and trust so deeply. I am glad, for Daddy's sake, that some such friends remained for him, people who never saw their love and trust betrayed.

The third person whom I hope will be able to give me information is Bob Lewis. He is the newspaper carrier who had found my father's suicide note. "I didn't see much of your father," he tells me. "He kept pretty much to himself. I delivered his paper to his box every afternoon."

Bob was startled to find the suicide note. He knew the handwriting was George's because his customer usually wrote a check and left it in the box to pay his bill. Bob went immediately to call the sheriff, and remembers a deputy promptly was sent to

George seemed to be a very rugged country man, who carried inside him both tremendous strength and a tender heart, as well as sadness and a great depth of loneliness.

Daddy and His Shadow

check on George. Bob gives me the name of the sheriff, and also suggests that the post office in town can tell me the names of neighbors who lived along the long upwardly-winding state road that led to Silent Valley.

At the post office, the mail carrier gives me these names, and I am able to call and make appointments to meet with neighbors who will fill in many of the pieces of these last four years of George Culbertson's life.

One of the neighbors, Dave Henderson, tells me that he remembers my father well because of his deafness. "George was friendly and easy-going," he says. "I used to meet him on the road, and I remember sometimes helping him out with my four-wheel drive pickup."

Another neighbor is Sheriff Roberts. I reflect to myself that even as Daddy was actively engaged in abusing kids, the local sheriff was residing just down the road. I ask him if he was the one Bob Lewis called about the suicide note. He tells me yes, and he was also the one who officially signed the suicide record in the sheriff's office. "I knew George more or less in passing, as a neighbor.

But the sheriff seems to be holding something back. I think back to the phone call I received when my father died, the call in which a strange woman told me about the rumors that my father was being brought up on molesting charges. I decide to ask him about the rumored incidents.

"I heard that my father's suicide might have something to do with his being charged with molesting a child," I tell him. "Do you know anything about that?"

"I guess I had wondered if you knew about his problems," the sheriff replies.

"Yes, I know that he molested lots of children, including mine," I answered. "He also molested me. I don't know many details about this last part of his life, though."

"You might want to call Sargent Wood," he says, giving me a phone number. "Also, you could check with the Teller County Sheriff's Office. I know they have more detailed information."

The Teller County offices are located in a cluster of trailers on a highway leading north of Woodland Park. There I am asked to fill out forms and provide my birth certificate and my father's death certificate. What I learn from this thirty-three page collection of typewritten and handwritten documents is new and startling, maybe because it is now printed on official documents, part of the public record.

In March of 1982, a warrant was issued in Teller County for the arrest of George Culbertson and the search of his property. The charges were "sexual assault on a child." The warrant was executed at Silent Valley by Deputies Marshall, Wood, Rogers and Potter.

INCIDENT REPORT

"Informant reported that a neighbor had talked his 9 and 11 year old daughters into getting into his pickup, that the man had no clothing on from the waist down. He took the girls to his residence, where he showed them pictures of naked children whom he called his grandchildren. He took pictures – naked – of them also, then made them touch him… ."

My stomach in knots, my heart frozen, I read through pages and pages of the two girls' description of what my father coerced them to do. My heart goes out to them, but my mind is elsewhere.

Photographs of Joe and Jenny! My own children, now used as bait to entice other little ones.

Jody Curtis, the eleven-year-old from the incident report, is talking with me by phone, sounding willing and even eager to tell her story. She is now a young woman in her mid-twenties. "Yes, I recall very well when George was our neighbor. We lived on the same road up in the valley. Sometimes we'd see him when he would stop and pick up his paper or when he would drive by in his truck. He was always friendly, waving at us and smiling.

"Sometimes George would pick us up at our bus stop," she continues, "and then take us to his place for treats before he took us home. We also used to go to visit him with other kids in the neighborhood, and he was teaching us sign language.

"One day, my sister and I were out walking the boundary of our property, and we saw George naked. He put on his pants, saying, 'Your mom and dad wouldn't like this,' then he invited us back to his cabin for a soda. After we talked and drank our sodas, he began showing us pictures of nude people, and telling us we could go skinny-dipping in his pond with him. He told us to take off our clothes and we did. He took all his clothes off too.

"Then he took pictures of me walking around his cabin naked, and asked me to take a picture of my little sister holding his penis. When we got dressed and ready to leave, George said, 'Remember, this is our little secret.' I was eleven years old when this happened. It makes me really angry, what George did! We were friends, and there was so much trust."

Jody says, "Since the time when I knew your father, as I've grown up, I have also had other experiences, both of sexual abuse as well as rape." She lives now with her fiancé of five years, and they have had a lot of therapy and sexual counseling.

I think predators know whom to abuse; they know how to find children who are vulnerable.

271

"Because of what's happened to me, I now want to become a therapist, to help children. I think predators know whom to abuse; they know how to find children who are vulnerable. I guess I feel they need to be castrated or locked up. What is important is that kids need to be protected! If they haven't been through it themselves, no one can really help a child abuse victim recover."

As a psychotherapist who is also a survivor, I can acknowledge how my life experiences have helped me understand the trauma that abuse victims suffer. However I have been helped by counselors, and worked with professional colleagues, who were not survivors, yet had superb skill and insight in aiding survivors. So while I can empathize with Jody's belief, I cannot agree with her final statement.

I next drove out to talk with Jack Buford, one of George's neighbors on the Silent Valley road, who knew all about the abuse of the Curtis girls:

"My three girls and the Curtis girls were friends. Jody and her sister told our children what George had done, but they were afraid to tell their own parents yet. My wife and I strongly advised them to inform their parents.

"I'm a retired private investigator; so when the police came out, they told me about what their search of George's cabin revealed. I had heard one other story from them, previously, that George drove around in his truck in the nude.

"They brought by photos of at least fifteen or twenty children, which they had discovered at the cabin. Of course, they were taped and everything, so you couldn't see the background, or bodies, or actions of the children. You could just see the faces. Neither my wife nor I recognized any of them. The police told me that this wasn't the first incident with George.

"I volunteered to speak with the Public Defender, more or less on George's behalf.

"I said to him, 'No, I don't think jail is the answer. That's no place for somebody like this. He probably needs some help. There must be somewhere more appropriate you can put him.'"

What Mr. Buford suggested never came to pass. Instead, in keeping with legal practices in the early nineteen-eighties, my father was found guilty and placed on probation, and again failed to receive treatment.

"I don't think your dad ever approached my kids," continued the investigator. "Once, after all this had happened, he drove up by the house, and I fired a shotgun into the air to send him a message. Another time, I found him down where our drive forks off the road to Silent Valley. I stopped and told him, 'This isn't your road, George, and you don't need to be down here.' He never came back again, so I never had any other experience with him."

On May 3, 1982, I learn from the next police report that a neighbor reported that George again was "hanging around the school bus stop." There were three girls at the bus stop, and George drove by three times, slowed down and came to a stop. All the girls ran for home. The officer advised that he would be in the area of the bus stop the next day, and that deputies would patrol the area. No further action was taken on this complaint. Again, even after being discovered by legal authorities, George cannot resist the impulse, which seems essentially like an addiction, to sexually abuse children.

A month later, in June of 1982, I learn that Daddy went to the Pike's Peak Mental Health Center and enrolled as a client. A letter from his psychologist states, "He came in very upset following his recent arrest. He felt very fearful, anxious and depressed, feeling that he needed help."

As I review this segment of the records, questions begin to occur to me. After being hospitalized for abusing me in 1958, had Daddy come to understand that "psychiatric consultation" could shield him from many legal consequences of his behavior? I know he had used this shield at least once since then, in 1965, to avoid charges by his Colorado Springs teaching colleagues.

Is this a third example of using such care for self-protection?

Or did he seek out psychiatric care in a moment of genuine remorse and clarity over the harm he had done to so many children?

On July 2, Daddy appeared before the Judge in Teller County on trial for photographing and molesting the Curtis girls, his neighbors down the road from Silent Valley. He entered a guilty plea to the charges of sexual assault on a child. The trial record notes little Jody's words about her parents' friend, George. "He told us not to tell anybody, because he loved us so much."

How many times, Daddy, and with how many children in the years between then and now, did you use these same innocent-sounding words, about love, to coerce and deceive and destroy?

The public defender noted that the defendant had voluntarily placed himself in the care of a psychologist and that he was remorseful about his behavior. The judge found Daddy guilty and placed him on probation for four years with the condition that he keep out of unsupervised contact with children.

The record shows the probation officer's name, and I obtain an appointment to speak with Mr. Frank Reese. Though fourteen years have passed, he remembers George well, describing him as a probation client who always did as he was directed.

"He was docile and easy to supervise, not like some of the violent and macho guys I had to deal with," said Officer Reese. "I felt sorry for him, his deafness... and he used that. Charm, I see now, was part of his persona. When I would check on him at Silent Valley, he was always cordial, never hostile. He was definitely the kind of guy kids would love. I would always visit him in an unscheduled way, be sure no kids were

My father was found guilty and placed on probation, and again failed to receive treatment.

273

with him, and I guess I thought he was pretty much okay. I never really feared he would re-offend while on probation.

"On the other hand, in my field George was what I call a "fixated pedophile," one who regularly re-targets kids who are the same age he was, if he himself had been abused as a boy. I mean, here he is driving around without pants, looking for kids. Yet now he has two separate felony convictions. He's what we call a 'bitch'... an habitual offender. He knew he'd be facing definite prison time – maybe even thirty years – if he offended again."

Still, my father had asked the judge to allow his grandchildren to make their annual summer visit, and that presented a problem. "The judge had serious concerns regarding George's pedophile charges and his avid nudism, and simply wouldn't consider letting your children come out," Reese told me. "That's when I telephoned you, Joyce. I told you the situation, but you said that since your aunt would be supervising the children, it was all right with you if they came.

"When I told this to the judge, he really thought it was strange. He said, 'Well, I guess it takes all kinds of parents...' and went ahead and signed the permission order."

I find myself feeling stunned and ashamed. What the parole officer has just shared has been spoken in a kind voice, a voice that's seen it all, a voice without blame. Yet I have absolutely no memory of that conversation with Officer Reese in the summer of 1982.

Recently, my mother, my friend Pat, and Joe and Jenny's father John, each have told me that they, too, questioned my sending the children to visit their grandfather. Until these recent confirmations, I had been completely blank about their warnings, too.

It sounds impossible! How could I have disregarded these warnings on behalf of my children? How could I have been so unaware?

I felt like a person who had just been given a fatal diagnosis from a physician... somber, numb, and incredulous.

Even today, writing this out, all the pain and disbelief I felt at initially learning of my children's six summers of abuse wells up and overcomes me once again.

When will this agony end?

In the sheriff's record about my father, I had seen a telltale note. Acting on a warrant issued on July 12, less than two weeks after his probation for assaulting the Curtis girls, Sheriff Wood picked up George Culbertson again, transporting him this time to the El Paso Jail in Lakewood, Colorado.

Again my father has been charged – this time on two counts – with sexual assault on a child.

Again, even after being discovered by legal authorities, Daddy cannot resist the impulse to sexually abuse children.

He was advised of his rights, detained in the El Paso jail on five thousand dollars bond, and was represented by the Public Defender in Court.

Here is the moment, the story Ruth had told me, how "all hell broke loose" when Daddy was jailed for molesting her and her little sister.

Here also is the moment, I now understand, when George's favorite niece, Karen, and her husband William, stepped in. On July 23, after he had been in jail for one week, he contacted them in desperation.

Short, energetic, and dark-haired, Karen was always my best friend during my childhood summer visits to Colorado. As we meet together in her suburban Denver condo to discuss her recollection of this period after so many years, she is still the outgoing, optimistic, and kind companion I knew as a girl.

"It was clear how humiliated George was when we picked him up from the jail," she tells me. "He had been stripped and searched, and was just so upset. According to his neighbor's children, he had coerced them into touching his private parts, but he told us, 'No, I was just giving the girls hugs, being affectionate. It was all just a huge misunderstanding.'

"William and I put up our home as bail collateral, and invited him to stay with us and our kids for a few weeks. I never told my mother Eleanor, or Aunt Elizabeth, about this, for fear of upsetting them, and I still don't want to share this incident about their brother with them. After all, they are old now. It would be too much of an emotional burden for them.

"The first night he was with us," Karen continued, "he was upset and despondent. I could hear him masturbating in his room. And sometimes he wanted to walk around nude inside the house, which made me uncomfortable. We had completely different philosophies about nudity, but I didn't want to discuss this with him, so I tried to ignore it.

"Joe and Jenny were due to arrive soon, Joyce, and I was embarrassed to bring up with you what had happened with your dad," said my cousin. "But I phoned you, do you remember? I was worried, wondering how or if they should come."

Once again, I have no memory of this warning.

"But the truth is," she continues, "I always loved Uncle George, no matter what he did. It was an enriching experience, knowing him. He really had more genuine love of children than anyone I ever knew."

Completing my investigation of events in 1982, I stop at the Pikes Peak Mental Health Center (PPMHC). PPMHC records actually indicated that George

He told us not to tell anybody, because he loved us so much.

Culbertson had a total of only six sessions with his therapist there, after which the psychologist suggested that he discontinue treatment.

When will

this agony

end?

The PPMHC microfilm Discharge Summary for George R. Culbertson is succinct:

> Began treatment on June 29. last contact August 9, 1982.
>
> Background information: chronic child molesting; prior treatment history with Dr. Brown at Colorado Springs.
>
> Summary of treatment: reestablished social networks, vocational interests to prevent isolation, contact with peers, etc. Also, re-educated in reference to the effects of behavior on victims. No longer depressed, increased social contact and support, increased self-esteem.
>
> Final diagnosis: #302-20 – pedophilia.
>
> Recommendations: continued contact with probation officer.
>
> No solitary contact with children.

On September 21, the sheriff's record shows a "suspicious vehicle" incident report on George, who was now on probation. This suggests that his neighbors are now much more concerned and vigilant.

On October 12, 1982, George Culbertson's attorney asked the Court to dismiss the charges of assault on Ruth in exchange for a guilty plea to the charges of assault on her stepsister, Sherry. The Court granted this request. The Judgment of Conviction states:

The Court grants defendant probation for four years. Special conditions:

> 1. Defendant to continue in regular Mental Health Counseling;
>
> 2. Defendant to refrain from any contact with victim or any child less than 16 years of age;
>
> 3. Defendant to refrain from public nudity except on own property and then only if not offending anyone.
>
> Meetings with parole officer to be done in Colorado Springs.

This time, as I reviewed his records from 1982, it felt as if the high, cold peaks of those Rockies were closing in around me and weighing down my spirit.

Clearly more and more isolated, my father was beginning to unravel. I have been able to piece together a basic time line of events in 1982:

February 28 – nude, and abusing two little girls, his neighbors; photos of my nude children and another nude little girl found in his cabin.

March 1 – arrested, charged, jailed, pleads guilty to sexual assault on a child. Between this date and October, 1984, he will appear in Court ten times regarding these charges.

April 7 – week-long visit with friends; spends each day nude with two daughters while parents at work; abuses both of them "because I love you."

May 3 – waiting at school-bus stop, tries to invite three girls into his truck; deputies alerted to patrol and interdict if he repeats this activity.

June 29 – enters therapy. Diagnosis: pedophilia; discharged after six sessions.

July 2 – arrested, charged, jailed, pleads guilty in another county to child sexual assault of his friend's children; placed on probation for four years and forbidden to be unsupervised around children; these friends never speak to George again.

July 3 – lies to his niece about reason for latest charges; she bails him out and takes him home to stay with her and her two young sons.

July 28 – Joe and Jenny arrive for one-month visit. He takes them on camping trips so he can avoid probation officer home-visits, and abuses them regularly.

September 21 – again seen/reported waiting in his truck at school-bus stop.

October 12 – In an adjoining county, George is placed on a second four-year probation.

I was just giving the girls hugs, being affectionate.

It's all real. Sheriffs', judges', psychiatrists' signatures and dates, so terse, clinical and impersonal there on paper. With pages and pages of photocopied documents scattered on my motel-room bed, the implications of my father's timetable for 1982 slowly seep into my body.

At last, he has been legally forbidden to have access to children. But these words on paper will prove insufficient to keep children safe. In reality, this legal action changed nothing, since I myself continued to deliver his own grandchildren into his hands in August of 1982, and again in the summers of 1983 and 1984.

Suddenly, like a slow-swelling tidal wave gathering force and volume far out at sea, it hits me. Since 1978, and especially after 1982, when his pedophilia had been prosecuted by Colorado courts, my son and daughter had been among the primary sexual assault targets of my father's pedophilia.

"Grampy molested me when I was a child." My words of disclosure to my child, in the bizarre setting, just after their grandfather's suicide, had eased flatly and calmly into spoken reality.

Joe and Jenny – their eyes meeting mine directly and then gazing out over Silent Valley – had answered my revelation with silence, and at the time I had been too tired, and too broken by events, to pursue the conversation further.

Now with brutal clarity and, finally, a painful fullness, I can understand my children's stony silence when they first learned about my own abuse following Daddy's suicide. They too had been numb. They were not yet able to tell me, but the cancer within our family had already spread to them.

Outside my motel, heavy snow has started to fall. There's a blizzard forecast on TV, and just like the mountains cloaked in whiteness, I too am becoming cold and frozen. I am alone, and I know I shouldn't stay here. Phoning for a last-minute reservation change, I maneuver my rented car into the snow and slush, and flee along the Interstate for safety, for home and Freeman, before I shut down and collapse.

Grampy molested me when I was a child.

Back in Virginia, I re-enter an old, familiar inner state: shock, depression, and constant grief. I set aside work on this book for nearly a year. I do laundry; I start cleaning out closets and the basement; I break down crying as I walk down grocery store aisles. My father's deeds have become so vivid, so horrible, so invasive. They are more than I can bear.

Even typing these words today I can feel nausea creeping into my stomach...hands clinching...forehead tightening. I am simply overwhelmed with grief.

I don't want to be here, to feel this anymore. It's just too hard.

Within a few months, feeling unable to write, or even to look at my notes, I resume weekly sessions with Ted, my ever-steady therapist. I casually recount my most recent trip to Colorado.

"It wasn't difficult," I say to him, "except for learning about the photographs the sheriffs found of Joe and Jenny."

Before I can continue, Ted raises his right hand, palm outward, to interrupt my conversation. Gently, and with a look of true compassion, he grasps his fingers around the handle of an imaginary knife, turns his hand, and moves it towards his chest.

You've been stabbed in the heart.

"You've been stabbed in the heart," he says.

Even though I don't believe I can ever feel blameless, I try to accept Ted's absolution. More to the point however, I too must learn to live with the consequences of my deed.

With Ted's help, I am able to finally encounter my tears, my grief, and my long-stifled remorse. And then I can admit the horror of facing my family history, and start to move on. There will be no proceeding with this work unless and until I am able to open my heart and make my spirit vulnerable – first to myself, to my terrible mistakes, and my terrible wounding; and then to my children and others like them; and perhaps, just maybe, someday, to my father.

Silent Valley

Daddy, Mom, Gary and Me

Chapter Seventeen

The Silent Shadow

(1944-1994)

"We've been taught that silence would save us, but it won't."

– Audre Lorde

After seven years spent exploring my father's life history and talking with numerous people, I discover that I am most intrigued with the rules, values and beliefs that were given by my informants as reasons for remaining silent. Everyone agreed that sexual abuse of children was wrong and should not happen. In examining the inter-relationships of these different groups of "actors," I realize their exists an actual "ecology" of child abuse, an environment that allows the abuse to flourish and perpetuate itself. Yet their silence effectively permitted my father to continue molesting additional children.

Here, in their own words, the ones I call *The Knowers* explain the silences they maintained.

The Knowers

My mother's sister Agnes says, "Although I never realized that George was a child abuser, I knew he was a womanizer. Not long after I was married, he wrote me this long letter telling how attracted to me he felt. It scared me.

How could he do this when it was my own sister he was married to?

I never told your mother. She was my sister. It would have hurt her so much, and ruined her marriage. You don't interfere in someone else's marriage."

"Then, when you were a baby, I noticed that when your father would change your diapers, sometimes I thought he was overly attentive to your private parts. That is all I really saw, but I was worried. I didn't really realize he was abusive or anything. That was unthinkable. People hadn't heard about child molesters much in those days. If they did talk about it, it stayed in the family. I mean, it should stay in the family."

Agnes admits, "After it all happened, and when George moved to Colorado to work in the school for the deaf, I wanted to write that school so badly and warn them. But I thought, I can't do it because they won't do anything. It was probably just as well to not tell the people at the school, because nobody understood (pedophilia); it was just unthinkable. It just couldn't happen. I felt like I had to warn these people, but I never did."

Agnes also reveals that, "My children didn't know about your father. When we brought you and Gary and Dorene to our house, we just said that George had suffered a nervous breakdown. I thought: 'It's not up to me to tell them.'"

Agnes remembers, "Once my daughter, Susan, told me that your Daddy was a 'sloppy kisser.' I don't think he had abused her in a sexual sense, but she had thought about that event, and she didn't like it."

Agnes also says, "You know, George wasn't a bad person. So many people are that way. There is so much that is good about them, but sexual abuse is one thing that is, to me, unforgivable. I hope everybody knows: you can't trust anybody these days."

Jane, my mother's classmate at Gallaudet, and her closest friend, says, "To my regret we did not understand the warning signs. While your family was living in Langley Park, your mother once asked me my opinion of George's insistence on going around the house naked, and having the children be naked. He said it was 'healthy.' I did not tell her what I really thought about this practice because I wanted to ease her worries. One other thing that should have alerted us was the fact that he insisted on sleeping alone, with the excuse that your mother's moving around disturbed his sleep. Of course, we later realized that he just wanted to be able to go into your room and molest you without her knowing!

"As for my finally realizing he was molesting you, it wasn't until your mother caught him at it when you were living in College Park! Lots of pieces fell into

Their silence effectively permitted my father to continue molesting additional children.

place after that when your mother opened up to me more on the topic. She told me that: the Rogers would not permit their daughter, Betsy, to ride in the car alone with him. She told me that you no longer had friends sleep over at your house, but she didn't realize why. She told me that the Dobsons' oldest daughter refused to baby-sit unless your mother, not George, drove her home."

"You must understand," says Jane, "that the subject was taboo. In our circle, fathers simply did not molest their children, so to the best of my recollection we avoided the subject entirely, but rallied around your mother. I did not tell my children until they reached adulthood, since I believed it best that they not know that your father was different...that he wasn't to be trusted."

Jane remains puzzled. "I heard that he was still molesting children in Colorado and, frankly, to this day, I cannot understand why he was never formally charged with molestation...perhaps because the families of his victims did not want to face the publicity and further upset the child."

My mother's brother Harold, who later assumed something of a stepfather role towards me, told me: "The first I knew of your father's molesting you was when our parents called me to come help your mother. Your mother told us what she had seen George doing, and absolutely nobody doubted her. If your mother said it, it was true. We did what we could to limit the damage. I didn't talk with anyone else about your father's problem, because I don't understand the whole topic of pedophilia at all. I don't think many people do."

Harold remembers, "After George was discharged from the hospital, he began harassing your mother to let him come back home, or at least to let him take you children for regular visits. He didn't want to have a divorce. When he saw that she was determined, he sent some vicious letters to me and to your grandparents, threatening to spread ugly rumors and even insinuating he might physically harm them.

I never told anyone, because "he was my friend."

"Because of his threatening behaviors, I was relieved when your mother was granted a divorce and George moved on to Colorado. I didn't want to gossip about him because I was afraid he might sue for slander."

Irene Johnson, my father's second wife, has a different set of explanations for not speaking widely about Daddy's condition. Irene says, "I really admired your father when I knew him at the Colorado School for the Deaf and Blind. He was a wonderful friend and companion, and we enjoyed watching football, basketball, and wrestling together.

Calvin, Daddy's long-time business neighbor, also didn't speak to anyone about his knowledge of George's arrest for sexually assaulting a child.

"My daughter was twelve when we opened our shop next door to George.

My wife had heard about him molesting the children of friends at the School for the Deaf. My wife didn't trust George and wouldn't let our children go places alone with him. I didn't agree with her.

Our family did lots of things together with George, and, yes, he did molest my niece, a girl about the age of my daughter. My daughter still has good feelings for George, although my niece is angry about what happened. I am sad he had this problem, but I think he was just lonely. My daughter says maybe we would feel different if George had molested her too."

Gary, Me, Daddy and Dorene

Calvin admits, "Once I even bailed George out of jail after he was arrested for molesting some neighbor children near his cabin. He and I didn't talk about what had happened. I never told anyone, because "He was my friend."

Dr. Payne, a professional psychologist and one of Daddy's neighbors at Silent Valley, says, "When George was arrested and charged with molesting the three girls of our neighbors up the road, all the neighbors were talking with each other about the incident. I don't doubt that the girls made a complaint, but the family went off 'half-cocked.'

"The mother was hysterical and was picking at her daughters for details. I knew (this lady) was often overly dramatic, and so I didn't pay too much attention. I just didn't believe everything she said.

"I often talked with George and, as a psychologist as well as a marriage and sex therapist, I realized he didn't have very good social skills. He also was not very realistic about his business ideas and other plans. He operated at about a seven-year-old level emotionally and what he did was normal for that age. For him, the girls were like playmates."

Mrs. Curtis, the same woman whom Dr. Payne had called "overly dramatic," says, "My children liked your father, and George tried to be nice to them. They were lonely after school, because my husband and I had to be at work. George would pick them up from the school bus and take them home for treats. He'd also take them snowmobiling. But

I got suspicious of the way he acted – overly friendly. A part of me knew it didn't seem right, a man who was always trying to be with children.

"Then one winter day, your dad took the girls up to his place on top of the mountain. That's when he had them undress, had them touching him, and took photographs of it. When Jody told me, I was just livid. We went to see the sheriff. They came up at once. I know they found a lot of photos of other kids, of his grandchildren, of some children from up around Denver, as well as the ones of my own girls.

"What also made me angry was that my husband didn't have time to bother with it. He was always so busy with work, and just wouldn't do anything about what happened to our daughters."

The silences of all those *Knowers* whom I spoke with, described above, have ended up casting shadows. Many of these silences facilitated Daddy's abusive behavior. Wrongly focused patterns of belief about marriage and family, respect, ownership and privacy, and social concerns such as embarrassment or rejection were also causes to refrain from speaking.

The Survivors

A second group of people I interviewed, the now adult *Survivors* of George Culbertson's abuse during their childhood, remained silent for different reasons. The silence of child victims is more familiar to us. It is a silence often based on fear, shame and guilt.

As a survivor, although I cannot place these words in the context of a full memory, in my mind I hear Daddy's words, "I'm doing this because I love you, but you can't tell anyone because they won't understand. They will think we're doing something bad." I would spend twenty years keeping the secret, believing that I had done something bad and that no one would understand.

My sister, Dorene, says that she never told about Daddy having her fondle his erect penis because, "It was about sex. Sex was embarrassing and shameful." Like me, she could not tell anyone about it.

Another child, the son of one of my father's friends, said, "I don't like to bring up bad memories. It's too painful." These two children give glimpses into a common difficulty for survivors of child sexual abuse. Talking about what happened repeats the pain of the abuse.

Carolyn, who often had gone with her parents' friend George in order to

What is lacking in these explanations for silence is a view of children as people with special, and sometimes, separate, needs.

284

escape the violence in her own home, said, "I've never told anyone what happened. I wouldn't ever tell about the oral sex and the other things. It's too shameful. Also, he never forced me, I had a choice." Like so many other children, Carolyn, who was already being abused by her own father, believes that she is responsible for her own abuse.

For another of my cousins' children, the silence came from affection and concern for her Uncle George. "He called me 'pretty.' No one else ever said that about me. And, he was fun to be with and made us lots of toys. He asked me not to tell what we were doing, so I didn't. I thought he was he was lonely. I feel sad he had this problem."

Jody, my father's eleven-year-old neighbor, says, "We were friends for three or four months before it happened. He told me 'It's our little secret.' I felt like he trusted me to keep the secret."

Another child, who felt love and affection for George, was Ruth, whose family had included George in their activities since the time of her birth. She says, "I always knew him and I trusted him. I still have no hatred for him. I remember him as being kind and loving and that is why it is all so confusing." She didn't tell her parents because, "I felt like everyone knew what was going on, so it must be acceptable. It was just part of my life."

Ruth says, "I think I was afraid that, if I told the secret, he would get into trouble and I didn't want him to get into trouble. I kept telling my stepsister, 'Don't tell.' Then, when she did tell, it was kind of like all hell broke loose.

"After the first upset, my Mom and Dad just never talked about what happened. Mom did write a letter to George telling how hurt and disappointed she was, but he never responded. It felt like we all tried to act like it didn't happen. I'm sure there was a lot of guilt. My parents had completely trusted George.

"And my mother, she had been sexually abused herself when she was young... by her brother. So I think that is why she never particularly wanted to talk about it.... When I got older and told her I didn't like sex, she would tell me that this was normal for a woman. She seemed to think it was even normal a girl would be abused."

As a teenager, Ruth once revealed her abuse to a counselor. When she told the counselor she did not like men, the counselor replied, "That is your own fault. You have no respect."

Ruth also noted that as an adult she found herself dating a guy she really did

I don't like to remember bad things – it hurts inside.

Joe

not like. "But he told me that (because of my abuse history) nobody else would ever want me; so I ought to marry him, because he would be the only one who would be willing to have me."

Ruth's stepsister, Sherry, says, "When I initially told my Dad, I was afraid that he may not believe me, since (when I was a girl) I had a tendency to lie. Also, we loved George. He was a great family friend, so I didn't want to tell (on him) because I was afraid of hurting our Dad. He and George were good friends."

Children have an enormous capacity for love, and their greatest fear is disappointing or hurting the people they love. Pedophiles use a child's desire to please to manipulate the child into submitting to the abuse.

My son Joe told me, "Grampy didn't threaten us. He would say something like, 'You can't have your dinner until after you take off your clothes.'

"Grampy was always real loving and real caring, saying, 'This is nice. I do this because I love you.' Then he would talk about how sad he would be if I stopped loving him. Sometime he would even cry. It was like the abuse and love were the same thing. So I never even necessarily thought about it as a bad thing." Joe always told Grampy he would never say anything. He would never tell anybody.

"But," Joe continued, "when my therapist asked me why I didn't tell my mother what was happening, I explained that Grampy said, if we stopped loving him and told our mother, "Your Mom won't understand and she won't let you come back out here. I'll be so lonely that I'll kill myself.' It wasn't until I saw the shock on my therapist's face that I realized how awful this was.

Joe is also shadowed by guilt. "I feel responsible about Jenny. Like, if I had told after that first summer on the motorcycle trip, then it wouldn't have happened to Jenny."

Clearly Joe is not responsible for keeping his grandfather from being lonely. He is also not responsible for Jenny's abuse. I am responsible for sending both Joe and Jenny to be with my father. Hearing these words from Joe, as well as from Daddy's other victims, is so painful and shocking.

My father had repeated to my own children the same reason he had given me to keep the secret – "Your mother won't understand." And Joe recalls words that clarify the deep feelings I have always carried, "I am having sex with you because I love you. This abuse is the same as love. If you stop letting me abuse you, that means you have stopped loving me. If you stop loving me I will be so lonely I will die."

What an impossible situation for a child! "Telling the secret means you betray our friendship. Telling the secret means you don't love me. Telling the secret will destroy me."

My daughter Jenny says it most powerfully. "Sometimes I still can see Grampy's blood splattered on his bedroom wall, all over a pretty design I had painted for him when I was eleven. Grampy said that if we told about the sex then you wouldn't let us visit, and he would be lonely and kill himself. So we didn't tell; but he killed himself anyway."

How I wish my daughter did not have those memories.

Survivors of my father's abuse displayed an entirely different set of concerns, including shame, pain, guilt and misplaced trust, as reasons not to directly address what had happened to them. Many had experienced traumatic amnesia, anxiety, and feelings of personal worthlessness and suicidal thoughts. I ask myself, "How can society expect these victims to speak, if we ourselves will not?"

Numerous childhood friends and neighbors who had frequent contact with my father, told me they did not remember him. There is no way to know if their lack of memory is because nothing significant happened or because something very traumatic happened.

Dissociation, the lack of "intact, integrated" memory, can prevent *Survivors* from talking about their abuse. Many of the survivors of my father's abuse, including Joe and Jenny and myself, do not have full memories of what happened. Nevertheless, these survivors remember enough to "know."

For example, I remember that something happened with my father. I can't visualize what happened, but I remember he used to say, "I'm doing this because I love you."

Joe, on the first night of the motorcycle trip, remembers that "Grampy gave me a backrub. After that I don't remember what happened, but the next day I was sick and throwing up. I remember other stuff he did to me later on the trip, but I'm sure it happened the first night, too."

You can't have your dinner until after you take off your clothes.

> *Grampy said that if we told about the sex then you wouldn't let us visit, and he would be lonely and kill himself. So we didn't tell; but he killed himself anyway.*

Ruth asked me to take her to see Silent Valley because, "I know what happened, and I remember some of it, but I don't remember most of the details." Ruth hoped that returning to the location of the abuse would help her "get back my memories."

One *Survivor* told me, "I hate to be naked. I hate men's bodies. I get anxious and nauseated when I see a penis."

Ruth says, "Even just seeing a nude body, in a movie or something, I get so upset. How could people be doing that?" As a teenager visiting a friend who would go around in her home in her bra and panties, she recalled how this caused her to feel horrified. "I don't mind intercourse, because George never did that," she says. "I just don't like taking my clothes off."

Another woman revealed that, "When I change my baby's diaper, I feel afraid I might touch her in a bad way. I don't want my own abuse to affect my daughter."

Avoiding sex and emotional intimacy are common responses for survivors of childhood sexual abuse. These traumatic childhood events cast long shadows across the years.

The Betrayers

My father's relatives had a variety of concerns and reasons for not speaking out about his abusive activities. When I asked them about secrets and silences, the responses were personal and distressed. I have chosen the word *"Betrayer"* to describe these members of my father's family whose silence betrayed their own children. I do not use the word *Betrayer* lightly. A *Betrayer* is someone who delivers us into the hands of the enemy. Because of divided loyalty, each of us delivered our children over to our loved one, who was also "the enemy." I include myself in this group.

When I was ten and my mother discovered my father molesting me, she was advised by her social worker to not discuss with me what had happened, because "it might upset Joyce." My brother, Gary, and my sister, Dorene, were not told the reason for our parents' divorce. My mother and I did not discuss my childhood abuse until forty years later.

Mother decided that she needed to obtain a divorce from her husband in order to protect her children. She informed George's two sisters of what he had done to his daughter. The sisters, Elizabeth and Eleanor, did not want to tell their mother, Hannah, what had happened. But when Hannah became angry

288

thinking my mother had caused the divorce, Elizabeth and Eleanor thought that knowing the real reason would help her understand.

When Hannah learned what her son had done to his daughter she went into a deep depression and died without ever fully recovering. Her daughters believed she "died of a broken heart."

George's older sister, Elizabeth, told her sons, Andy (age eighteen) and Scott (age thirteen), what had happened because she worried that there might be some genetic problem and wanted to warn them not to act on "impulses." However, she mentioned it only once, when they were young. Elizabeth says, "It was never mentioned again."

Elizabeth also says, "I didn't tell our daughter Liz, because she didn't need to know and think about her Uncle George that way. Why should she carry around a memory like that of her uncle whom she always loved?"

Liz, tells me, "When I was twelve, George came to California to visit us. Mom didn't tell me what he had done to you, but she was protective. She didn't let me hug, stand too close, or sit on his lap. No touching inappropriately. She was vague, and said, "You know how men get." I knew there was "something."

When Liz moved back to Colorado with her three young children, they enjoyed numerous visits with Uncle George. Liz recalls, "I think my mom told me about George molesting some kids and told me to be careful of my children around George, but I forgot. What do you call that? Repression? I've asked my kids about George and they all say they don't remember anything, so I haven't mentioned it. I like everything to stay calm. I don't like to make waves."

Liz's youngest daughter, Stephanie, does not remember Uncle George. Liz's oldest child, Charles, and her daughter, Nancy, were both abused by George, but each kept this secret.

Aunt Elizabeth later wrote to me. "I understand that it is important to talk about abuse to help protect children, but why do you have to make it personal and talk in our family? Do you really have to tell my children? What good will it do? I know your memories are painful but can't you go to a psychologist, who can help you get it all out and vent your anger? Then you can begin enjoying your family and your future life ahead. We know you are suffering, but how is publishing this book going to help your very worthy cause of trying to prevent sexual abuse of children? Wouldn't it be better for you to forgive and forget?

I don't want my own abuse to affect my daughter.

"Every time I read it in the paper or hear on TV about child sexual abuse, I get angry enough to hit them. The memory that George did this too, it hurts so deeply. When I heard about what your father had done, I was so shocked and hurt. I felt sorry for your mother and you, and so angry with my brother as a man who would do such a thing to his little girl. The memories are painful. I'd rather let go of them and I wish you would."

After receiving this letter from my aunt, I wrote back and told her I was puzzled. "I know that in your family, you have experienced divorce, alcoholism, suicide and other difficulties. Why is it possible to talk about those events but not about what my father did?"

"Because," Elizabeth, replied, "incest is so much worse. Can't you give your burden over to the Lord and forget it? Please try, dear."

Her letter was signed: "We love you and always will, no matter what. Aunt Elizabeth and Uncle Andrew."

Eleanor, my father's younger sister, told me, "You can't imagine how hard it's been on Elizabeth and me, hearing in the news about what these men do to little children, knowing our brother was one of them. I never told my children about what your father did to you. They loved Uncle George. What good would it do to destroy a child's faith in someone? I hope you can understand."

Eleanor's daughter, Karen, invited me to her home during my first trip to Colorado. We talked for several hours. I told her about the purpose of my trip and about my recent discovery that my father had molested my own children.

Karen's husband, William, was dismissive about any concern regarding Daddy's deeds. During an interview on the same visit to Colorado, he recalls, "We bailed your father out of jail. I think he hated himself but couldn't stop what he was doing. Today I'm fine with it."

Unfortunately, it would later be discovered that their son Paul had not only been abused by my father, but that he would himself become an abuser.

On behalf of Joe and Jenny, a relative also makes a plea for silence. "Pedophiles and child molesters make me sad and angry. I feel helpless," he said. "Let your father rest in peace. He has nieces, nephews, sisters. If you are the relative of a pedophile, people use such a thing against you. There is shame. It's a crime, it's evil, and people cannot accept it.

"I believe you first need to protect Joe and Jenny; you don't know where their lives are going; you don't know where the culture is going. Many pedophiles,

Why is it possible to talk about
divorce, alcoholism, suicide and
other difficulties, but not about
incest?

and their protectors, have a lot of power. What you write today is going to come out someplace later. Somebody is going to trace it.

"Be careful. Protect our families and children. We're not the ones at risk, they are. It's a shame you have to be so careful, but you can't take the emotional and social risk. Consider the impact your speaking might have on our children."

We must tell what we know.

What my relatives did is what most of us do when faced with the shadow's impact upon our lives. But these acts have a terrible ripple-effect. They create lifelong consequences upon the lives of the next generation.

This is our light of truth.

I believe we must tell what we know. We must tell it actively. This is our light of truth. This is our most powerful ray of healing. Only this kind of speaking can greatly diminish the intensity of the silent shadow.

If we decide to speak out about incest, we cannot avoid embarrassment and discomfort. We cannot assume that respecting marriage and family is best for children. We cannot afford to remain silent.

We need to become educated about child development, about children's needs and rights, about human sexuality, and especially about the traumatic effects of abuse, so that our beliefs will be based on fact. We need to find the strength and the courage to make protection of children our most important value.

As all of these stories from friends, family and survivors clearly show, childhood sexual abuse is not over when it's over. We all live together in its dark and silent shadow.

Chapter Eighteen

Leaving Silent Valley

(1994-2002)

Me

"Fountain of sorrow, fountain of light.
You've known the hollow sound of your own
steps in flight.

You've had to struggle,
you've had to fight.
To keep understanding
and compassion in sight."

– Song by Jackson Browne

My father once told his sister, Elizabeth, "I'll never be in a rest home. I'll know what to do." In late November of 1985, his pedophilia cost him the irrevocable loss of his only remaining circle of friends. The Central Colorado Outdoors Association broke apart in sorrow, shock, anger, and disbelief over what George had done to one of their children. Some were horrified to realize that over the past eighteen years he may have also abused other children during their frequent hikes at Silent Valley. Others, however, refused to believe that he had done anything wrong at all.

Daddy had "desperately wanted to regain a degree of self respect," and, faced with this final shame, he had known what to do. Just as his own abuser, his uncle Ralph, had done decades earlier, he chose to take his own life.

To his children, Daddy addressed a brief postscript to his suicide note: "I love you all so very much and I'm truly sorry; I feel that what I'm about to do is necessary and best. Please don't regret – just forgive." For many years, these few words would be all the solace I had, my only road map for laying to rest the hurt of his many invasions of my own and my family's life.

But the rebuilding of my world was soon to start. After several years of courtship, Freeman and I celebrated our marriage, on a crisp, red-leafed fall day on the lawn of "Mountain Magic," our new Virginia home. Our parents and nearly forty of our friends were there with us. We created a blended family, with my children Joe and Jenny becoming elder siblings to Freeman's sons, Daniel and Gabriel.

I changed my professional focus from child psychiatric nursing to specialization as a licensed psychotherapist, and began a decade of teaching and private counseling practice.

I am no longer alone with my incest, alone with Daddy's suicide, alone with Gary's death, alone with my shame, anger, and grief.

Immersed in a new life, with a supportive husband and a job I loved, I was able finally to break the silence with my own mother and ask her to attend counseling with me. This speaking collapsed the huge wall that had existed between us.

In 1997, Joe, Jenny and I drove up into Silent Valley together again, along the same curved and rutted dusty road we traveled after Daddy and my brother, Gary, died. This time though, twelve years later, we are not alone.

My husband, Freeman, who now has been Joe and Jenny's stepfather for ten years, is with us. Mom – Joe and Jenny's Grammy– is with us, too, as is Henry, Mom's husband of two years.

We have come to Silent Valley together, the six of us, to let Mom see the place where Gary died, and we have planned to have a small memorial ritual, some acts and words performed together that will bring closure to all the pain our family has endured.

When we turn off the main highway and begin the series of turns that will lead us higher into the mountains and forests where Silent Valley is hidden, Joe and Jenny and I find ourselves searching our memories to recall how to find this long-ago place. We all remember the dramatically beautiful array of red rocks at the entrance, rocks which, when younger, we had named and even claimed.

"The Turtle, that's my favorite, it's mine!" In my mind, I can hear the childish laughter and shouts of my siblings, and later those of my children.

Finally we see the sign, a hand painted wooden arrow marking the entrance to "Silent Valley." We come to a clearing, and there before us is Silent Valley itself. It is, as always, overwhelming, both in its beauty and in the pain it evokes.

The moss-covered stone and cedar-shingled cottage that George so skillfully built is still there, across the stream – the home of Daddy's dreams and Gary's death. As we park the car and prepare to walk toward the cottage, Joe and Jenny indicate that they prefer not to participate in the ritual. Instead, they move in the opposite direction, walking off together in what must be a poignantly familiar way, to climb up to the top of the tall rocks, the same place I used to go to find solitude in my summer visits to Silent Valley.

Mom and Henry, Freeman and I walk quietly toward the cottage. We explore around the outside and peek in a few windows. I point to the kitchen. "That's where Gary and I had our soup together before he went to sleep. There in the living room, that's where Joe and Jenny were watching TV. Through the door back there – that's where Gary's bed was. That's where he died and where we found his body in the morning."

Freeman, Me and Mom by the Fire

Mom is quiet, nodding her head, holding Henry's hand. "I feel better," she says. "Gary died in a beautiful, peaceful place."

We each write brief notes on paper to Gary and to Daddy, telling them our losses and our hopes. I write, "Gary, I wish you were here with us today. Silent Valley will always be a part of my memories of you, but you are never gone from my life."

To my father, I write, "Daddy, I'm sad for all the suffering – yours and ours. I hope you have a way to help and participate in the healing. God bless you."

Freeman has built a small fire, sheltered by some rocks from the cold wind that is blowing. As we gather around the fire and read our messages to Daddy and to Gary out loud, to each other and to them, it begins to snow!

It had snowed the night Gary died, but that was in November. We are gathered here together on an afternoon in early May. I am convinced that Daddy and Gary found a way to let us know they were watching and listening.

After each message is read it is placed in the fire to be burned to ash and to blow across the valley. We close our eyes for the holy and healing silence, and our tears blend with the snowflakes that are melting on our cheeks.

As we turn to look across the valley, we can see the small, distant figures of Joe and Jenny seated on top of the high rocks. Between us, unseen, I sense the presence of family and friends, and others whom we do not even know, as all the ashes of their stories blow out of Silent Valley one last time.

I recognize that Silent Valley is forever changed for me by this moment. I am no longer alone with my incest, alone with Daddy's suicide, alone with Gary's death, alone with my shame, anger, and grief. By speaking my story and listening to others, by allowing myself to return to the pain and allowing others to come in with me, and especially by risking and discovering the blessing of safe and loving relationships, my experience and my memory of Silent Valley from now on will be one of intimacy, support, and change.

Jenny and Joe

Mom and Henry walk hand-in-hand across the valley; Freeman and I walk with arms around each other; Joe and Jenny walk down from the rocks, not young children this time but strong, wise adults.

We are all silent, but no longer locked into the silence of secrets. For the moment, there is simply nothing more to say. As we meet each other at the car the snow stops, the wind calms. We look around once more at a place that will always be the location of some of our saddest memories, but no longer is a cause of fear or shame.

We drive out, three generations of a family, together. I remember when Jenny, Joe and I had driven away from Silent Valley the last time the radio was playing, "Freedom's just another word for nothing left to lose." Now I understand that actually it is the loss of fear that creates real freedom. In letting go of fear – in being willing to encounter and immerse myself in the pain – I have discovered the greater freedom of truth.

As we reach the place where the road bends away from the valley, Joe and Jenny ask Freeman to stop the car and help them remove the arrow pointing the way to Silent Valley. They all take turns pulling and twisting, laughing together about how solid the arrow is and how firmly anchored it is in the ground. Joe and Jenny remember their grandfather's workmanship and competence as a builder, but with a final tug the arrow is loose and they toss it into the car. There is a sense of accomplishment and completion.

It's easier to find our way out. After all, this is the road where three of us, as children bumping along in Daddy's old truck, each had learned to drive! We come to the field dotted with the red rocks. "I like that big one in the middle," I say. "I think I'll call it 'The Lighthouse.'"

"You can't have that one," Jenny laughs. "That one belongs to me."

Holding the sign that Grampy made, Joe keeps his eyes on the road. I see that he is smiling, too.

Joe is living in New Mexico now, working a project examining links between teen pregnancy and sexual abuse. With summer days that easily reach over one hundred degrees, Joe has learned to wake early for his morning run with his two dogs. With our two-hour time difference, we have found mornings a good time to talk by phone as we each drink our black coffee from equally large mugs. So, despite the early Sunday morning hour, when the phone rings, I answer, knowing already that it will be Joe.

"So," he says, "are you excited? What's it like to get a new father when you're fifty-six-years-old?"

"What's it like for you to get a new grandfather?" I answer

Today, Father's Day of 2001, Dorene and I will be adopted by our stepfather, Henry. We have already completed the legal process but this morning there will be a "ceremony of commitment" at Mom and Henry's church.

Joe is unable to join us in person, but he is clearly with us in spirit. We reflect on the coincidence of Mom meeting Henry during the same year that Joe and Jenny disclosed their incest by their Grampy.

"Remember," I tell him, "Elisabeth Kubler-Ross says 'There are no coincidences.'"

In the time since I got his letter saying he "wanted to talk about what happened during the summers in Colorado," Joe's life has taken a number of turns. He had wandered somewhat uncertainly and unsettled for a few years, in a manner reminiscent of my brother, his uncle Gary. By 1997, though, Joe began to chart a course for himself and settled in New Mexico, one of the wildest and most appealing landscapes he had discovered on his travels.

Joe had married a delightful young woman in Albuquerque whom he had known only briefly. A few months thereafter he had begun to have intense sexual abuse flashbacks and emotional responses, and had participated with her in marriage counseling. Realizing he had married for the wrong reasons and could not continue, he had divorced less than a year after the marriage.

For the past two years, while obtaining a Master's degree, Joe also began therapy to deal with the effects of his abuse. Joe began to work weekly with a trained therapist and also enrolled in a support group for male survivors. At age thirty-one, his self-awareness surprises me. He and I have become able to talk openly and honestly about our family and our feelings.

Today he tells me how happy he is that Freeman and Henry have joined our family, and that he has these new father and grandfather models. "I've always had my Dad on Father's Day, but I never could really think about Grampy. I wish I could be there with you today. Give everybody my love."

Dorene, Henry and Me

As the summer morning birdsong reaches its peak and the hummingbirds dart eagerly to their feeder, I settle with my coffee into my porch rocking chair. I'm sorry Freeman is not able to be here today. His mother is ill and he is visiting her, but last night we talked on the phone and celebrated the excitement of this year's Father's Day.

Freeman and Henry share the bond of being nurturing men for this wounded family. Freeman and I, in our now fourteen years of marriage, have encountered the usual challenges about household roles, child discipline, and financial priorities. But he has also patiently accompanied me on this long and often painful journey to learn more about my father's pedophilia.

Besides Joe and Freeman, the other family member who will miss the adoption ceremony is Gabe, my youngest stepson. Now nineteen years old, he is in Costa Rica for the summer, working on a rainforest regeneration project as part of his college's Environmental Studies internship.

Joining me on the porch this morning, instead of Freeman, is Jenny. Last evening she drove in from her home almost two hours away so she could be with us for the adoption ceremony. Like Joe, Jenny has been making her own moves toward maturity and independence. She has not encountered the type of emotional shock-waves from the abuse that Joe and I experienced, and so has not been inclined toward therapy or support groups.

Rather, she has focused her attention on the empowerment and job skill needs of "at-risk" youth, and women prisoners. Jenny is pursuing a Masters Degree, planning to work in the non-profit community action sector. She also is working with a group of women in a local prison. She has become well aware of the high proportion of women in jail, with drug problems, or on welfare, who have a history of childhood abuse.

This morning though, before the adoption ceremony, we are not focused on the sexual abuse of others, or our own. We are deciding what to wear to church. Jenny has brought her light blue dress with white flowers, and I will wear a burgundy dress with cream-colored flowers. We decide that it is sufficiently hot to go in sandals.

Daniel, Freeman's older son, now a tall, muscular twenty-five-year-old, will meet us at the church in a little while, joining us from his apartment in town. Dorene and her husband, Rick will be meeting us there.

The church where we will have the adoption ceremony is the same church where Mom and Henry met, and where they were married in 1995. There is a small group of deaf members who worship regularly with the rest of the congregation and all of the services, including the songs, are interpreted into sign language. This church provides a warm, caring community for its deaf members.

Jenny and I finish dressing and eat a quick breakfast, saving room for the Father's Day buffet at Henry's favorite restaurant planned for after the ceremony. Driving to church, I feel inside the sense of grace and blessing which has been so inexplicably woven into our family's pain and tragedy of the past seven years.

In many ways, my family died when I was a little girl. My father was not caring for me as a parent. He forced me into secrets I could not share with my mother or my siblings, nor with my grandparents, aunts or uncles. I was alone in the world.

I remember a statement by Dr. Kubler-Ross, as she addressed an audience at the National Cathedral in Washington, DC: "Incest is the worst experience of grief. At the moment when the incest first occurs, the child's entire family dies."

When I was trying to be a mother to Joe and Jenny, part of me remained alone and deadened. My children, too, grew up with the "death" of their family, without being able to share their real life with their mother or other relatives.

For Christmas of 1993, Jenny placed photos she had taken of Freeman and me and of herself and her three brothers into a collage frame. On the back she wrote, "Thanks for making us into a family."

This new sense of "family" – Freeman and me committed to our marriage, both parents committed to all our children, children respectful of each other – is what I believe created a solid foundation and became the basis of our survival.

When Joe and Jenny revealed their secrets in 1994, they had joined Mom and me for several sessions with our counselor, Ted. All four of us were able to speak and to listen to the guilt, anger and grief that was flooding us.

Mom explained to Joe and Jenny what had happened in her marriage to their

Daddy forced me into secrets I could not share with my mother or my siblings, nor with my grandparents, aunts or uncles.

I was alone in the world.

Grampy. They were able to ask questions and hear honest answers. Afterward, Jenny wrote a letter to her grandmother:

> "I want to say thank you for dealing with all this Grampy stuff. I know it has been really hard and really painful, but I thank you for finding the strength to do it…I hope you know that no one holds you responsible for what Grampy did. He was a very sick man, and you did everything right…Whenever I feel powerless or weak, I remember that I come from a family of strong women, and that I am really strong too. Thank you for that strength, and for all the loving you have taught me."

Once during a counseling session with Ted, Jenny confronted me. I listened to her anger at how I was "always trying to talk about it" and how I needed to "stop being so weird." With Ted's support, both my children told me they were tired of hearing me go on and on about their "terrible childhood."

"You know," Joe said, "Jenny and I do volunteer work and we see lots of families with problems. No one in our family has dropped out of school, is on drugs, has an unwanted pregnancy, or is in jail. I think we have the best family I know of."

Knowing that I had sent my children to many summers of their own abuse, this felt like surprising news: that, even so, they thought our family had lots of positive and valuable strengths. The generous, straight-in-the-eye look they gave me when they said they could forgive me for what I did helped us transition into a family willing and able to deal with truth, and to experience and express the accompanying emotions which sad, hard truths may bring.

We have had our time to keep silence. We have claimed our time to speak.

During the ensuing years, as my intention for writing this book took shape and followed its own almost inevitable course, each member of the family found a way to speak, to participate in the healing.

Our community, like many others nationwide, has an annual Vigil for Survivors of Child Sexual Abuse, sponsored by our local Sexual Assault Resource Agency. Freeman has accompanied me to these vigils each year since we moved here in 1987. In 1994, after learning about her grandchildren's abuse, Mom also attended the Vigil with us. However, in 1996, when I asked Mom if she would actively participate in the Vigil with me by speaking about the healing that had occurred in our relationship, she said shyly, "Oh, I couldn't do that."

Henry, her new husband and my new stepfather, reached across the lunch table, took her hand, and said, "Yes, you can. I'll help you. We have to talk about it. Don't you remember when parents used to be ashamed of their deaf children? We can't be ashamed to tell what happened in our family."

I had begun to understand that Henry was our family's good father, but I was still surprised and touched by his offer to interpret at the Vigil. It wasn't until a year later, when he accompanied us all to Silent Valley that one last time, that my heart was able to feel the depth of his taking care. In our last ritual, he never criticized our Daddy. He gave unconditional love and help to my Mom, and to her children and grandchildren.

And so, at the Vigil that April, Mom signed as Henry interpreted for her, speaking about the guilt and pain of learning her daughter had been abused. She ended by saying "My daughter is a survivor and, as the mother of a survivor, so am I."

Me, Mom and Dorene

Two years later, at the 1998 Vigil for Survivors, Joe asked Jenny to come with him. With Freeman and me sitting on one side and Jenny on the other, he mustered his courage to walk up front and speak publicly for the first time about his pain.

Joe and Jenny's stepbrothers began speaking, too. Daniel had talked to college friends about his family. Some of them had confided their own abuse secrets to him. He was able to understand and give them open and heartfelt acceptance.

Gabe found a different way to be involved. With close friends at his high school, he began participating in a group called "Voices for Interpersonal Violence Alternatives" (VIVA). This frank, outspoken group of teenagers developed a performance which they put on for high school audiences throughout our area, helping their peers learn to identify and speak out about power issues in relationships – whether in school or at home. The message was clear – it is not OK for someone to treat you badly. You can tell someone. You can ask for help. Gabe performed with VIVA for two years.

While our Virginia family was beginning to speak about incest and get involved in various activities, my sister, Dorene, continued to live in Ohio, feeling that she was not really involved. When I first interviewed her for the book, she could only say she wanted me "to go away, so she wouldn't have to think about it.

Not long afterward, I received a videotape of an Oprah Winfrey in the mail. On the program Oprah interviewed parents who had not realized their child was being molested, who told how they made the discovery and what actions they took. Dorene had taped it for me. My sister's gesture felt like her way of saying, "I'm on your side."

After Dorene's youngest son graduated from high school and moved to his own apartment, she and her husband sold their home in Ohio and came to live in Virginia, near Mom and me.

Dorene was no longer "outside" the family. We were sisters anew, and friends, too.

By now, in 1999, I was in a second semester of a writing Fellowship at VFH All these years of talking, writing, day after day focusing on incest and sexual abuse. Sometimes I am tired, sometimes overwhelmed. I have learned to take care of myself in so many ways. Other members of the family are doing that too. We see therapists when we need to unravel emotional and relationship knots. We have come to value bodywork – massage, movement, yoga; spiritual and intuitive practices like meditation, healing energy, and dream work. When the incest history seems to affect our marriage, Freeman and I see my counselor. From time to time I still see Cathie, my own gifted therapist and healer. Joe is still connected to his support group. Jenny is pursuing yoga and art.

My therapist said once, "Your family has been a stagnant lake. It needs truth and tears to cleanse it."

A year ago, in spring of 2000, I completed my Fellowship and began the final revising of this long-time-coming book. It had taken seven years. It could not have happened faster, and it could not have happened in a better way. I am convinced that by paying attention to what hurt, honestly naming and expressing our fears and angers and sadnesses, that every one of us in my family have become stronger and healthier in these years.

Now, on this June day in 2001, Father's Day, we are coming together to honor our new father and grandfather. This story is almost like a fairy-tale, with its happy-ever-after ending. The blessing of Henry coming into our lives, marrying our mother, adopting us as his daughters, was never imagined. I know it is not likely to happen to many other survivors.

We are remarkably fortunate.

Henry does not replace our father. Like every adopted child, Dorene and I will always have our "biological" father and our "adopted" father. Our lives will always have the mark of George Culbertson, for better and for worse.

We are leaving Silent Valley.

For so many years, our family's attention has been focused on the past, focused on my father. We have had our time to keep silence. We have claimed our time to speak. "To everything there is a season"… a time to heal, a time to break down, and a time to build up.

Today, our family conversations include discussions of favorite music, car maintenance problems, whose turn is it to cook or wash the dishes. Sitting together around the dinner table – some of us survivors of sexual abuse, and some who are not – our talks help remind me: sexual abuse is not all of who we are. It is just a part of our life – woven into the whole. It is still noticeable, but no longer prominent.

We are leaving Silent Valley.

Epilogue

A Family Legacy

Paul

"He's somebody's brother, he's somebody's son.
Don't sit and pass judgment
for the things he has done.
His life didn't turn out the way that he planned,
But he's somebody's brother,
He's somebody's friend."

– Song by Anita Holt

In the winter of 1998, I received a phone call from my cousin William. "I have to talk with you," he said.

I could tell it was going to be something bad.

"It's about our son, Paul," William continued. "When he was about twenty-one years old, he came into my bedroom one night. He had been drinking, and he was crying, saying he wanted to tell me something. He said that your father George had molested him – fondled him, masturbated him, had oral sex with him – all through his childhood. At the time, I told Paul I was sorry, but these things are part of life. We didn't talk about it again after that night."

"Well," William went on, "Now something else has happened. Paul is in jail. He's in jail for molesting his own sons. I'm calling to ask if you think that what your father did to Paul might have something to do with why Paul did this to his own boys?"

With a deep, sad sigh I answered, "I'm so sorry, William. This must be so painful for you. Yes, I think all the abuse might be connected. I wish it had ended when my father died."

I could tell it was going to be something bad.

I ask for Paul's address and say I am available to talk with him about anything, anytime. As we say goodbye, I tell William, "I hope you'll share with Paul how concerned I am for him. When you talk with him next time, please tell him I would love to hear from him if he'd like to speak with me. Maybe it would help to talk with someone who understands what he's been through."

When William hangs up, my mind is reeling. I thought it was over. I don't want to know this. Oh, God, No, Why?

My body is rigid, electric. For now I see a five-generation heritage of child sexual abuse, woven throughout my family's history. Not four generations. Now it's five. Five generations of hardworking, devoted, responsible family members doing unspeakable and unnameable things to children.

Great-uncle Ralph, abusing my father during the nineteen-twenties and thirties; Daddy continuing it with his own children, nieces, and nephews through the forties, fifties, sixties, seventies, eighties; and now one of those nephews, Paul, abusing his own two boys in the nineties. Nearly a century in silence, in shadow. A one hundred year family legacy of pain.

I have inherited many wonderful gifts from my father. We who are his family are blessed with intelligence, good humor, a love of the outdoors, dedication to family, a sense of adventure, physical and emotional strength and, not least, excellent health. But a correct accounting of the wealth and debt of my family must include, as well, a legacy of incest and betrayal.

I wait to hear from my cousin's son, Paul, this thirty-one-year-old young man who is the same age as my son Joe, and who spent summers at Silent Valley with Joe and Jenny.

Paul is in jail for molesting his own children. Is he innocent like my children or is he guilty like my father? The bleakest chapter in my father's legacy of betrayals has waited eleven years before emerging from the shadow cast by his suicide.

Days later, the voice on the phone is Paul. He has called me from a jail detention room, and other men are in line waiting to use the phone.

I tell Paul I am glad to hear his voice. He is concerned that I might not want to talk with him, since he has done the same thing to his children that my father did to me and to my children, Joe and Jenny.

Part of me agrees. I do not want to know any more. I want this story to end, to be finished. Wanting to not know, wanting to not hear about it, wanting it to not be true – of course I feel that way. That is how so many relatives and friends have felt as our family incest tragedy has been revealed.

Five generations of hardworking, devoted, responsible family members doing unspeakable and unnamable things to children.

304

But into the phone I am able to say, "We're family, Paul. We don't know each other very well, but we have a lot in common. I'm so sorry that my father molested you, and I'd be glad if you and I could talk about it openly. You know, my father molested me, and also Joe and Jenny, but today I work with survivors of child sexual abuse. I'm willing to listen to anything you'd like to talk to me about."

"I'm sorry I lied to you, Joyce," Paul replies. "When you visited me two years ago researching your book, I didn't want to talk about it. But it's true. When I was a kid, George would make me masturbate him, and then he did the same to me. He liked to be nude, and used to do stuff to me 'til my parents got home. I never told anyone about what happened with George and me.

"Then when I was nineteen or twenty, one night I was pretty drunk. I guess you could say there's been alcoholism all over my family, Joyce. Dad and I were drinking together the night before my brother's wedding. Anyway, I had a few strange behavior patterns, and my dad started asking me questions about me using drugs, the troubles in my marriage – he knew something was wrong with me.

"It seemed like my dad was always questioning me about George. This time, finally, I told him bits and pieces. He knew, or guessed the rest, and got what had happened out of me."

"'Was it George?' Dad asked me. When I told him, 'Yes,' Dad said, 'I knew it, damnit!' But after that one time talking about it, the whole thing became a forbidden subject. We never mentioned it again."

Paul tells me he can remember, as a child, Daddy being nude when visiting his home in Denver. "Back then, my mom just said, 'That's his thing,'" said Paul. "And when we'd be up at Silent Valley, George would wake me and Joe up and tell us, 'It's a beautiful day to be naked outdoors.'

"Once when I was ten, he visited, and (in the back room) he always would have his penis hanging out of his shorts. So I told mom. I know I wanted George to get in trouble, but when she confronted him about it, I ended up looking like a little tattletale. Belts were popular in our family, and mom began slapping and hitting me because I had told about George.

"About a year and a half later, George came in the bedroom and began to fondle me," Paul continued on the phone. "There wasn't any oral sex; I don't know why I even let him do it. I felt manipulated."

Paul had only known one other report of Daddy abusing children during the time he stayed at their home. His mother was crying as she talked with George in the living room. Later she told Paul, "George is in trouble for being naked in the mountains with two little girls."

I never told anyone about what happened with George and me.

"I wonder why, if Mom knew George's history, she would have let me go to be with him so much?" said Paul. "I guess when I was a kid Mom wasn't home a lot."

It's funny, but I still love him.

Paul and I agree that he will telephone me whenever he is able to, that Freeman and I will always accept his calls, and that I want to continue to support him. He concludes our conversation with a final reminiscence about Daddy:

"He was one heck of a guy, your dad. It's not like he was a hard-ass, he was a good man. He and my dad always got along. It was just fun, being with George – volleyball, snowmobiling, motorcycle rides, swimming; I always had a real good time." Paul pauses, then concludes, "It's funny, but I still love him..."

I realize how important it will be to stay in as close touch as possible with Paul. First and foremost, I feel tremendous compassion for this young man, both for the suffering of imprisonment he must now go through, as well as for the grief he is bearing about the breakup of his family, the hurt he has done to the sons I know he loves.

And there is a second reason I must give Paul all the support I can. In a strange way, he has become the unwilling inheritor of George Culbertson's lifetime practice of inflicting emotional and physical harm on children. Due to substantial changes in the legal consequences of pedophile offending, Paul will endure the substantial time behind bars that Daddy chose to avoid by committing suicide.

I must do everything I can to learn about the treatment available for helping him, and, with Paul's agreement, resolve to find a way in which his story too can contribute to our breaking the silence that surrounds the subject of child sexual abuse.

Periodically, over the years between this first phone call and the present, I will talk with Paul many times. The phone will ring one evening in the quiet kitchen of our peaceful mountain home, and when I pick it up a cold, metallic voice will recite, "You have a collect call from an inmate in the Colorado State Penitentiary. To decline this call, press 2. To accept this call, press 1."

As we come to know each other better, he will share, with remarkable honesty and courage, the process of his prison-mandated psychotherapy and treatment plan. Paul tells me he has flashbacks sometimes, and replays what he did to his children. "I know what I did to my stepson, but also, that I was a good father. I was always there for him. I just always liked children. It was like I was considered the best dad in the neighborhood, and all the kids used to come over to my place to play. I knew better, but didn't understand the consequences. My kids still love me, but now I can't see them anymore."

During the succeeding years, Paul will share his feelings about a variety of topics related to his own changing internal perceptions about himself as an abuser. He reveals more of his father's efforts at controlling abuse of alcohol, and admits his upbringing involved a lot of shoving and physical punishment from his parents. He spent a lot of time alone as a boy, and admits he is still a loner ("It keeps me out of trouble in here.").

Another time, we discuss how his family has continued to respond to the offenses Paul is charged with. "Granny Eleanor and my Mom are angry with you, Joyce, for writing your book. They told me, 'Now the whole world's going to know about our family.' "Its funny, my Mom is more upset with me for what I did to my kids than she is with George for what he did to me all those times."

As our years of sporadic phone talking goes on, Paul's sentence will become extended to seven years. The parents of neighbor children, it develops, have also brought abuse charges against him. His concern becomes focused, more and more, on treatment possibilities.

"I've finally been accepted by the Fremont program, Joyce," Paul tells me when I pick up the phone one evening in 1999. "I'll be transferred to Cañon City, near where Granny lives. It's a large state operation called the East Colorado Correctional Complex, and is specifically set up for SO's (sexual offenders)." He has been waiting a long time for this news, and I can hear the excitement in his voice. Paul will spend from six to eighteen months in the Fremont program, and the treatment will be intensive and difficult.

Finally, in October of 2000, Paul became a candidate for the Arrowhead Facility, the beginning of Phase Two of his treatment. He was still in prison, but successful completion of this stage, plus Paul's submission of an "approved living plan" on the outside, could lead to his release and parole. "This segment won't be easy," Paul told me. "The program is really hard on us; only sixteen of us from Phase One have qualified for entry. You don't realize how hard it is even to get into the Fremont program. Just to get on the waiting list took years of work."

Paul tells me he is beginning to think about his final project, part of the requirements for his probation, which he now forecasts may come in September of 2002. "This project lets the parole board know who you are, and also let's me know who I think I am. It will show I am totally out of denial, and will never re-offend. I guess I am deeper into the program than I ever thought possible. Most SO's never even attempt to go through this sort of therapy. They just wait in jail for their sentence to be up."

In the fall of 2000, I attend the Association for the Treatment of Sexual Abusers (ATSA) annual conference in San Diego, accompanied by Freeman. I arrange my return flights so I can stop off in Cañon City, Colorado, where Paul is now incarcerated. For several years, it has felt important, despite the geographical distance separating us, that I visit him face-to-face. On the phone, Paul is

I was considered the best dad in the neighborhood, and all the kids used to come over to my place to play.

enthusiastic about the possibility and makes arrangements to get permission for a "special visit." I will be allowed to see him during Sunday visiting hours.

I arrive at the guard station at eight a.m. and there are already a number of people ahead of me. Following the simple signs and direction, I fill out my visitor's form, hand it to a guard, have the computer verify that I have been approved for my "special visit," put a ten-dollar bill into a change machine, place all my quarters and my drivers license and my car keys into a plastic bowl, walk through a metal scanner, open my mouth for inspection, remove my shoes for inspection, retrieve my driver's license and quarters, leave my car keys, and board the yellow school bus marked "Correctional Facility."

It will show I am totally out of denial, and will never re-offend.

As our bus approaches, I note the movie-like setting – high concrete walls, with double rolls of razor-sharp wire. As I step off the bus, to the right is a sign that announces that if I enter the prison I must consent, if asked, to a body search by a same-sex guard. Inside the prison, we repeat our security check. Finally, the entrance door to the visiting room is opened by a guard.

I see Paul enter and wave my hand. We walk toward each other, share a big hug, and return to our seats at table seventy-four. We will have two hours now, and after a lunch break, three more hours this afternoon to share time together.

In many ways I hardly know this young man, but in other ways I know so much. He is thirty-one now, the same age as Joe, but Paul is taller and he has a neatly trimmed mustache. He looks healthier and calmer now than when I saw him near his workplace five years ago. "No cigarettes, no drugs, no alcohol, regular working hours, and lots of time to think things over and accept 'what I cannot change,'" he explains.

For five hours, Paul and I talk. We exchange stories, jokes, tears and yawns. Paul gives me a photo of himself. As time comes for me to leave, he says, hesitantly, "There is one question I've been wanting to ask you – if you don't mind?"

"I'll talk about anything," I remind him. "What do you want to ask?"

"I just don't understand. If George abused you when you were a child, why did you let Joe and Jenny visit him? Why did you let me visit him?"

To this day, I am still heavily burdened by Paul's question. Why do we, ever, allow a child, whether our own or someone else's to be unattended in the presence of a pedophile?

I told Paul, "Nothing I can say can take away what happened to you. I was so numbed by my own abuse, so confused and unaware of its effects on me, that I didn't protect you, or Joe and Jenny. You each needed and deserved to have your family keep you safe. I'm sorry I wasn't able to do that."

"That means a lot to me," Paul replied. "Thanks for your honesty."

Following that visit, Paul and I talked every few weeks. In June, 2001, I had another chance to visit him.

As we sit at our own table in the prison's family visiting area, it is astonishingly hard to see the "criminals" in this room. A laughing toddler runs around the tables playing peek-a-boo with her father, who is dressed in prison green. Another inmate walks around the edges of the room, one hand on his adolescent son's shoulder. The room is filled with noise and emotion as families and friends greet their loved ones who are serving sentences in this minimum-security facility. Young couples hold hands and look longingly, sometimes tearfully, into each others' eyes. The incarcerated fathers throw foam rubber footballs with their sons, bounce daughters on their laps and follow toddlers as they walk or scoot by on riding toys. "Children may not be left unattended at any time," a sign on the wall warns.

When I last visited Paul, he was in Phase One of the Sex Offender Evaluation and Treatment program, located in the Fremont unit. Paul spent one-and-a-half years in this medium-security prison. The demands of the program were rigorous. Out of the sixteen men with him in his original group, Paul was the only one left.

Now, five months after his transfer to Phase Two, Paul describes a busy schedule of daily work in the prison greenhouse, structured meals and recreation activities, ten hours a week of sex-offender education and therapy groups, and 24-hour-a-day supervision, feedback and confrontation in his "therapeutic community."

His description of the program reminds me of well-planned, well-run, well-staffed psychiatric programs: clear rules and consequences; firm boundaries between staff and clients; steady emphasis on language and behaviors which both teach and require the individual to take responsibility for thoughts and emotions.

Paul describes keeping a journal, writing concept papers, developing his "plan for change," making disclosures, confronting other community members, and giving a talk in front of the almost one hundred-man community about his progress.

His seven-year prison sentence will end September 2002. He wants to successfully remain in this treatment program, to learn as much as possible about how he began to offend, and how he can avoid ever repeating this behavior. He is learning about assertiveness, anger management, manipulation, coercion, cycles of behavior, "triggers" for acting, out, and how he can use humor to "stay in the comfort zone."

"Wouldn't it have been great if you could have learned all this in high school before you started offending?" I ask.

"I wouldn't have listened to anyone then," he says. "It was already too late. I was

You each needed and deserved to have your family keep you safe.

lying and manipulating and in complete denial of my feelings. I would have had to be taught much younger."

Pointing to two little children playing at a table across the room, I say to Paul, "Look at those kids. Wouldn't it be great if we could start teaching children about their emotions and behavior choices when they're little and cute like that?"

Rather than joining in my enthusiasm, Paul tells me matter-of-factly, "I can't look at the children. If I do we might make eye contact. I need to avoid any facial expressions that would encourage them to interact with me."

"Really?" I say. "You can't even make eye contact?"

"It's better if I don't ," Paul explains. "If I do I have to file an addendum and disclose it in therapy tomorrow. If I don't disclose the contact, I can flunk out of the program, or be put on temporary suspension.

"I can never have contact with children again. I'll be on probation for the rest of my life. Of course, I can't entirely avoid being in situations, but when I need to be, like a grocery store or an airport, I will always need to notify my support system."

Remembering the heart-warming vignettes we have been seeing all day, fathers with prison numbers printed on their green shirts hugging and playing with their children, I ask Paul about his own son and stepson.

"No, I don't think I'll ever be allowed to see them again until they are adults, over eighteen," he says. "Just through our contact, my therapists say, I would be re-victimizing them. I can't even know anything about them – their health, school, nothing. That's called 'secondary contact.'

I can never have contact with children again.

"I'm learning to live with losing them. I know it's my fault. It's because of what I did. But it's still hard."

"I'm so sorry," I say to Paul. "I know you love your boys and they love you."

"Yes," he says, softly. "Yes. But I have to let them go. Can't get stuck in that denial.

"Every morning our group repeats a motto. I used to think it was kind of corny, but now I understand it's really important. 'We are all our brothers' keepers, and our goal is no more victims.'"

Five generations of incest – my father's uncle abused him; then my father abused me; then he abused my children, his nieces and nephews and their children; and now one of the nephews my father abused has himself molested his own children.

What can I do with this tragic family legacy? I am writing a book. I am speaking out about the silences and betrayals, including my own. I want the speaking out to become a part of my children's legacy, and of those who follow. Then maybe the incest will stop.

The time for my visit with Paul is coming to a close. I am struck again with how much he is like my son Joe, the same age, height, and build. My father sexually abused both when they were young boys. Both are in therapy to heal the emotional, psychological, sexual, and spiritual effects of their abuse. Paul is sexually aroused by children and Joe is not.

No one knows why it turned out this way. What if it had been the opposite? Imagining my own son as both victim and offender seems incomprehensible. Yet my father was both victim and offender. Not either-or. Not black-white. Not good-bad.

I think of the words to a song I have meditated over many times. During the last few minutes of my visit I sing to Paul:

> *"He's somebody's brother, he's somebody's son.*
> *Don't sit and pass judgment for the things he has done.*
> *His life didn't turn out the way that he planned,*
> *But he's somebody's brother, he's somebody's friend."*

"Yep," Paul smiles.

"That's me."

We are all our brothers' keepers, and our goal is no more victims.

Joe, Me and Paul

Timetospeak.com

I challenge and encourage all of us to approach the national epidemic of child sexual abuse in a more effective and more holistic way. We must examine what I call the "ecology of abuse" – the inescapable connections that exist among perpetrators, families, the community, victims and survivors.

We must construct a system that contains and creates consequences for perpetrators, a system that not only works for the friends and family who love these abusers, but a system that also really protects children.

It is not the purpose of this book to explore the causes, varieties or treatments of pedophilia and child molesting. Research in this field is developing slowly because there is not a willingly available population to study. Because child sexual abuse is a crime as well as a psychiatric problem, pedophiles and other child molesters usually do not seek out treatment or volunteer for research studies.

Mom's Friends

Legal issues are also outside the scope of this book. Child sexual abuse is generally a crime without witnesses, a crime without evidence, and a crime without a legally competent victim, due to the child's young age. There is a growing controversy about how to protect children responsibly, without violating the constitutional rights of alleged perpetrators.

Because I Love You raises issues which I am convinced our national community must begin resolving now. It shows us clearly that sexual abuse of children has far-reaching consequences. It's not over when "it's over." At the same time, its victims and perpetrators are not "the Other." They are in the same family or community, the same system, as the rest of society. The vast majority of abusers usually

Using Sign Language to Speak

function as "good people." Our keeping silent about their abusing is based on societal beliefs, rules, and values about respect, authority, and family sanctity. It is our silence which allows, even promotes, the abuse.

We often hear child sexual abuse described as "the ultimate taboo." The writer Florence Rush has pointed out, however, that child sexual abuse is not taboo. It has been an intimate part of the human condition since history began. What is actually taboo is speaking about incest, pedophilia, and other sexual abuses.

What are we afraid would happen if we simply speak what we know? Time after time, as I interviewed and shared pieces of this book – with both friends and strangers alike – I encountered people amazingly, and immediately, ready to engage with me in conversation about the sexual offenders and child violations of which they personally knew.

It was as though our words, spoken together, had created a sudden light that simply dissipated the shadows cast by our guilt, shame and embarrassment about sexual abuse. It was as though our flow of words could begin washing away the fragile power of the perpetrators in our midst, could begin healing wounds inflicted upon us all.

"What do you think would happen," I asked, "if you began sharing exactly what you are telling me now with the people in your own circles of extended family and community?"

It is not enough that we create "Safe Touch" classes in our schools. It is not enough to ask abuse survivors to tell their stories. It is time for the rest of us to speak.

To that end, I have created **www.timetospeak.com**, a place where all of us can join in a new kind of conversation.

What is it like to live in a family, or to be friends with, people who don't talk about the child sexual offenses they know of?

How do the silences, about survivors or perpetrators you know, look? Do they have a texture or shape?

How do they feel?

*Our children
are our most
important
responsibility.*

How have these silences affected you?

What keeps you from speaking?

What do you fear or imagine would happen if you spoke?

Whom does your silence protect?

What has happened to other people who did try to speak about the secret?

If you have spoken, how did this affect your life and the lives of those you love?

I invite you to visit the Message Board at timetospeak.com and see how others have answered these questions. Here you can talk anonymously and experiment with engaging in your own time to speak. And if you don't have web access, mail your comments to: Child Development Resource Center, P. O. Box 4222, Charlottesville, VA 22905-4222. I will be glad to post your contribution to this new, and so necessary, national conversation.

Since our children are our most important responsibility, it is time for us to say: "Because I love you, I am speaking to you about incest and child sexual abuse."

I do have some memory fragments of my experiences, which I describe as pieces of a jigsaw puzzle.

"The existence of child sexual abuse is going to change
when we all decide we want it to change,
when we realize that every person's child is our own child."

Oprah Winfrey

Attributions

p. 5   Ecclesiastes 3:1 & 7 King James

p. 10   Excerpt from "Phizzog" in GOOD MORNING, AMERICA, copyright 1928 and renewed 1956 by Carl Sandburg, reprinted by permission of Harcourt, Inc.

Chapter 1   *Return to Silent Valley*

p. 23   "Lonesome Valley," a traditional song.

p. 32   "Amazing Grace," a traditional hymn.

p. 32   "Me and Bobby McGee." Words and music by Kris Kristofferson and Fred Foster © 1969 (Renewed 1997) TEMI COMBINE INC. All Rights Controlled by COMBINE MUSIC CORP. and Administered by EMI BLACKWOOD MUSIC INC. All Rights Reserved. International Copyright Secured. Used by permission.

Chapter 2   *The Journey Back*

p. 33   Dr. Elisabeth Kubler-Ross, lecture On Death and Dying, Washington National Cathederal, 1988. Used with permission.

p. 44   Young Man Luther: A study in psychoanalysis and history, by Erik Erikson. Reprinted with permission of W. W. Norton, Co. Copyright 1962.

Chapter 3   *From Ruffian to Wrestling Champ*

p. 45   "Man of Constant Sorrow," a traditional song.

p. 59   The Colorado Index. Colorado: Colorado School for the Deaf, Fall 1930. Reprinted with permission.

p. 60   Culbertson, George. "The Washington Bicentennial," The Colorado Index. Colorado: Colorado School for the Deaf, May 1932. Reprinted with permission.

p. 62   Culbertson, George. Report in "How the Holidays Were Spent," The Colorado Index. Colorado: Colorado School for the Deaf, Winter 1933. Reprinted with permission.

p. 64   Bishop, Gerald. Report in "How the Holidays Were Spent," Colorado Index. Colorado: Colorado School for the Deaf, Winter 1932. Reprinted with permission.

p. 71   Essay, "'38 25 Years Hence," from The Buff and Blue: Gallaudet Yearbook. Washington, D.C.: Gallaudet College, 1938. Reprinted with permission.

Chapter 4   *Ahead of His Time*

p. 73   "On The Sunny Side Of The Street." Lyric by Dorothy Fields, music by Jimmy McHugh. Copyright © 1930 Shapiro, Bernstein & Co., Inc., New York and Cotton Club Publishing for the USA. Copyright Renewed. All Rights for Cotton Club Publishing Controlled and Administered by Universal – MCA Music Publishing, A Division of Universal Studios, Inc. International Copyright Secured. All Rights Reserved. Used by Permission.

p. 81   "Byron," poem by Joaquin Miller (Cincinnatus Hiner Miller). In the public domain.

Chapter 5   *Roller Coaster at Ocean View*

p. 87   "You Are My Sunshine," by Jimmie Davis. Copyright 1940 Peer International Corporation. Copyright Renewed. Used By Permission. All Rights Reserved.

p. 88   Ecclesiastes 3:1. King James

p. 88   1 Corinthians 12:1-13

p. 98   Allan, Joyce. "Roller Coaster." Copyright 2001.

Chapter 6   *Father Knows Best*

p. 113   "The Great Pretender," by Buck Ram. Copyright © 1955 by Panther Music Corporation. Copyright renewed. Used by permission. All Rights Reserved.

Chapter 7   *The Atomic Bomb*

p. 127   Excerpt from THE LITTLE PRINCE by Antoine de St. Exupery, copyright 1943 and renewed 1971 by Harcourt, Inc., reprinted by permission of the publisher.

Chapter 8   *Rebuilding from the Rubble*

p. 137   "Only a Dream." Words and Music by Mary Chapin Carpenter © 1992 EMI APRIL MUSIC INC. and GETAREALJOB MUSIC. All Rights Controlled and Administered by EMI APRIL MUSIC INC. All Rights Reserved. International Copyright Secured. Used by permission.

Chapter 9   *Queen for a Day*

p. 148   "Doing My Job," song written by John McCutcheon, from album titled Doing Our Job." Copyright 1995 by Appalsongs. Used by permission.

Chapter 10   *Hiding Out in High School*

p 156   "Secrets," Words and Music by Terri Allard. Copyright BMI, 1993. Reprinted with permission.

p. 165   The Columbine. Colorado: Colorado School for the Deaf, October 1958. Reprinted with permission.

p. 169   Tolstoy, Leo, Anna Karenina. In public domain.

p. 169   Culbertson, George. Report from The Colorado Index. Colorado, Colorado School for the Deaf, October 1959. Reprinted with permission.

p. 169   Report from The Colorado Index. Colorado, Colorado School for the Deaf, January 1960. Reprinted with permission.

p. 171   Report from The Colorado Index. Colorado, Colorado School for the Deaf, January 1962. Reprinted with permission.

Chapter 11   *Filling in Blank Pages*

p. 177   "Crazy," copyright © 1961 (renewed) Sony/ATV Songs LLC. All rights administered by Sony/ATV Music Publishing, 8 Music Square West, Nashville, TN 37203. All rights reserved. Used by permission.

Chapter 12   *Just Playing Roles*

p. 196 "He Thinks He'll Keep Her." Words and music by Mary Chapin Carpenter and Don Schlitz © 1992 EMI APRIL MUSIC INC., GETAREALJOB MUSIC, BMG SONGS, INC. and NEW DON SONGS. All Rights for GETAREALJOB MUSIC Controlled and Administered by EMI APRIL MUSIC INC. All Rights Reserved. International Copyright Secured. Used by Permission.

p. 204 George S. Kaufman. Quote used with the kind permission of his daughter, Anne Kaufman.

Chapter 13   *The Earthquake*

p. 213 "Free to Be You and Me," song by Bruce Hart and Stephen Lawrence. Reprinted with permission. Courtesy of Free To Be Foundation, Inc.

p. 222 "Free to Be You and Me," song by Bruce Hart and Stephen Lawrence. Reprinted with permission. Courtesy of Free To Be Foundation, Inc.

p. 227 "Free to Be You and Me," song by Bruce Hart and Stephen Lawrence. Reprinted with permission. Courtesy of Free To Be Foundation, Inc.

Chapter 14   *Dancing in the Dark*

p. 231 "La La Rosie Goes" - Words and Music by Terri Allard from Loose Change and Spare Parts, courtesy of Reckless Abandon Music, Copyright BMI, 1998.

p. 245 "Free to Be You and Me," song by Bruce Hart and Stephen Lawrence. Reprinted with permission. Courtesy of Free To Be Foundation, Inc.

p. 256 "Nuts," a film based on a play by Tom Topor. Reprinted courtesy of Warner Brothers.

Chapter 15   *Hitting Bottom*

p. 257 "It's All Right to Cry," by Carol Hall. Copyright © 1972 Free to Be Foundation, Inc., Assignment 1999 Otay Music, Corp., and Daniel Music (ASCAP). All rights reserved. Used by Permission.

Chapter 16   *Stabbed in the Heart*

p. 267 Conrad, Joseph. Heart of Darkness. New York: Random House, Inc., 1901. In public domain.

Chapter 17   *Silent Shadow*

p. 280 From the Cancer Journals by Audre Lorde, reprinted by permission of the Charlotte Sheedy Literary Agency Inc., © 1980 by the Audre Lorde Estate.

Chapter 18   *Leaving Silent Valley*

p. 293 "Fountain of Sorrow," by Jackson Browne. © 1974 Swallow Turn Music. All Rights Reserved. Used by Permission. WARNER BROS. PUBLICATIONS U.S. INC., Miami, FL 33014

p. 297 Dr. Elisabeth Kubler-Ross, lecture On Death and Dying, Washington National Cathederal, 1988. Used with permission.

p. 299 Dr. Elisabeth Kubler-Ross, lecture On Death and Dying, Washington National Cathederal, 1988. Used with permission.

Epilogue: *A Family Legacy*

p. 303 "Somebody's Brother," song written by Anita Holt. Reprinted with permission by Aubrey Holt, Tulipland Publishing –Broadcast Music, Inc. (BMI). Copyright 1999.

p. 311 "Somebody's Brother," song written by Anita Holt. Reprinted with permission by Aubrey Holt, Tulipland Publishing –Broadcast Music, Inc. (BMI). Copyright 1999.

Timetospeak.com

p.316 Oprah Winfrey, on The Oprah Winfrey Show, August 1999. In public domain.

p. 319 "Go Tell It On The Mountain," traditional song, rewritten by Joyce Allan.

Illustrations and Photos

Color Plates:

Details from paintings by Trisha Orr. Copyright 2000 Trisha Orr. Used with permission.

Front Piece: *The Only Secret*

p. 32/33   *Choose One*

p. 112/113   *Floating World*

p. 176/177   *Schoolroom of the Sky*

p. 256/257   *Rumor of Delirium*

Back Piece   *Too Bright*

Photos:

p. 65 "Our 1933 Basketball Teams." The Colorado Index, March 17, 1933, Number VII, Volume LIX, page 1. Photo reprinted with the permission of the Colorado School for the Deaf and the Blind.

p. 136 Courtesy of Spring Grove Hospital, Catonsville, MD.

p. 315 "Putting the Pieces Together," essay by Joyce Allan, photo manipulation by Angela Daniel SilverStar, SilverStar Graphics. Sacred Bearings: A Journal About Surviving, Vol. 2, No. 1. p. 14. The Virginia Foundation for the Humanities, Charlottesville, VA. Copyright 2001. Reprinted with permission.

Go Tell It

Go tell it on the mountain
Over the hills and everywhere
Go tell in on the mountain
So child abuse will end

Go tell it to your mother
Tell it to your father
Your sister and your brother
Go tell it to your best friend
So child abuse will end

Go tell it your grandma
Tell it to your grandpa
Aunts and uncles too
Go tell it to your cousins
So child abuse will end

Go tell it to your teacher
Tell it to your scoutleader
Tell it to your preacher
Go tell it to your neighbor
So child abuse will end

Go tell it on the TV
Tell it on the radio
Tell it everywhere you go
Go tell it on the mountain
So child abuse will end

© 1995 Joyce Allan with apologies

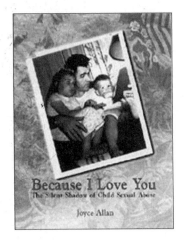

BECAUSE I LOVE YOU:
THE SILENT SHADOW
OF CHILD SEXUAL ABUSE

by Joyce Allan. The emotional,
physical and spiritual damages of
incest will affect one in four of us
before the age of eighteen. Forces of
patriarchy and taboo forbid us from
talking about this topic, says Allan, a
child psychiatric nurse/therapist.
Using the story of her pedophile
father's life, extensive interviews, and
statistics, she encourages us to break
the social silence that permits abuse to
pass down through generations. A
book to heal and transform the heart.
Because I love You, pbk **$19**

To order:
Because I Love You
through our distributor,
please fill out and mail
this form.

Sacred Source

PO Box 163, Crozet, VA 22932

for faster service, order online:

www.SacredSource.com

We're here to take your order
Mon–Fri 9am to 5pm, E.S.T.
24-hour answering system
800-290-6203
or 434-823-1515
24-hour fax: 434-823-7665

Person ordering _____

Street _____

City _____ State _____ Zip _____

Daytime Phone Number: _____ **E-mail:** _____

Ship to (if different from person ordering): _____

Street _____

City _____ State _____ Zip _____

Payment: ☐ Check / Money Order ☐ MC/VISA/Diners/Discover/AMEX ☐ COD ($6.00 addt'l. charge)

Credit Card Number: _____

Expiration Date _____ Signature _____

Number of copies	Item Description	Price Each	Total
	Because I Love You	$19.00	

Shipping and Handling

If Order Totals:	Add:
$00.01—$24.00	$5.00
$24.01—$35.00	$6.00
$35.01—$60.00	$7.00
$60.01—$75.00	$8.00

Subtotal	
Shipping & Handling	
TOTAL	

☐ Send the above order as a **gift**, with a card saying: _____

_____

_____

A portion of the sale of this book goes to support the Sexual Assault Resource Agency (SARA)
and other organizations that serve survivors of child sexual abuse.